Introduction to
MANAGEMENT
INFORMATION SYSTEMS
A User Perspective
Second Edition

James W. Vigen, Ph.D.
Professor
Management Science
California State University, Bakersfield

Hossein Bidgoli, Ph.D.
Professor
Management Information Systems
California State University, Bakersfield

Kendall/Hunt
Publishing Company
Dubuque, Iowa

CONTENTS

PART 1.   INTRODUCTION TO COMPUTER BASED MANAGEMENT INFORMATION SYSTEMS

Introduction.. 1

   Wysong, Jr., Earl M., "MIS in Perspective," **JOURNAL OF SYSTEMS MANAGEMENT**, October 1985, Pgs. 32-36........................... 7

   Raho, Louis, E. and Belohlav, James A., "Discriminating Characteristics of EDP, MIS and DSS Information Interface," **DATA MANAGEMENT**, December 1982, pgs.18-20.......................... 12

   Baxter, John D., "Line Managers Move From MIS to DSS For Decision-Making Help, **IRON AGE**, September 28, 1981, pgs. 71-73... 15

PART 2.   IMPORTANT ISSUES

   Introduction... 18

   Corney, William J., "Human Information Processing Limitations and the Systems Manager," **JOURNAL OF SYSTEMS MANAGEMENT**, March 1985, pgs. 28-33.. 23

   Rao, K. Venkata, "Graphics in Business Information Systems," **JOURNAL OF SYSTEMS MANAGEMENT**, July 1985, pgs. 18-21........... 29

   Collins, Joanne A., "Continuous Security Control Clamps Down on Abuse," **DATA MANAGEMENT**, May 1985, pgs. 56-59.................. 33

   Landgarten, Harris, "Beware of Security Risks When Implementing Micro-Mainframe Links," **DATA MANAGEMENT**, April 1985, pgs. 16-18.. 37

   Keim, Robert T. and Janaro, Ralph, "Cost/Benefit Analysis of MIS," **JOURNAL OF SYSTEMS MANAGEMENT**, September 1982, pgs. 20-25... 40

   Carter, John C. and Silverman, Fred N., "Establishing a MIS," **JOURNAL OF SYSTEMS MANAGEMENT**, January 1980, pgs. 15-21........ 46

PART 3.   DEVELOPMENT AND IMPLEMENTATION OF A CBMIS

   Introduction... 53

   Page, John R. and Hooper, H. Paul, "Basics of Information Systems Development," **JOURNAL OF SYSTEMS MANAGEMENT**, August 1979, pgs. 12-16... 58

Shevlin, Jeffery L., "Evaluating Alternative Methods of Systems Analysis," **DATA MANAGEMENT**, April 1983, pgs. 22-25............. 63

Green, Gary I. and Keim, Robert T., "After Implementation What's Next? Evaluation," **JOURNAL OF SYSTEMS MANAGEMENT**, September 1983, pgs. 10-15... 67

PART 4. DATABASE: A CRUCIAL COMPONENT OF CBMIS

Introduction... 73

Snyders, Jan, "Let's Talk DBMS," **INFOSYSTEMS**, December 1984, pgs. 36,38,40,42,44.. 77

Robichaux, Rory C., "The Database Approach," **JOURNAL OF SYSTEMS MANAGEMENT**, November 1980, pgs. 6-14............................ 82

Burlingame, Andrew, "Matching a DBMS to User Needs," **MINI-MICRO SYSTEMS**, October 1981, pgs. 165-168............................ 91

Wood, David, "Relational Systems Meet the Real World," **DATA MANAGEMENT**, July 1985, pgs. 10-15............................... 94

PART 5. TELECOMMUNICATIONS AND DISTRIBUTED DATA PROCESSING

Introduction... 99

Burch, John G., "Network Topologies: The Ties That Bind Information Systems," **DATA MANAGEMENT**, December 1985, pgs. 34-37, 51.. 103

Rushinek, Avi and Rushinek, Sara, "Distributed Processing: Implications and Applications for Business," **JOURNAL OF SYSTEMS MANAGEMENT**, July 1984, pgs. 21-27.............................. 108

Smith, Jonathan, "Distributed Data-Processing 'Nightmares' Offer Valuable Lessons," **DATA MANAGEMENT**, September 1985, pgs. 20-24.. 115

Lederer, Yvonne, "Planning User Needs Determine Final Shape of Local Area Networks," **DATA MANAGEMENT**, November 1986, pgs. 10-14.. 120

Thackeray, Gail, "Telecommunications: Trouble in Paradise," **THE OFFICE**, November 1984, pgs. 49, 57............................ 125

PART 6. APPLICATIONS OF MIS AND DSS

Introduction... 127

Chandler, John S., Trone, Thomas and Weiland, Michael, "Decision
Support Systems Are For Small Businesses," **MANAGEMENT ACCOUNTING**,
April 1983, pgs. 34-39... 132

Dressler, Michael, Beall, Ronald and Brant, Joquin Ives, "Why
Marketing Managers Love DSS," **BUSINESS MARKETING**, April 1983,
pgs. 77, 78, 80, 81... 138

Chan, K. H., "Decision Support System for Human Resource Management," **JOURNAL OF SYSTEMS MANAGEMENT**, April 1984, pgs. 17-25... 142

Attaran, Mohsen and Bidgoli, Hossein, "Developing an Effective
Manufacturing Decision Support System," **BUSINESS**, October -
December 1986, pgs. 9-16.. 151

PART 7. FUTURE: THE CHANGING ENVIRONMENT

Introduction... 159

Diebold, John, "Six Issues That Will Affect the Future of
Information Management," **DATA MANAGEMENT**, July 1984, pgs.
10-12, 14.. 163

Chang, Alec, Leonard, Michael and Goldman, Jay, "Artificial
Intelligence: An Overview of Research and Applications,"
INDUSTRIAL MANAGEMENT, November-December 1986, pgs. 14-19...... 167

Andriole, Stephen J., "The Promise of Artificial Intelligence,"
JOURNAL OF SYSTEMS MANAGEMENT, July 1985, pgs. 8-17............ 173

Oxman, Steven W., "Expert Systems Represent Ultimate Goal of
Strategic Decision Making," **DATA MANAGEMENT**, April 1984, pgs.
36-38.. 183

Lin, Engming, "Expert Systems for Business Applications:
Potentials and Limitations," **JOURNAL OF SYSTEMS MANAGEMENT**,
July 1986, pgs. 18-21.. 186

PART 8. CBMIS: AN INTEGRATED VIEW............................. 190

PREFACE

After consulting in the area and reviewing introductory Management Information System textbooks for the past few years, we are of the opinion that these texts have not adequately addressed some of the important areas, in particular, information system design, implementation, and the utilization of Computer Based Management Information Systems (CBMIS.) In many cases the texts have not been able to keep up with the contributions related to the growth of computer technology or, more specifically, have not addressed the user and designer views in dealing with CBMIS. In general, most of the texts have emphasized the technological aspects of CBMIS. Because we had not found texts which introduced CBMIS from a user/designer perspective, we decided to develop a textbook utilizing readings related to the current state of the art to present an introduction to CBMIS from a user point of view. The technological aspects of the topic have been deemphasized and only those which are necessary to put a particular topic in prespective are included in the text.

Prior to the development of the first edition and for the past year, we continued to class test the material in the text. Based on an analysis of these tests, we have eliminated seven articles and have replaced them in this second edition with six new articles. The new articles relate to computer security, data base, local area networks, expert systems, artificial intelligence, and an application in the manufacturing area. We feel these articles will strengthen the reader's understanding of this dynamic and complex subject.

To develop a successful CBMIS several different dimensions should be carefully monitored. The computer and the user of CBMIS are two of these dimensions. In particular, the users are a very important dimension in the whole process of design, implementation and utilization of CBMIS. CBMIS design has experienced many failures and most of these failures are due to the lack of communication between DP personnel and the end users. Traditionally, CBMIS has been designed by DP personnel with very little or no input from the users. Successful cases in CBMIS design and utilization have exhibited heavy involvement of users in the whole process of CBMIS design. This is why we have chosen the user perspective in this text.

This text throughout the eight parts, presents several dimensions in CBMIS design and utilization. In each part readings specifically address the important factors related to users of CBMIS. Understanding these important issues should help in promoting designs which are more "user-friendly" and decrease the number of CBMIS failures.

Part I contains a comprehensive presentation of electronic data processing (EDP), Management Information System (MIS) and Decision Support System (DSS). The section also includes a historical review of EDP growth and a highlighting of some contributing fields to MIS. The presentation in this section should prepare the reader for the understanding of materials throughout the text.

1

In Part II, different aspects of CBMIS development are addressed. First, we start with the "human information processing limitations." This article addresses some very important issues in designing more effective CBMIS. After this important topic, the readings address several other important issues for CBMIS development. Security in CBMIS environment, planning, control and cost/benefit analysis of CBMIS are addressed. Finally, this section ends with an article highlighting the process of establishing a CBMIS.

Part III focuses on important issues dealing with CBMIS implementation. The life cycle of CBMIS from different dimensions is presented. The user's role in the whole process of CBMIS design and implementation addressed. Several different tools and techniques for structural systems analysis and design are introduced. Different format for successful information delivery including graphics and exceptional reporting, are explained. This section ends with some guidelines for successful implementation and post-implementation of CBMIS.

Part IV focuses on database as the heart of CBMIS. The evolution of database and unique advantages of database are presented. Different database models and their advantages/disadvantages are explained. How to choose a database and DBMS which fit closely to specific users' requirements are introduced. Since relational database is becoming the standard of the future, we have emphasized this type more than the others.

Part V highlights telecommunications and distributed data processing (DDP). Distributed data processing and its applications in CBMIS environment is fully discussed. Important issues of security in DDP environment is examined. A couple of readings in this section are devoted to the local area networks (LAN). What is LAN and what is its impact on CBMIS is discussed.

Part VI presents several applications of CBMIS which build on the five part introduction to CBMIS. These CBMIS applications include examples from small business, marketing, personnel, and manufacturing.

Part VII focuses on different dimensions of the future of CBMIS. Artificial intelligence, and expert systems as a new methodology for system design are presented. The readings in this section should provide the readers with relatively a clear picture about the future.

In the last part of this text, we present a conceptual model for CBMIS. This model explains different components of CBMIS. This serves as a framework for design, implementation and utilization of CBMIS. The included readings have directly and indirectly addressed different components of CBMIS, however, this wrap-up section should pull everything together. The reader has two options regarding this final part, either he/she can read this part first as an overview of the subject and progress or use this part as a review of the important aspects of CBMIS.

Hossein Bidgoli   James W. Vigen

PART I

INTRODUCTION TO COMPUTER BASED MANAGEMENT INFORMATION SYSTEMS

LEARNING OBJECTIVES:

- Be able to understand the historical development of MIS.

- Be able to define the terms EDP, MIS and DSS.

- Understand the system characteristics inherent in EDP, MIS and DSS.

- Have an understanding of the basic components of MIS.

- Be able to recognize some of the contributing disciplines to MIS.

INTRODUCTION

The three articles included in this section bring together the salient aspects of three functional areas which have roots in systems theory and have evolved in the development of CBMIS. These functional areas, which basically follow in parallel with computer technology development during the past forty years, are Electronic Data Processing (EDP), Management Information Systems (MIS), and Decision Support Systems (DSS).

Historically, many disciplines have contributed to the current state of the art of CBMIS. Some of these disciplines and fields are psychology, mathematics, economics, accounting, management science, and computer science to name just a few. However, for our purpose in developing an introduction to CBMIS, we have limited our focus to the three functional areas listed above because we consider them the most important in terms of identifying the major changes that have taken place during the past forty years.*

During the late 1940's and early 50's the term Electronic Data Processing (EDP) took on significant meaning. In conjunction with the development of the first (vacuum tube) and second (transistor) generation computers, the term EDP was defined as the collection and processing of data and transformation of data into transaction reports. Most of the data were collected on the internal environment of the firm and a very limited amount collected on the external environment. The kinds of reports, transaction reports, were related to those which are generally considered routine in the operation of the organzation. This mode of processing was a reflection of the technological data processing environment. Volumes of routine data were starting to be collected and application of this data were largely limited to the financial area. A framework relating to programs for managerial decision making was not available and emphasis was placed on the creation of large data files and operational efficiency. This period has been classified as one in which the programmer became the key element and procedures dominated.

In the middle to late 60's hardware and software advances led to new applications of the computer. These advances were mainly in the form of a new generation of computer, the third, which was characterized by semiconductor technology which replaced transistors. At this time there were also significant advances in data storage capabilities on the computer. The factors which had prevailed during the 50's in terms of computer tehcnology and which had inhibited the shift in focus from the automation of the clerical processing function to managerial support, were changing. A shift began in which dominance was shifted from the programmer to the manager. In terms of technology, most computer operations were run in the batch mode. Software development became very important and became an issue to be dealt with, however, hardware was recognized as a major constraining factor. Computer applications grew from those mainly related to the financial area to marketing and production. The concept of MIS emerged. MIS had many meanings but it generally related to not only the transformation of data into reports but encompassed all the information used for decision-making in the operation and management of an organization. Hence, the concept of decision making was formally recognized as it related to the computer data processing function. Emphasis which had previously been directed toward the operational level of the organization was now being directed at both middle and upper management. Computer applications were now being focused on decision problems relating to both structured and semi-structured tasks. Teams began the development of information systems and this added to the complexity of the systems being developed. This complexity also led to a significant increase in the cost of software development. Also, many of the MIS undertakings were not immediately adopted for implementation and in many cases, adoptions led to failures. Many factors contributed to these failures. In many cases, the degree of computer literacy related to the organizational decision makers was seriously lacking. In other instances, the MIS projects undertaken were too ambitious for the organization and, consequently, many failed. However, the MIS concept was born and many large organizations continued their MIS efforts. Also, educational institutions initiated research programs in this area and began the development of curriculum designed for MIS practitioners.

During the late 60's and early 70's a new theme was born which is being carried on today. This theme reflects the continuing development of computer technology in regard to integrated circuits, storage devices, especially those relating to secondary storage, communications and networks. The advances in hardware led to lower cost per unit in terms of computer processing power and at the same time, witnessed a shift in costs from hardware to software development. At this time, there was also a recognition that an information system must provide information for all levels of managerial decision making -- supervisory, tactical and strategic. Where MIS had addressed the clerical efficiency in providing reports for managerial decision-making from an organizational perspective, a new concept, DSS, came into being. DSS was oriented toward the individual manager at all levels in the organization. DSS oriented itself toward managerial effectiveness as opposed to the clerical efficiency attacked by EDP and MIS development. Because of the continuing development in computer technology, DSS shifted emphasis from structured and semi-structured problem environments to those relating to an unstructured environment. In essence, the emphasis was directed toward the end users of information. With DSS end users could specify their needs for information in the form of a unique unstructured report. They would have the ability to interact with the system to generate reports from large data bases and through the use of user friendly software.

At the present time there is no unique working definition of MIS or DSS. Throughout this text we have defined CBMIS as:

A well-organized integration of people, machines, facilities and procedures designed to assist a decision maker in making decisions -- or better decisions -- at all levels in an organization.
This definition indicates the components of CBMIS as:

People to include users, designers, programmers and maintainers.
Machines include all the computer hardware.
Facilities include all the other supporting technologies excluding computers such as telephone, telex, air conditioning, etc.
Procedures include all the written descriptions, materials and computer software.

A CBMIS with the above definition could be used in any of the organizational levels. However, if it is mostly used at the upper level of the organization we would call it DSS, otherwise it is either MIS or EDP.

Although a CBMIS for any functional area of the organization may include the same components, the goals and the objectives of the system may be quite different.

In the sixth part of this text we will present examples of MIS for different functional areas of a business organization.

* For an additional reading on the historical development of this topic area and an analysis of the significant events see Gary W. Dickson, "Management Information Systems: Evolution and Status," Advances in Computers, Volume 20, 1981, Academic Press, and Franz Edelman, "The Management of Information Resources--A Challenge for American Business," MIS Quarterly, March 1981, pp. 17-27.

DISCUSSION QUESTIONS

1. What is EDP?

2. What is MIS?

3. What is DSS?

4. Define "Systems Approach" and its relationship to EDP/MIS/DSS.

5. Mention four distinguishing characterisitics of each field.

6. Is DSS really a new field? If yes, why? If no, why?

7. What characteristics a CBMIS should have in order to be called DSS?

8. What types of information may be generated by MIS in a department store?

9. What is the CEO role in MIS design?

10. Why CEO should participate in MIS introduction and design?

11. What is the difference between systems analysis and systems design?

12. What are some of the criteria for MIS evaluation?

13. What is the relationship between OR and MIS?

14. In what stage of MIS design OR techniques may be the most useful?

MIS In Perspective

BY DR. EARL M. WYSONG, JR., CSP, CPA, CISA, CM

■ For years, the term "management information system" or "MIS" has been a subject of conversation and/or correspondence. In the 1960s, it was heralded as the answer to all business ills and management problems. Later, when organizations attempted to implement MIS, it was doomed to failure. Why this apparent disparity? Just what is a MIS?

Some people think of MIS as a transaction recording system that generates reports that must be important to somebody. Others, in recent years, think of MIS as a system to support managerial decision-making, a decision support system (DSS). Still others think of MIS as a system to support their day-to-day activities in their individual functional areas. This author believes it is all of the above.

To place in context the role of MIS within an organizational structure, perhaps it would help to look at the three terms involved: management, information, and systems. Since most everyone agrees that it is a "system," we will discuss that term first.

Systems

Systems is a word that appears everywhere, both in our writing and in our speech. A great many publications, conferences, symposia and courses have been and will continue to be devoted to systems. The "systems approach" plays a dominant role in a wide range of fields that includes virtually every discipline. Daily references are made to such systems as heating systems, solar systems, weapons systems, school systems, etc. In one way or another, systems must be dealt with in all fields.

There are certain models, principles and laws that apply to systems in general irrespective of their particular type, components and relations. The universal principles that apply to systems have led to a discipline called General Systems Theory.

DR. EARL M. WYSONG, JR., CSP, CPA, CISA, CM

Dr. Wysong is a professor of accounting at Loyola College in Maryland. He also provides consulting services in the systems area. He has presented speeches and conducted seminars on systems on numerous occasions throughout the Western Hemisphere and in Europe and has contributed many articles to professional journals. He is co-editor of a book, *Information Systems Auditing*, North-Holland Pub. Co. 1983. He has recently completed writing a textbook, *Management and Control of MIS* from which this article was adapted. Besides ASM, he is also a member of AICPA, AGA, IIA and AAA.

General Systems Theory is the study of the principles which apply to systems in general regardless of whether they are physical, biological or sociological in nature. Similar concepts, models and laws appear in widely different fields, independently and based upon totally different facts. General Systems Theory is an interdisciplinary science which has provided significant contributions in the fields of applied science, technology and behaviorial sciences.

From the study of General Systems Theory, we find that all systems have the following five fundamental implications:

— A system is designed to accomplish a certain objective.
— The elements of a system have an established arrangement.
— The individual elements of a system have a synergistic interrelationship among each other.
— The process itself is more important than the basic elements of a system.
— The objectives of the system are more important than the objectives of its elements.

A few characteristics that are common to all systems are organization, interaction, interdependence, integration and a central objective. *Organization* implies structure and function that arrange the components of a system in such a way as to allow a function to aid in achieving specific objectives. *Interaction* refers to the relationship of the various elements of a system to each other. *Interdependence* carries interaction a bit further and means that the elements of a system mutually satisfy the needs of other parts. *Integration* emphasizes a synergistic effect among the parts of a system that makes the whole more valuable and productive than the sum of the individual elements. The *central objective* of a system provides the means of measuring a systems performance.

There are certain elements or components that describe a system's relationship with its environment. The first element is the environment itself. Although the environment is not an internal element of a system, it is the reason for the system's existence. It is often called a supra-system because it is the setting in which the system exists. It constitutes the ecology of the system and is composed of all the elements related to the system. A system has no control over the behavior or characteristics of the environment but, conversely, it must react to such behavior and characteristics.

Common to all systems are organization, interaction, interdependence, integration and a central objective.

The major internal element of a system is its outputs. The basic objective of any system is to provide an output that has value to its environment. Regardless of what that output may be, it must provide some utility or satisfaction to the environment through a transaction which transfers the output from the system.

Inputs to a system are transfers from the environment to a system that are used to produce the outputs. They provide the resources that are applied in the output production process.

The element that provides the transformation or conversion process of inputs to outputs is the processor. The processor performs the operations in a system to modify the inputs to add value and produce the outputs.

Subsystems are elements within a system that are necessary to accomplish the system's objectives, but may have their own unique and identifiable functions as well. Each subsystem performs a function within the processing operation to contribute something to the conversion of inputs to outputs.

Parameters of a system provide the system's identification and boundaries. They describe the relationships of systems with other systems through interfaces. Parameters are limitations needed to define system objectives and provide for interfacing with other systems or subsystems for inputs and outputs to accomplish the objectives.

A control element is required in any system to connect the input, processor and output together with the environment. Control provides the guidance for the receipt of input resources, the processing of those resources into output products and their subsequent transfer to the environment.

Communication is the element that provides the channels for movement of resources through a system. It is the means by which the transfer of resources is made between the system and its environment and within the system itself. The communication element is closely related to the control element.

A feedback element provides a means to measure system performance by comparing output with certain standards. It measures any variances of the output product against the desired output. The feedback element, therefore, relies heavily on the communication and control elements. The relationships of the elements of a system to each other and to the environment are illustrated in Figure 1.

Elements of Systems

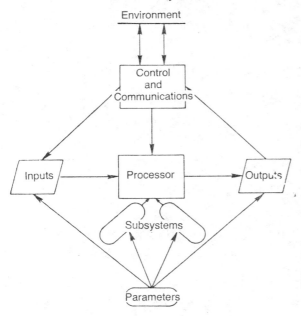

Figure 1

The word "system" implies a routine operation of a set of planned procedures to accomplish a specific purpose. It further implies a coordinated body of methods within an overall scheme or plan. A system is an orderly and organized chain of events. The first event involves an input into a planned process in which there is a processor that performs certain operations over the input. The processor provides output which may serve as input to other processors

or as feedback to a measurement process. Controls monitor the processor performance by comparing output to some predetermined standards or criteria. The feedback loop reacts to deviations from the standards to maintain established limits of the imposed controls.

In our discussion of the terms contained in MIS, we must continue in an orderly and organized fashion. Since we started with the word "system," we shall continue in reverse order with the word "information."

Information

Information consists of a body of knowledge that reduces uncertainty about future happenings. It must be communicated, received and perceived. Information can be either historical or predictive or a combination of the two.

Information results from the transformation of basic facts or data. Information also may be used as data in another level of knowledge. The general connotation of information is that it is the result of gathering, classifying, recording, analyzing, sorting, interpreting and presenting data selectively in a format that is useful and timely.

Information is used to measure performance and responsiveness

---

The information produced by a MIS must be such that it aids decision-making and helps managers execute their responsibilities effectively. This means that information must contain the following qualities:
— reliability and consistency,
— timeliness and availability,
— accuracy and relevance,
— comprehensibility and usefulness.

Information is necessary for day-to-day operations and performance measurement as well as for tracking progress toward long-term strategic goals. It is an important resource in the business world and, therefore, must be managed as a resource. Successful organizations recognize this fact and structure information as efficiently as they do other assets. Such organizations use information to make changes in plans in order to mazimize the cost-effective use of resources. Information is used to measure performance and responsiveness as an adjunct to profitability measurements. Information, therefore, must be considered as a vital component of an organization.

Management

The term "management" generally implies a process by which certain basic functions are performed. It also implies the people who administer the process. The management functions themselves have been classified and categorized in various ways by students of the theory.

Planning and control generally are considered as the two principal functions of management. Planning is primarily a decision-making activity involving the selection of alternative courses of action. Control ensures that the plans are executed properly.

In the development of any MIS, there are some general axioms for consideration. First, the system structure should relate to the organizational internal structure so that its results can be viewed the same as management views the business. Second, the system should tie in the planning and budgeting process to provide the basis for comparison and control. The system should provide management with the following information:

- that which is necessary to exercise control over operations,
- that which will provide early warning of developing problems and indicate remedial action required,
- that which will enable correct interpretation of financial and other statistics,
- that which will enable effective allocation and efficient use of organizational resources.

Management Information Systems

Now that we have discussed the terms involved in MIS, just what is a MIS? One reason many managers were unsuccessful in implementing MIS in the past was because they viewed the MIS as a product (thing). This author believes, however, that a MIS *is not a product; it is a concept.* If viewed in this light, it will perform effectively as it is refined and enhanced over time.

Then how can we define MIS? The concept of MIS is all-inclusive from an information standpoint. It is an information producing system using a network consisting of interrelated intelligence and transaction recording systems which deal with data of an interdisciplinary nature.

The literature on the subject reveals a number of definitions that have been proposed by various authors. The definition of MIS that relates most closely to the conceptual viewpoint is one that was expounded by Walter J. Kennevan in a September 1970 article, "MIS Universe," in *Data Management.*

"A management information system is an organized method of providing past, present and projected information related to internal operations and external intelligence. It supports the planning, control and operational function of an organization by furnishing uniform information in the proper time-frame to assist the decision making process."

Figure 2 illustrates how the above definition

MIS Wheel

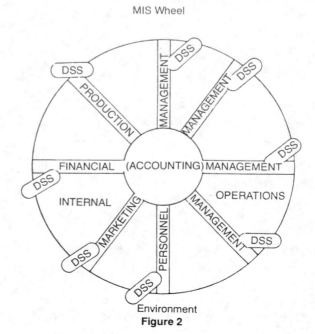

Environment
Figure 2

can be integrated with the conceptual viewpoint. The MIS is depicted as a wheel that encompasses the various functional information systems with decision support systems (DSS) interacting with the environment. The hub of the MIS is the Financial Management Information System for two basic reasons:

— It interacts closely with all other information systems for the gathering of data and reporting financial statistics.
— It drives the organization to maintain and improve its financial position which is its life blood.

The development of sophisticated computer and communications technology in recent years provides the basis for the realization of the conceptual viewpoint of MIS. Functional managers require information about their operations, both historical and predictive, for planning and control purposes. Additionally, they must be able to interact with other functional areas to achieve the overall goals and objectives of the organization. Finally, top management must be in contact with the environment to be able to direct the organization effectively and to establish realistic goals. Current technology provides these capabilities.

Summary

In this article, the words which comprise the acronym "MIS" — management, information and system — were discussed individually. After discussing some of the concepts of systems from General Systems Theory, the requirements for information, and the functions and needs of management, the logical conclusion of MIS as a concept is reached.

An organization's MIS must provide managers at all levels of management the information they need in performing their functions of planning and control. Such information is produced internally by the organization and obtained from the external environment. The information must be both historical and predictive. A MIS is an integrated and interrelated collection of functional management information systems and decision support systems. As such, it cannot be a "thing;" it is a concept that involves many "things."   ●jsm

Discriminating characteristics of EDP, MIS and DSS information interface

by Louis E. Raho and James A. Belohlav

Some 30 years after the development of the computer, many managers are wondering what is more perplexing—all of the fast paced organizational changes, or the systems that are supposed to help them with these changes?

Discriminating between electronic data processing systems, management information systems and decision support systems will help a manager to cope with the dynamic environment he or she is in.

Business people are being confronted by an increasing number of internal and external challenges. From outside the organization, more "competitors" are surfacing—governmental bodies as well as businesses. Within the organization, virtually every functional area of management is experiencing drastic changes. Planning and control, organizational structure and managerial leadership styles have all undergone significant and continual changes.

A significant outgrowth of these changes has been the development of better and faster communication systems. Information is being generated at geometric rates, and that information is being placed into the hands of more people than ever before.

The flood of information presents both a threat and an opportunity for the manager. The threat arises from the information overload that can inundate a manager at any organizational level. However, more information means managers have more at their disposal to make better decisions—even though the decision-making environment has become more complex.

The effective transformation and movement of information throughout the organization is a function of the data processing-management information-decision support systems interface. How well these systems are used will determine the effectiveness of each system and the organization as a whole.

Only after the distinguishing characteristics of each of these systems are understood by the manager, can an integrated and useful decision framework exist.

Each of the three types of processing systems will be discussed from four different perspectives:

- Focus on the entity of interest of the system
- Target group who receives the processed material
- Output characteristics of the processing system
- Initial impetus leading to the establishment of the system

Electronic Data Processing (EDP)

Data is of primary interest in an EDP system. Data is simply a collection of "raw facts" on internal and external events. The function of the EDP system is to change the data into a form where relationships can be drawn. The sequence of ac-

---

What's needed—raw facts, interrogative reports or interactive reports?

---

tivities within an EDP system that creates this transformation are: The collection of data from appropriate primary and secondary sources, the validation of the acquired data and the final processing of the data.

At this lowest level, the processing of the data occurs from the technical perspective of optimizing computer hardware performance rather than from identified organizational information needs.

Once the data is processed for a particular application, the material is delivered to an individual who usually functions at the operational level. Because of EDP's main emphasis on processing data for specific applications, the operational processing procedures are characterized by rigid structures focusing on manipulating individual transactions at a central facility.

The internal output of an EDP system consists mainly of declarative reporting and summary reports. The outputted material serves as a snapshot of what has occurred in a particular application and makes little effort to relate common business functions of the recipient of the output across different applications.

The initial impetus for the creation of an EDP system is frequently generated by the observation of an excess volume of data. That is, management becomes inundated with too many transactions. Thus, EDP has been used primarily as an *expedient* method to an increasingly frustrating problem, rather than as a part of a systematic channel of information throughout the organization.

Most EDP systems have emerged having a conceptual design based on the synthesis of manual and automatic data processing (ADP) methods. The underlying philosophy for this design is management's predilection toward the continuation of past processing activities.

Management Information Systems (MIS)

The first step in moving away from viewing the information system in terms of expediency was MIS. In contrast to the EDP system, a MIS views not just the transformation of data but how it can be turned into useful organizational information.

In a MIS, information is data which has been processed in such a manner that the integration and presentation of individual bits of data become meaningful to a variety of potential users, primarily middle and upper management. The preparation of information in a MIS is performed by operational procedures which provide managers with the capability of interrogating data bases and generating reports from diffused data processing facilities.

The processing procedures are semi-structured because of the need to provide multiple points of access for input and output of the system. Because of the general nature of a MIS, the end user is provided with more information that is necessary— sometimes everything that has been processed. Thus, a MIS places the burden on the user to select the meaningful information and discard the remainder.

The main output of a MIS is composed of standardized reports and interrogative reporting. The standardized reports emphasize a need for common information and a standard information flow. The interrogative reports highlight the diffused processing capabilities of MIS to process related information in an organization's integrated data files.

In general, MISs have been created from recognizing that the processed materials from an EDP system are fragmented. For a processing system to be meaningful to management, an integration of information produced from specific applications must take place so that overall managerial efficiency can increase in all functional areas. MIS is designed from an organizational perspective rather than from a business transaction perspective.

Decision Support Systems (DSS)

In DSS, the focal point is not on data or information *per se*, but on the end product—the manager's decision. A DSS is a vehicle to help managers to make more informed

(and hopefully better) decisions. Therefore, a DSS is oriented to *the individual manager*. For individuality in a DSS, the system must be driven by the manager's personal decision-making methodology. That is, while EDP and MIS receive managerial input, the system builders and operators develop the structure. In DSS, the manager not only provides the input but the structure as well.

Since DSS can be used at all levels of management in the organization, DSS emphasizes a system strategy of localized processing which is user friendly and flexible since the emphasis is on developing a rapport with the manager who must use the system. The operation of the system is necessarily semi-structured to unstructured because the system must be initiated and controlled by the individual decision-maker.

The information produced by a DSS consists mainly of interactive-iterative reports and unstructured reports. In the search for supporting

Figure 1. Summary of system characteristics

SYSTEM

EDP — MIS — DSS

	EDP	MIS	DSS
Focus	• Data	• Information	• Decisions
Target group	• Operational level	• Mostly middle and upper management	• All levels
System strategy	• Designed from technical perspective • Application oriented • Synthesis of manual and ADP methods	• Designed from organization's perspective • Business function oriented • Synthesis of EDP and information dissemination methods	• Designed from manager's perspective • Individual manager oriented • Synthesis of MIS and MS methods
Operations	• Centralized processing • Emphasizes transaction processing • Computer hardware optimization • Rigidly structures procedures • File driven system	• Diffused processing • Emphasizes structured information flow • Inquiry and report generation optimization • Semi-structured procedures • Integrated files and data-base driven system	• Localized processing • Emphasizes user friendliness and flexibility • User initiation and control optimization • Unstructured procedures • Personal managerial decision methodology driven system
Output	• Declarative reporting • Summary reports	• Interrogative reporting • Standardized reporting	• Interactive-iterative reporting • Unstructured reports
Impetus	• Expediency • Excess volume genesis	• Efficiency • Information fragmentation genesis	• Effectiveness • Complex variable interaction genesis

EDP, MIS and DSS

information in a specific decision situation, the user may be required to make iterations of particular reports, adding and deleting selected variables deemed to be important components of the individual's decision-making procedure. Reports involving complex relationships such

---

A DSS won't make a decision for a manager.

---

as portfolio management, budget analyses and risk analysis are typical products of a DSS. However, these reports only represent a fraction of the potential output from a DSS.

DSS have been developed as a result of managers trying to cope with decisions that include complex variable interactions. To study the situation, the decision-maker must be able to combine the existent variables pertaining to the decision-making responsibility in an effective manner.

In DSS, effective decision-making is paramount to efficient decision-making. A DSS is designed from an individual manager orientation synthesizing the aspects of MIS with management science techniques. The ultimate objective of a DSS is to help support a manager in making a decision. It should be noted that a DSS will not make a decision for the manager, therefore, managerial decision-making judgment is an integral component throughout the decision-making process.

Getting the right fit

As an organization grows and matures, managers must be able to select the informational material provided by the information system that best fits their decision-making goals and responsibilities. They must be able to distinguish the reports that will be needed and the information arena within which they must operate.

The intent of this article is to help serve the manager by comparing the different characteristics of EDP, MIS and DSS, which are summarized in Figure 1. Each manager can then

select the most effective combination of reports and interfaces that flow from these different information systems. This selection ability is not easily acquired unless the manager can first differentiate between the three systems presented and then recombine them to effectuate and extend his or her decision-making capability in a dynamic environment. ∎

About the authors

Raho is assistant professor of management at the University of Louisville. Belohlav is assistant professor of management at DePaul University, Chicago. — Ed.

References

1. Alter, S., Decision Support Systems: Current Practice and Continuing Challenges, Addison-Wesley Publishing Co.: Reading, MA, 1980.
2. Dearden, J., "MIS Is a Mirage," Harvard Business Review, January-February 1972, 90-99.
3. Newman, S. and Hadass, M., "DSS and Strategic Decisions," California Management Review, Spring 1980, 77-84.
4. Sprague, R. H., "A Framework for the Development of Decision Support Systems," MIS Quarterly, December 1980, 1-26.

LINE MANAGERS MOVE FROM MIS TO DSS FOR DECISION-MAKING HELP

Decision Support Systems are the 'in' thing as Management Information Systems seem to fade. In DSS, the line manager is 'king.'

By John D. Baxter

Line managers who have been around long enough, remember the golden promises made to them back in the 60s that the computer was going to change their lives. It was going to completely change the way they managed their companies.

They were told that the age of push-button management was just around the corner.

Well, here it is in the early 80s, and push-button management is a long way off. Maybe, it is further off than ever. As one about-to-retire top executive noted recently, "Doing a good job of managing seems tougher than ever these days. Companies are more diversified, the economy is more jumbled, the constraints on management are tighter and the competition comes at you from more sides than ever."

So, where is that great promise and buzz word of the 60s—Management Information Systems (MIS)?

In a word, it seems to have flopped. As one information systems expert now puts it, "The MIS craze of several years ago ended—for all practical purposes—in expensive failure."

The key reason for the failure of MIS is cited by information systems consultant John M. Thompson.

"Initially," he says, "people looked at MIS as an outgrowth of the computer's transaction process function and experience—the automation of payrolls, accounts receivables, inventory controls and so on. The attitude was that a great pile of corporate data had been amassed, so why not have executives use it for managing."

"But," he adds, "this information simply was unsuited for management use in making decisions. Managers were left data rich and information poor."

Mr. Thompson is a vice president of Index Systems, Inc., a Cambridge,

MA, consulting and systems development firm.

So, management today, in the opinion of a number of experts, instead of standing triumphantly atop a mountain of data with a clear overview and control of all company operations, finds itself buried under that very mountain of data.

"Suffocation by statistics" is the autopsy report on MIS made by one management systems 'pathologist.'

Where does all this leave management today?

"Unlike MIS, the starting point for DSS is the line manager and his job."

Enter DSS—Decision Support Systems. DSS is now pushing onto center stage in the evolving drama of the computer in industry.

A skeletal description of DSS in practice is where a company line manager identifies for a data processing manager the most critical on-job decisions he makes. The data processing manager then sets up an on-line computer program of relevant information to specifically give support to the line manager in making those decisions.

Notably, DSS can help managers at all company levels and in companies of just about any size.

Is DSS just another buzz word, or another failure about to happen?

That's for managers in industry to determine—by testing in the field. That's where claims and performances are sorted out. That testing is now going on, and reportedly, is picking up steam. DSS use is growing, more companies are turning to it, and

quite a few are said to be finding it a significant improvement over MIS in giving on-job, decision making support to line managers.

Thomas P. Gerrity, president of Index Systems, and one of the pioneers in the development of DSS at the Massachusetts Institute of Technology, says, "I have been involved in DSS for the past 15 years or so, but it is only in the last two or three years that it has really taken off. After a long, slow growth, it has suddenly gone straight up."

Mr. Gerrity explains that there is good reason for the recent surging interest in DSS.

"The technology is there now," he says. This is in reference chiefly to distributed data processing (a network of local data processing terminals tied into a central computer), and on-line information capability (where a 'dialogue' between user and computer is possible).

"And very importantly," he adds, "the pressure has been mounting on managers to make sense out of the overwhelming amount of data they are buried under these days. The time for DSS is right."

Mr. Thompson defines DSS as "a blending of information technology and management judgment which provides an understanding and a decision-making capability better than either could reach independently."

The key point there, he stresses, is "decision-making capability."

Mr. Thompson quickly adds another key point: "DSS starts with the line manager and his job."

The consultant makes a quick sum-up of differences between MIS and DSS:

"MIS informs you about what **has** happened; DSS is a learning tool that helps a manager get a handle on what **is** happening in his particular area of responsibility. MIS is summary data;

Basic Kinds of Decisions

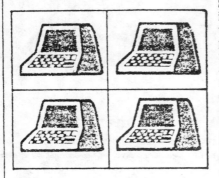

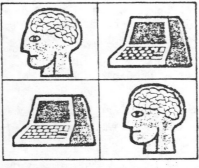

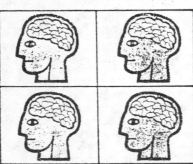

Structured Decisions—These largely involve situations where no choice, or very little choice or alternative, is possible. The decision situation here is largely self-evident once the facts and numbers are known. Managers make these decisions chiefly in areas of operations, rarely in cases of strategic planning. It is in dealing with the more highly structured decisions where MIS has been used mostly in recent years—"where a bunch of numbers crank out the answers," notes one information analyst.

Semi-Structured Decisions—These involve both data and a manager's intuition and judgment and are the kind most commonly faced by line managers. Examples: In operations control, decisions on expediting; in management controls, decisions on master scheduling; in strategic planning, decisions on optimum plant size and location. DSS can greatly assist line managers in making these kinds of decisions; MIS can help but little.

Unstructured Decisions—These involve no data reference source. They represent decisions based entirely on a manager's intuition and judgment. These kind of decisions are involved mostly in the area of company strategic planning, not often in areas of management operations and control. Line managers face unstructured decisions chiefly in dealing with people—workers, other managers, bosses and so on.

a three or four-month time frame—so that we can see something working in the system. It may not be the ideal thing, but a line manager can actually interact with the data on the terminal and get out some useful information to support him in decisions he faces."

Mr. Crescenzi reports that both the line managers and the executives who have to approve budgets to cover DSS costs, like the prototype approach. Line managers, for their part, see some results quickly, and the budget-approvers are in a position to say, We are giving DSS a try, and at the least amount of cost. If we want to throw it out four months from now, we can throw it out and we haven't made too big an investment."

Many companies settle on the prototype. Mr. Crescenzi states that in the last two cases he used a prototype DSS approach in manufacturing companies, "the prototypes became the permanent systems." He adds that that is not unusual.

A key element in a company DSS program—following proper indoctrination by those who are to take part in it—is a meeting between a line manager and a representative from the company's computer services group. (See box here on the DSS cycle.)

The purpose of this meeting, and usually a number of others to follow, is to pinpoint those decisions and goals most critical to the line manager's job responsibilities. Also pinpointed, is the information support needed by the line manager to help attain these goals. The essence of the meeting is in-depth questioning of the line manager by the data processing specialist.

There are variations in such meetings as to techniques used to uncover a line manager's goals and information needs. The consultants at Index Systems frequently use the popular interviewing method called, Critical Success Factors.

"This method," explains Mr. Gerrity, "is triggered by interviewing a line manager to gain his or her idea on what is 'critical' to the success of his job responsibilities. It is a common-sense method of seeing needs and setting goals."

He says examples of critical success factors might include such things as pricing tactics, fast product development cycle and product reliability. In other words, it is anything a particular line manager may perceive to be a critical factor on his job.

"This method is simple and fast," says Mr. Gerrity. "And regardless of

DSS is interpretive—what's going on **behind** the numbers.

"MIS is static—it consists of reports a manager uses every Monday morning. DSS is evolutionary—as a manager learns more of his job and the way he makes decisions, he changes the system. MIS tends to be internal—it looks at just internal company data and gives summary results. DSS looks at a blend of internal and external data."

The starting point in a DSS program in a company is indoctrination into such systems for those who are to take part in it.

Indoctrination in a company comes usually from a consultant or from an information systems specialist or manager who has had DSS experience or courses in 'B' schools or seminars.

Notably, a number of experts who have set up DSS programs in manufacturing plants stress that the task does not have to be costly and long-drawn-out. Too, they point out that results—at least on a limited basis—can be quickly realized. These points are so because it is possible—and often even preferable—to get into DSS in a toe-wetting prototype approach.

A man highly experienced in setting up DSS programs in manufacturing companies is Adam Crescenzi, a vice president of Index Systems. He notes that "very properly" the attitude of line managers he approaches on DSS is "show me first before I believe it."

In two recent DSS programs set up with his help in manufacturing operations, the first step was to build a prototype of a system.

"Prototype," he explains, "means something we can do rather quickly—

The Decision Support System Cycle

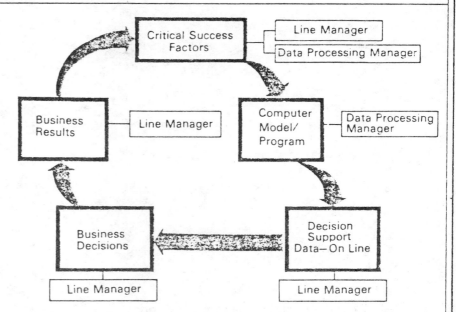

1. Line Manager and Data Process Manager (or other information specialist) confer. Data manager questions line executive in depth to assist that executive in pinpointing goals most critical to success of Line Manager's job. Also pinpointed, is the information support needed by the Line Manager to help attain these goals. (Typically, at start of a DSS program, a limited number of goals and data are sought).

2. The Data Process Manager compiles needed information data and sets up a computer model or program for on-line access to that information by the Line Manager.

3. The Line Manager draws on the on-line computer model/program for decision support information as he requires it.

4. The Line Manager blends the decision support information now provided him with his judgment and intuition to make decisions relating to the critical success factors of his job.

5. Results of Line Manager's decisions are usually improved when he uses a soundly-conceived Decision Support System. The system, typically, evolves into a larger, more comprehensive management tool as feedback from results of past decisions is evaluated.

The system is flexible: inputs are expanded or changed as critical success factors of Line Manager's job change.

Note: This is a highly simplified illustration of DSS and does not purport to include all the steps and procedures involved in developing a sound DSS program—ranging from setting of priorities to measurement of program costs and benefits.

---

the outcome of the total DSS implementation, the fact is that the interview process is almost always a valuable experience for the parties involved."

Mr. Thompson adds that a knowledge of the three basic kinds of decisions that managers face can be helpful to those involved in DSS. (See box on basic kinds of decisions.)

Notably then, the DSS process starts with—and centers on—the line manager. In DSS, the manager is king, information technology is his silent servant. This is unlike the case in MIS where in-place technology—hardware and software—governs what is fed back to line managers.

A somewhat typical case might illustrate the DSS process.

The interview (line manager and data processing specialist) uncovers, that in the judgment of a line manager, pricing is a critical success factor. After agreement on the most pertinent data needed in making decisions on pricing, the data processing manager might then build a price-change program or model. This program/model might well be based on past company price changes, their magnitude and so on, and include data on company sales, production and inventories following previous company price changes. Also included, might be data on competitors' prices following past company price changes.

This is, of course, a simplified DSS illustration. But DSS is not a greatly complicated technique. And it is flexible and evolves easily and naturally.

It is getting easier than ever for companies to get started on DSS. One reason is because of a fast-growing, commercially-available information service termed, End User Programming.

A number of vendors have produced systems that allow users to create a data base, generate information and process information from that data into a computer terminal in what Mr. Thomson calls, "a very flexible and user-friendly way. You don't have to be a programmer to use it."

He also terms development of these program packages as "new and exciting." They have been available in most cases for less than a year.

What is strikingly new, according to the consultant, is the rapid acceptance of these software kits. But he points out that these kits are not DSS. They are only tools to help a user to build a DSS program.

It is easy to see that the technologies and procedures of DSS could readily be expanded to cover aspects of management beyond decision-making. In fact, the original idea of those who pioneered DSS was a full management support system—MSS.

Says Mr. Thompson, "When we ask what are the critical things that a manager needs support on, and what can we do to supply that support, that's management support, not just decision support." He sees DSS as "clearly, a sub-set of MSS.

"It depends on what a manager's job is, and what he needs for support," sums up Mr. Thompson.

So, start looking beyond DSS to MSS. That latter may be the ultimate blending of a manager's judgment and intuition and the power of the computer.

But still, push-button management is a long way off. Today, nobody is saying that DSS or MSS looks anything like a magic push-button. But those things can be a big help to managers. □

LEARNING OBJECTIVES:

. Be able to understand some of the most critical factors involved in establishing of a CBMIS.

. Be able to understand the significant difference between data and information.

. Be able to understand some of the issues related to security of CBMIS.

. Be able to establish a conceptual model for the development of CBMIS.

. Be able to understand the human issues involved in CBMIS development and utilization.

. Be able to establish a clear picture of costs and benefits of CBMIS development.

INTRODUCTION

The six articles included in this part relate to major considerations involved in establishing a CBMIS and each article addresses a significant dimension. Before the actual development and implementation of a CBMIS, these issues must be clearly identified and carefully analyzed.

One significant issue, which is important to both the user and especially to the designer of CBMIS, is the difference between data and information. This issue covers a broad range of considerations regarding such items as organizational policies related to data collection and utilization, and formal and informal information systems within the organization.

Every organization develops and operates an information system whereby data are processed and converted into information which, in turn, is used to satisfy specific requirements of users. The amount of data processed and information generated has grown significantly, in fact, during the past thirty plus years we have witnessed an explosion in both data acquisition, processing, and information generating capability within organizations. Increased movement in these activities generally parallels growth of the organization. Within the firm, organizational policies relating to meeting consumer demand for quality products while at the same time facing increased competitive pressures from both domestic and international sources, places significant pressure on the firm for quality information. Technological changes, which affect the design of goods and services and how they are to be produced, also add to the need for information. Along with the internal needs of the organization, external factors also exert pressure on the organization for more quality data and information. These pressures relate to a number of factors. For example, numerous changes in the legal environment of the organization impose increasing demands for information relating to taxation, energy, safety, etc. In essence, these factors add to the complexity of the managerial function for planning and control and, in turn, require more information for the decision-making function.

Other organizational considerations in the conceptual development of a CBMIS relate to the relative size of the organization, the purpose for which the entity was organized, the style of management supported by the organization, and the internal structure of the organization in terms of organizational design. For example, in regard to the size of the organization, as the organization grows, the information requirements change from a basically informal to a more formal structure. Also with growth, the information systems tend to develop along functional lines. Management style, in terms of the planning and controlling function, will impose specific requirements on the system.

The concept of organizational structure and needs for information within the structure may be in conflict. That is, current technology allows extremely large data bases to be developed and utilized at all levels of management for information generation. However, as one proceeds from the operational level to the strategic level, the information requirements become less detailed in nature. Hence, there is a filtering process involved as information is generated for higher levels of management. Given the information requirements at the various levels and the ability of users to handle that quantity of data in a particular mode of presentation, one may ask if too much data are being collected relative to the information that is generated. For example, if one uses the 80/20 rule which states that twenty percent of the data collected and processed can generate eighty percent of the information required, the cost of excess data becomes apparent.

Data processing and information functions within the firm are support functions to help the organization attain its goals and objectives. Hence, in designing an information system, we need to make the information generated compatible with the organizational goals and objectives and be aware of human limitations in terms of how information is processed. Behavioral facets of the system are as important as the technical components in the development process. Those involved in the development process must recognize that users are information processors interacting with an organization, and as such, the CBMIS design must recognize this fact. Decision making in most organizations involves interaction among persons in a dynamic setting. Decision makers are also affected by the availability, amount, and usefulness of the

19

information in setting a strategy for problem solving in the complex environment of an organizational setting. The form in which the information is presented and the experience of the decision maker will also affect the strategy developed.

Another important factor which must be considered in CBMIS development is the security issue. This may include physical security, environmental security, and overall hardware and software security. The designer of CBMIS should consider a variety of factors related to this matter. Data sabotage, unintended disclosure, and hardware/software failures have created significant problems for many organizations. A sophisticated CBMIS design must provide some safeguard for each factor.

The increase in quantity of both data accumulated and information produced by the firm and the increasing use of micro-mainframe links, brings about an increased demand for security of both data and information. A computer based information system is particularly vulnerable to breaches in security and the organization must assess the risk inherent in their system and take steps to minimize the incidence of data and information theft from both internal and external sources.

Another important issue in CBMIS development is planning and control. The planning and development of a CBMIS requires the involvement of top management at the inception. Traditionally, this has not been the case. All too often, the information system department was not included in strategic planning. However, today more and more firms are realizing the value of information as a resource and that the information function is as much an integral part of the organization as accounting, marketing, finance, etc. In the past, planning in the information systems area revolved around hardware and software acquisition and failed to include all facets of the function including communications. Strategic planning for a CBMIS must take into account efficient resource utilization, coordination of future developments, better integration of functional areas, and a criteria for evaluating the information system. Along with strategic planning, control mechanisms must be developed as they relate to the many facets of a CBMIS. That is, control mechanisms with regard to the relationship between hardware, software, personnel, procedures, and standards for evaluating these entities in terms of performance in generating quality information for management.

To cope with the growing technology, organization should establish an EDP plan. The EDP plan should include both short and long term objectives regarding computer utilization within the organization. An effective EDP plan should also clearly express the philosophy of the EDP organization. The relationship between the EDP department and organizational goals and objectives should be well delineated and control mechanisms established. The control mechanisms could include a series of predefined standards. That is, they may include computer operating standards, documentation standards, project control standards, and systems development standards. Although there are pros and cons regarding the utilization of standards, we believe that the positive aspects of standards outweigh the negative aspects.

In developing an information system, the mode of presenting the information has gained an importance. Computer technology has advanced to the level whereby graphic displays, as opposed to tabular and written documents, are providing a greater latitude for human understanding of the information presented. Advances in this area, coupled with affordable prices, now bring application graphics to a number of functional areas including manufacturing where computer aided design and manufacturing (CAD and CAM) are now becoming common place. Management has also benefited in terms of learning and information utilization based on graphic analysis and presentation. Given the limitations on human information processing, computer graphics will increase in significance in terms of support within the organization's information system.

Once a decision is made to establish a CBMIS, the actual development of a conceptual system starts with the identification of organizational goals and objectives. From this base a system which will provide managers with the relevant, timely, and accurate information which they need for decision making regarding planning and control requirements, can be developed. The system must relate information to the purpose for which it is to be used. That is, to identify the purpose in terms of generating reports, monitoring performance, forecasting, long and short-term planning, etc. The identification of needs will also provide a framework for the development of a database. The determination of data requirements provides a basis for identification of alternatives regarding the time and cost of building a database. Since the system is to be used by managers, their direct involvement in the development of the conceptual system is deemed highly important. Without their involvement, the system may not be responsive to their needs and, thus, have very little utility.

To develop a successful CBMIS, a close cooperation among users, top management, and DP specialists is absolutely needed. The cooperation among these different individuals is generally accomplished by establishment of a task force. A CBMIS which has been designed in this fashion has a great chance for success. Users should be involved in all phases of systems analysis and design. The CBMIS must be responsive to different needs and styles of different users.

The final consideration before the actual implementation of a CBMIS involves a careful cost/benefit analysis. Development of a CBMIS involves a variety of cost factors. These costs should be offset by the benefits generated by the CBMIS. Although most of benefits do not have monetary value, the designer should be able to approximate the net value of the CBMIS.

DISCUSSION QUESTIONS

1. How do you differentiate data versus information?

2. What is an informal information system?

3. Is a CBMIS formal or informal system?

4. What is computer system security?

5. What is data sabotage?

6. How do you protect deliberate penetration in CBMIS?

7. How do you define planning in EDP environment?

8. What should be included in EDP plan?

9. What are some of the advantages and disadvantages of standards in CBMIS?

10. What is the difference between managerial approach and technical approach in CBMIS development?

11. How do you differentiate between the computer specialists and the computer users?

12. How do you integrate CBMIS design methodologies with behavioral issues?

13. Users may react negatively to the new CBMIS. How do you reduce these negative reactions?

14. What is cost/benefit analysis in CBMIS design?

15. How do you quantify intangible costs and benefits of a new CBMIS?

Human Information Processing Limitations and the Systems Manager

BY WILLIAM J. CORNEY

WILLIAM J. CORNEY

William J. Corney is an Associate Professor of Management Information Systems at the University of Nevada in Las Vegas. He is a former practicing electronic engineer and is the author of over 30 articles.

■ The systems manager is faced with a formidable task. Not only is he responsible for a system with the capability to efficiently produce the desired results, but he must also insure that it is accepted and properly used by the organization's personnel. The term "user friendly" is often used to signify a system that has been designed with the user in mind, encouraging its effective application. A full understanding of this term requires a knowledge of the user's cognitive information processes and the inherent limitations that exist during processing. Only with this knowledge can plans be developed for a system that will truly reflect the needs and information processing capabilities of the user.

Human Information Processing Model

When information is presented to an individual, a distinct process for information handling takes place. Figure 1 provides a model of this process.

When information is made available, it cannot be used unless the individual is receptive to the stimulus. It is necessary to be attentive or "tuned in" if the information is to be assimilated. Further, information that is received must be recognized if it is to be useful to the receiver. This is accomplished by comparing the stimulus with information previously stored in long and short term memory. The stimulus is perceived both as a whole entity (gestalt) and in terms of its individual features. Once the stimulus has been identified, it is held in short term memory. This memory has a limited capacity and can store information for only a few seconds. If proper conditions exist (to be discussed later), the information can be committed to long term memory.

Both short term and long term memories offer

Figure 1. Information Processing Model

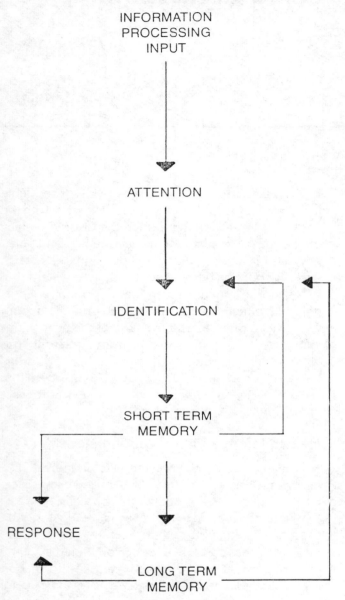

INFORMATION
PROCESSING
INPUT

ATTENTION

IDENTIFICATION

SHORT TERM
MEMORY

RESPONSE

LONG TERM
MEMORY

more than a simple means for holding information. Complex mental structures appear to exist which allow for search and retrieval within the memory mechanisms. It is extremely important to understand that user reactions to computer based information systems can be suboptimal because of inherent limitations in the way humans process the information input to them.

The problems that users have with information can be classified into three major areas; (1) quantity of information, (2) mode of presentation, and (3) timing of information.

Quantity of Information

Capacity

Users of information have a severe capacity restriction for retention in short term memory. Research has shown that the average number of symbols that humans can store is somewhere between five and nine.[1] If more than this number is presented at one time, an overload condition may develop, resulting in a possible degradation in decision making ability.

Knowledge of this limitation is of extreme importance in planning for the design of real time systems. Visual displays of information, from which immediate decisions must be made (e.g., military applications, air traffic systems, medical information systems, communication systems) are extremely vulnerable to problems resulting from this limitation. Many of these real time systems also involve user fatigue which may further lower the user's ability to "absorb" the information presented.

24

The system must insure that the information presented does not exceed the capacity of short term memory. Fortunately, the previously stated symbolic limit of between five and nine exist with respect to psychological units and not simply individual characters of information. The entire word OXYGEN, for example, represents only one symbol, since it is perceived as a whole and not simply a stream of individual characters.

Sample Sizes

If the information presented to a user of a management information system is based on a sample, misinterpretation of the information often results. Research has found that people place much more faith in small samples than they should, and tend to reach unwarranted conclusions from the data presented.[2] The sports world provides numerous examples of this psychological limitation. Many people falsely believe that one game (e.g., Superbowl) or even seven games (e.g., World Series) actually indicates which team is "best". Statisticians know that such small samples cannot provide reliable ranking information. Considerably larger samples of information (i.e., more games) would be necessary to yield good estimates of which team is actually "number 1", "number 2", etc. While this limitation can be accepted in spectator sports games as being of little real consequence, management information systems that have serious applications may be less forgiving. Important decisions may be incorrectly made based on data from just a few cases or time periods.

For small samples as these, the tentativeness of the data must be presented to the user along with the data itself. The best way to accomplish this is through the use of statistical confidence intervals, which indicate the degree of faith that the user should have in the estimated information provided by the sample. If intervals cannot be presented, at minimum the size of the sample should be clearly identified for the decision-maker. If, for example, an average sales figure is presented, the number of periods which were used to create the average should also be presented (e.g., "this average is based on two months data").

Unused Information

The perceived value of unused information is still another concern. Just as many people save old magazines that are never looked at again, many decision makers feel the need to enter and store vast quantities of data that have a low probability of future use. This can be especially distressing for on-line applicatons, where the user wants to have everything on disk storage for immediate possible retrieval. This desire tends to be a psychological one rather than one based on economic factors. The system plan should incorporate low cost storage (e.g., microfilm, tape, paper) or reconstruction procedures as alternatives for satisfying the end user while reducing the burden of high design and storage costs for infrequently used information.

Mode of Presentation

The mode or manner in which information is presented can have a profound influence on how it will be perceived and processed. A number of different limitations exist.

Confusion

In order for information to be used it must capture the attention of the recipient and be properly identified (Figure 1). The way in which information is presented can enhance or degrade these processes.

If information does not attract the attention of the user, it will not be processed further by him. This does not usually present a problem, as the user typically seeks out the system information or at minimum is ready to receive it. Attention is already fixed and the information can be identified and used. However, in those situations where vast amounts of data are generated by a system and truly important information occurs infrequently, it becomes necessary to take positive action to attract the user's attention when the important information is presented. This can be accomplished through the use of flashing characters, oversize characters, reverse video, colors, color changes, or sounds.

It has also been found that humans tend to interpret information within the context of that which is already known to them. Accountants, for example, expect to see numbers presented in certain consistent formats. Assets, liabilities, debits, credits, and so forth are expected to be displayed in a manner consistent with certain conventions. Similar situations exist with respect to financial managers, engineers, and others. To avoid confusion, the system must adopt the important conventions of the user, even though they may not represent the most logical or efficient approach from the designer's standpoint.

Not only may the arrangement of the data lead to confusion, but visual and verbal similarities in information may as well. For example, the symbols 3 and 8; F and E; O, C and G, may be confused. Also, because most people repeat symbols they see as silent sounds in their minds, it is possible for confusion to result from 3, and T; M and N, and others. In these cases, the system must, where possible, take care that situations involving symbols that can be easily confused do not occur. This can usually be done through changes in output formating or through the use of word and numeric substitutions. The use of graphs or pictorial representations may also help.

Weber's Law

Weber's psychological law of judgment provides another example of how the human information processor can be influenced by the way in which data is presented.[3] According to this law, the human information processor makes judgments concerning differences in a special way. In psychological terminology, the difference that is noticeable is a constant proportion of the stimulus. Mathematically, this can be represented as:

$$\frac{\Delta C}{C} = K \text{ For All C}$$

For example, if $1/5$ pound is a sufficient difference to distinguish between two ten pound weights, then $(1/5)/10 = 1/50$. Then, for a 20 pound weight, the noticeable difference would be, $x/20 = 1/50$; or

$x = 2/5$. In a management information system setting, this means the user considers numeric differences to be significant when judged by their size relative to the base rather than the absolute amount. For example, a $5,000 variation in a budgeted sales expense of $100,000 has the same significance in terms of noticeable difference as a $500 variation in a $10,000 budgeted sales expense (both are 5%). This behavioral mode of processing information can lead to a devaluing of absolute amounts when large numbers are developed in a management information system. Both governmental and large corporate systems are susceptible to this problem. A ten million dollar shortage may hardly be noticed as it may not seem as significant when reported as a 3 percent shortage, or when the amount is displayed adjacent to the much larger base value. If the significance of the absolute amount of a variation or difference is to have its full impact, it is necessary to provide it as a full numeric value (not a percentage of another number) and apart from the base value. All significant differences in absolute terms should be highlighted by the system.

Representatives

The human information processor often improperly attributes characteristics of an entity based on evidence received in a limited setting. This often leads to highly biased representations of true characteristics. For example,

"Bank presidents are usually surprised when the black suited bank teller absconds with the funds and is found living it up in Tahiti. To the extent that role and situational factors produce behavior that can be labeled as conforming, hostile, thrifty, brave, clean, or reverent, observers are likely to see the individual as being a conforming, hostile, thrifty, brave, clean or reverent person."[4]

The representativeness bias is a major concern for systems that have data bases that are used for management decision making purposes. It is essential that the scope of the information in the data base be encompassing enough to yield information that will properly support the actual decisions to be made. For example, if a system is being designed to support the decision process involved with matching stock and bond purchases to individual clients, the system must store information that includes all major attributes of the securities (e.g., price, volume, relative strength, dividends, safety, etc.) and also the important client attributes (e.g., income, net worth, years to retirement, etc.). The total volume of storage in terms of bytes is not the issue, the important factor is the breadth of attributes (scope) that are made part of the system.

Summarization

Information can be presented in summarized form (e.g., totals, averages, ranges, indexes) or as raw data. In many systems there is no choice but to provide summarized information, owing to the volume of data stored and/or requirements of the user. Unfortunately, summarized data can cause problems of interpretation. It has already been mentioned how unwarranted conclusions can result from small samples that have results given in summarized form. Beyond this, there are other problems that relate to summarized information. Research has found that individuals having an analytic cognitive style (i.e., are quantitative in their approach to decision making) prefer to look at raw data so they can reach their own conclusions through data manipulation, while those with a broad style are more interested in summary measures than in the raw quantitative data itself.[5] If analytic individuals are included in users of the system (engineers, technicians, etc.) the system should be designed to provide a means for allowing the user to easily obtain the data from which any summary measures were generated. This will allow users the option of making their own analysis, thereby increasing their confidence and satisfaction in the system. The raw data can be presented along with the summary measures, or if this is not feasible owing to data volume, the user can be provided with a programmed option of whether or not to have the raw data output by the system.

Timing of Information

Not only is the interpretation of information dependent upon what is presented and how it is presented, but also on *when* the presentation is made.

Periodic Information

A management information system can provide information on a periodic basis (e.g., daily, weekly or quarterly reports) or on a basis other than periodic. Although periodic reports are extremely common, the very fact that they are periodic can lead to suboptimal usage.

There is a basic psychological principle that states that if rewards are given out periodically, they rather quickly lose their power to motivate. If a child receives a $10.00 gift from his or her grandmother on the first of each month, it will soon become an expectation on the childs part, and its power to surprise and make the child appreciate the gift will diminish. A random schedule of rewards, however, can create a greater level of attention. Weekly system reports, for example, can soon become expected and routine to the point where they may not be read. Reports generated only when major changes occur or on some other non-periodic basis, will attract far more attention and may be used to a greater extent, while reducing overall system costs. The system plan should differentiate between which reports actually required on a periodic basis and those which are not. All those not essential for periodic output should be placed on a non-periodic schedule.

Availability

Beliefs concerning the occurrence of an event are often distorted by the recent occurrence of a similar event. In psychology this is known in more general terms as the Availability bias. This bias occurs because individuals tend to reduce complex judgments to simpler ones. Judgments about the future are made in terms of the ease to which relevant instances or associations come to mind. Strength of association becomes a surrogate for the judgment of past frequency. In some cases this approach works well since events that happen frequently are often easier to imagine than infrequent ones and events that happen infrequently may be more difficult to recall than those that happen often. Major errors occur, however, when factors that are unrelated to the frequency of occurrences affect the ease of recalling similar instances.

A study by Tversky and Kahneman[6] indicates how such errors might occur. Subjects were required to judge whether the letter K was more likely to appear as the first letter of an English word or as the third letter. Despite the fact that K is three times as likely to appear as the third letter, most subjects judged it more likely to appear as the first. When the subjects made their judgment, they tried to bring to mind words that start with the letter K and words that have K as their third letter. It is easier to think of words that start with K, and this acts as a cue on which the subjective judgments can be made. Words beginning with the letter K were, therefore, thought of as more probably than those having K as the third letter. In general, the easier it is to recall instances of an event, the more probably the event is believed.

A management information system that produces data across time periods runs the risk of promoting this bias, especially if the information produced reflects emotional issues. Recent data reflecting bankruptcies, deaths, injuries, airplane crashes or tornados on the negative side, or windfall profits, prize winners, and cancer cures on the positive side, will tend to make the information receiver feel that future events of the same or similar kind are more likely than they really are. For a management information system that directly supports management decisions, this bias could have deteriorating effects on decision quality. To reduce the chance of this effect taking place, attempts should be made to place data of this type in its proper context, and not present it alone. The form of the context will depend on the situation and may include lengthing the data time frame, increasing the type of cases or instances recorded, and expanding the scope of the data collected.

Associations and Causality

When something happens, it is natural for an individual to wonder why it happened. One major method used to find the cause of an event is to look for something else that happened at the same time, just before it, or in some way associated with the event in question. It is unfortunate that this approach often leads to false conclusions concerning causality. This can be especially troublesome for systems that yield graphical output. System users may see a lovely graph which clearly shows, for example, how profits in the company have risen as the number of employees has increased. Does this mean that, if the company hires more employees, profits will increase even more? The system should insure that association is not encouraged to be confused with causality. This can be done through user education and by means of warning labels (e.g., "causality not implied") on all regression or associative graphical outputs.

Conclusion

Developing an information system that is truly effective is not easy. The many information processing limitations and biases discussed, if not addressed in the planning phase, can cause problems long after the system has implemented. It is unfortunate that the subtleness of the effects of these problems often makes their detection and cure difficult.

Table 1 summarizes the important information processing issues and possible corrective actions.

Table 1
Summary of Information
Processing Issues and Corrective Actions

	Issues	Actions
QUANTITY	Capacity	Present information intended for short term memory in groupings of 5 to 9 units maximum.
QUANTITY	Sample Sizes	Information based on small samples should be accompanied by confidence intervals and/or a statement of data quantity.
QUANTITY	Unused Information	Use low cost storage (microfilm, tape, paper) or develop reconstruction procedures.
MODE	Confusion	Take care in formatting the system output
MODE	Weber's Law	For changes in large values avoid solitary percentages. Highlight all absolute significant differences
MODE	Representativeness	Increase the breadth of attributes that support each decision type
MODE	Summarization	Develop a means to allow for raw data to be presented
TIMING	Periodic	Reports not essential to periodic output should be made non-periodic
TIMING	Availability	Information that may evoke emotional responses should be provided only in a system that also gives context data.
TIMING	Association	Provide information indicating that causality is not implied.

REFERENCES

1. G. A. Miller, "The Magical Number Seven, Plus or Minus Two: Some Limits on our Capacity for Processing Information," *The Psychological Review*, V. 63, n. 2, March 1956, pp. 81-97.

2. A Tversky and D. Kahneman, "Belief in the Law of Small Numbers," *Psychological Bulletin*, v. 76, n. 2, 1971, pp. 105-110.

3. G. E. Davis, *Management Information Systems: Conceptual Foundations, Structure and Development*, New York: McGraw-Hill Book Co., 1974, pp. 70-71.

4. E. Jones and R. Nisbett, "The Actor and the Observer: Divergent Perceptions of the Causes of Behavior," *General Learning Press*, 1971.

5. H. C. Lucas, Jr., *Information Systems Concepts for Management*, New York: McGraw-Hill Book Co., 1982, pp. 20-22.

6. A. Tversky and D. Kahneman, "Availability: A Hueristic for Judging Frequency and Probability," *Cognitive Psychology*, v. 5, 1973, pp. 207-232.

Graphics in Business Information Systems

BY K. VENKATA RAO

■ Mode of presenting information is an important management information system (MIS) design variable. Computer generated tabular outputs still dominate most MIS designs. In sharp contrast to these impersonalistic and formal modes of presentation, there are alternative approaches to more personalistic forms of information presentation, e.g., graphics. Feeling and Intuition types find personalistic modes of presentation more acceptable than information in the form of hard data[9]. It constitutes a vital human-computer interface in the design of MIS. It is as significant as the value attributes of information, such as relevance, timeliness, accuracy, etc., because the value of information depends a great deal on the understandability of information. The format in which information is presented plays a key role in inhibiting or facilitating comprehension.

Studies on Information Presentation

Several studies on the alternative forms of information presentation and their effect on decision making have been reported in the MIS literature. Dickson et al studied the effects of printed tabular reports versus CRT displays, and presentation of summarised reports as against detailed reports. They also suggested further experimental studies.[3] Schutz carried out some experimental studies on graphics and notes that line-type graphs produced greater accuracy and speed of performance then vertical bar or horizontal graphs.[12] Another study by Hitt shows that color coded and numerically coded graphics are by far better than several other coding methods.[6] Zmud compared tabular, bar chart and line-type graphical modes of presentation. He found that graphical presentation was preferred over others because they are more relevant, accurate and readable.[15] Benbasat et al found that the use of graphical displays produced cost-effective decisions.[1] Scott Morton et al, in their studies on decision support systems (DSS) note that graphical displays are more useful in problem solving process than tabular reports containing numbers that lack pattern and are difficult to grasp and comprehend.[13] In a descriptive

study, Gerrity notes that graphical display functions have an attraction for the user.[5] Lucas observes that a graphic mode of presentation would result in greater learning or performance than tabular presentations. He, however, suggests that further studies are required for a better understanding of the graphical forms of presentation.[8] A recent experimental study by Watson et al focused on the effectiveness of presenting three dimensional graphics on recall abilities. The study concludes that the use of three dimensional graphics did not result in any superior recall abilities on the part of subjects as compared to the use of tabular forms of presentation.[14]

Computer Graphics

The last five years witnessed significant advances in computer graphics technology. and both graphics hardware and software are now available at affordable prices. Applications of computer graphics can be classified into three broad areas:

(a) Computer Aided Design (CAD) and Computer Aided Manufacturing (CAM)
(b) Computer art — stills, animation etc.
(c) Management — analysis and presentation

The application of graphics in business is generally known as Business Graphics. Some view business graphics as a branch of computer graphics. There seems to be no clear definition of business graphics. It means different things to different people; the only common factor seems to be the application of computer graphics in businesses. According to this view, it includes every conceivable use of computer graphics technology in business — CAD/CAM applications, artistic productions, video games, slide preparation and so on. Lehman refers to business graphics as the use of graphics by managers in an organization.[7] According to this interpretation, CAD/CAM, commercial art and similar applications of graphics are excluded. Business graphics, then, is the graphics support to management in two major fields — presentation and analysis. Presentation is a form of communication, and analysis is the basis for decision making. Both comrhunication and decision making are the two vital functions performed by management in organizations.

People in business have been using graphics in many ways. Graphics are used in (i) management reports to indicate trends and patterns, (ii) making presentations at seminars or meetings, (iii) showing actual *versus* planned performance, and (iv) analysis, planning and scheduling. The types of graphics used in business are text, time series charts, bar and pie charts, scatter diagrams, maps and layout charts, hierarchy charts and sequence charts.

Although computer graphics mostly produce the same type of graphics as in manual systems, there is no comparison between the two in terms of speed and cost. These two factors have significant implications from a management standpoint. Not only the management charts displayed can be up-to-date, but they (computer graphics) also permit that different formats, scales, colors etc., can be tested out economically to see which format gives the best comprehension of the information for a particular chart. The high speed and low cost of generating computer graphics allows the management to explore alternate scenarios by seeking answers to a variety of feasible 'what if' questions. New charts can be quickly generated and displayed.[2]

Graphics Support for Presentation and Communication

Presentation, as mentioned earlier, is a form of communication. Graphics for presentation demands more formatting flexibility when information is communicated at business meetings or seminars in the form of instructional visual aid. Graphics software for presentation should have a wide range of formatting capabilities — more creative color combination, variety etc. These software packages must be designed with the objective of helping users to quickly perceive and contribute effectively in the discussions. Presentation of information in an attractive and colorful and effective form is currently the most commonly associated function of business graphics. This represents the automation of previous manual systems, namely art production and slide preparation. Computer graphics software is fairly developed and supports this area of communication. Chart Master, Super Chartman II, Superchart, APPLE Business Graphics, Business Graphics System and several other software packages belong to the category of computer graphics for presentation.[10]

Another area of communication which can be supported by computer graphics is in organizing the activities of large complex projects. Gantt charts and Network charts are the popular management tools. These tools, no doubt, use graphical displays which are, in some cases, automated. As the project progresses and as new data becomes available, the network charts need frequent updating to reflect current status of the project. PERT/CPM computer software packages generate a wide variety of reports on schedule and cost performance for use by managers at different levels. Graphics support in this area is beginning to emerge and seems to hold promise as a vital aid in project management[7].

A third area of graphics support to communication is in group decision making. Group decisions are usually made at meetings, and many of the activities usually carried out at these meetings can be transacted more economically and with fewer scheduling problems *via* computer conferences. The support of graphics facilities to these computer conferences would enhance the usefulness of these 'electronic meetings'. The problems involved in providing graphics support to these electronic meetings cannot be underestimated. Each of the members, located at different places geographically, must not only have compatible graphics hardware and software, but must also be connected *via* a suitable network.[2]

Graphics Support for Analysis and Decision Making

Graphics support for analysis is for the managers or their staff assistants. Analytical graphics packages used by those performing analysis are screen oriented and designed for speed and data management. Usually, analytical graphics software packages do not offer the wide formatting flexibility as in presentation graphics. Analytical software packages like LOTUS 1-2-3, IFPS/Personal, Context's MBA offer pie charts, bar charts, histograms etc., purely for the purpose of analysis, rather than the razzle-dazzle colorful presentations.[10] Although the graphics provided by many analytical graphics packages are crisp and attractive, they are no match to the capabilities of presentation graphics software packages.

Graphics software for decision-making depends on what aspect of human information processing system is supported or automated by a decision aid. There are three aspects in human information processing — short-term memory, long-term memory and processing.

K. VENKATA RAO

Mr. Rao is a senior lecturer in the School of Accountancy and Business Administration at the University of Singapore. Prior to joining the University in January 1976, Mr. Rao was at the Administrative Staff College of India, Hyderabad, where he held positions as Management and Computer Consultant. He is the author of two books—Introduction to Quantitative Techniques & Data Processing (Publishers: S. Chand & Co., New Delhi, 1975) and Introduction to Business Information Systems: Analysis & Design (Publishers: Times Books International, Singapore, 1979). Mr. Rao has published over twenty five papers in professional journals.

Short-term Memory: Short-term memory serves as a 'temporary storage facility' and its limited capacity, usually about seven chunks, is a major bottleneck in any human information processing activity. However, short-term memory can be enhanced in three ways. One way is to expand the short-term memory capacity by providing external memory. A computerized version, modeled on the use of scratch pads in manual systems, represents multiple screens or windows, and these facilities are now offered by many graphics software packages. A second way is to improve the method of fitting information into existing capacity. This is accomplished by a process called chunking (fitting more chunks or elements of data). Instead of individual elements or chunks of information, the entire presentation is considered as one chunk. Standard graphs and multidimensional displays represent the graphics version of chunking. Standard graphs and multidimensional displays represent the graphics version of chunking. Standard graphs include line charts, bar charts, pie charts, spatial charts and block charts. Most graphics packages offer the first three forms of standard graphs. Spatial charts are diagrams or maps and only few graphics packages (GADD) offer this facility. Graphics support in the form of multidimensional display is required when managers have to solve problems that involve multidimensional data. Multidimensional display techniques include Chernoff faces, Snowflakes, Metroglyphs, Multiple line graphs, Multiple bars, Subdivided bars and so on. These are the graphics substitutes for the statistical methods, factor and cluster analysis. And finally, the limited capacity of short-term memory can be overcome by better structuring and utilization of its limited capacity. This can be achieved by providing status indicators, display alternatives or reserved locations[7].

Long-term Memory: Long-term memory enhancement consists of extending, structuring and transferring of information. The extension of long-term memory facilitates the use of external sources of knowledge such as on-line reference materials. The structuring of long-term memory allows easy access to the contents of memory required for a given problem. Graphical support for better structuring of long-term memory takes the form of planning decision trees and prototype trees. Information stores in long-term memory needs to be transferred to other parts of the information processing system to enable the utilization of such information. Currently graphics does not support the integration of information and data base retrieval. This is an area which is currently engaging the attention of researchers in computer graphics.

Processing: Processing involves the generation and evaluation of hypothesis. It can be generated by syntactic decomposition which consists of generating novel configurations of possbilities, matching patterns between the current situation and established prototypes. Evaluation of the hypothesis can be supported by automating the computational algorithm based on the application of management science or statistical techniques. Graphics support to statistics is available with most statistical packages (SOSS, SAS etc.), while graphics support to management science techniques is slowly emergeing.

Graphics Hardware and Software

Hardware for graphics consists of both input and output devices. Graphics input devices include keyboard, game paddle, joystick, mouse, digitizer (also referred as graphics tablet) and light pen. Digitizer allows tracing or drawing a picture on the surface of the tablet and the corresponding lines are displayed on the monitor. Most digitizers support only two dimensional displays. Light pens, connected to the computer by a thin cable, are used to indicate locations on the display screen. It contains a sensor that measures the intensity of the electron beam shot from the rear of the monitor toward the screen. Graphics output devices can be divided into two categories — display devices and equipments like printers, plotters and film recorders. The last three are used to produce copies on paper, plastic or 35mm film respectively. CRT (cathode ray tube) is still the dominant display device; flat panel displays such as LCD (liquid crystal display), AC plasma and others are becoming popular. The quality of display device is termed 'resolution' which means sharpness. The quality or resolution is expressed in terms of picture elements (called pixels). For hard copies of these high resolution graphics images, printers and plotters are used. Plotters are now available at reasonable prices and there are three types of plotters — flat bed plotter, drum plotter and a roller bed plotter. There are numerous varieties of printers. The output device for recording on a 35mm film or video tape consists of a camera and an interface.

Business graphics software packages offer the tools to transform a wide variety of numerical statistics into multicoloured charts and graphs. These can be applied to a wide range of business applications such as market analyses, business forecasts, comparison of trends or stock prices, business planning etc. For example, the general-purpose Business Graphics Software generates three types of graphs — line charts, bar graphs, and pie charts with several variations. Bar graphs can be positioned vertically or horizontally, pie charts can be produced as whole or partial pies, and line charts with solid, dashed or dotted lines. The individual charts can also be merged to form complex graphics conveying information on a variety of related statistics.[4]

Graphics Standards

The link between application program and the graphics software is called interface and the need for developing standard interface is gaining acceptance. A programmer level interface between the application programs and graphics software was developed in 1970s in West Germany as the Graphics Kernel System (GKS), which is emerging as a standard interface. The Virtual Device Interface (VDI) is another standard that interfaces graphics utilities to the software that controls the operation of device drivers. Another standard, endorsed by AT&T for the transmission of text and graphics over tele-communication lines is known as NAPLPS (North Atlantic Presentation Level Protocol Syntax). These three standards are complementary interfaces, and these have particular significance to software writers who wish to develop graphics software programs that can be run on various systems.[11] Standard programmer level interface such as GKS provides source-code portability and logical interface that allow application programs to control the flow of graphics data between devices such as raster-scan displays, plotters etc. VDI provides object-code portability allowing a multitude of computers to run the same graphics program.

Conclusion

Business graphics has a significant role to play in providing support to management in businesses. This support can broadly be divided into two categories — communication and decision-making. Computer graphics software packages for presentation and analysis are designed to serve these two areas. There are other aspects of management communication and decision making which need graphics support.

Advances in business graphics hardware and software and their availability at reasonable prices on most microcomputer systems has opened up immense possibilities for a wide range of business applications. However, the potential buyers of business graphics packages for management support must carefully scrutinize the various features offered by a package in order to match with the management functions that need graphics support. Business graphics software should be application driven rather than technology driven.

References

1. Benbasat J, and Schroeder R, "An Experimental Investigation of Some MIS Design Variables", *MIS Quarterly*, Vol. 1 No. 1, March 1977, pp. 37-49.

2. Canning R.G., "Computer Graphics for Business' *EDP Analyzer* Vol. 20 No. 2, February 1982, pp. 1-12.

3. Dickson G., Chervany N., and Senn J., "Research in MIS: The Minnesota Experiments", *Management Science*, Vol. 28 No. 9, 1977, pp. 913-923.

4. Edward J., "Graphics Punch for Low Cost Computers", *Popular Computing*, November 1983.

5. Gerrity T.P., "Design of Man-Machine Decision Systems: An Application to Portfolio Management", *Sloan Management Review*, Vol. 12 No. 2, Winter 1971, pp. 59-75.

6. Hitt W.D., "An Evaluation of Five Different Abstract Coding Methods", *Human Factors*, Vol. 3 No. 2, July 1961, pp. 120-130.

7. Lehman J.A., "Computer Graphics for Management", MISRC Working Paper WP-83-05, MIS Research Center, Univ. of Minnesota, Minneapolis, 1983.

8. Lucas H.C., "An Experimental Investigation of the Use of Computer-based Graphics in Decision making", *Management Science*, Vol. 27, No. 7, July 1981, pp. 757-768.

9. Mason R. and Mitroff I., "A Program for Research on Management Information Systems", *Management Science*, Vol. 19 No. 5, 1973, pp. 475-487.

10. McClain L, "A Guided Tour of Business Graphics", *Popular Computing*, November 1983.

11. McClain L., "Graphics Standards: Where Do We Stand?", *Popular Computing*, November 1983.

12. Schutz H.G., "An Evaluation of Methods for Presentation of Graphic Multiple Trends", *Human Factors*, Vol. 3 No. 2, July 1961, pp. 108-119.

13. Scott Morton M.S. and Keen P.G.W., *Decision Support Systems: An Organizational Perspective*, Addison-Wesley, Reading Massachusetts, 1978.

14. Watson C.J. and Driver R.W., "The Influence of Graphics on the Recall of Information", *MIS Quarterly*, Vol. 7 No. 1, March 1983, pp. 45-53.

15. Zmud R.W., "An Empirical Investigation of the Dimensionality of the Concept of Information," *Decision Sciences* Vol. 9 No. 2, October 1978, pp. 187-195.

Continuous security control clamps down on abuse

by Joanne A. Collins, Ph.D.

Confidentiality and accuracy should be an essential management control function. Many experts, however, maintain this is not fact today, citing the emphasis on earnings by upper management and the difficulty of cost-justifying security measures for viewing security as a lower priority item.[1]

Nevertheless, you do not have to look far to find examples of abuse. A Dallas consultant became suspicious when he discovered his computer was being used between 11 am and 3 am for several weeks during July and August, 1983. Computer hackers (individuals whose avocation is to crack computer codes) from the Milwaukee area had successfully accessed his computer; a rude awakening.[2]

The consultant has company. Four 13-year-olds from a New York private school cracked a computer network used by numerous corporations, including a soft beverage company, and attempted to divert cases of soft drinks to their address. The thirsty "kidlets" successfully gained access to the confidential files of another company before they were poplessly apprehended.[3]

A utility company's inventory data base was accessed with only a terminal and a few programs. The outsider ordered parts shipped to a preselcted location and instructed the computer not to issue a bill. He then sold the parts.[4]

Employees in the data processing department of a mailorder firm copied the tape files that held the company's most valuable asset: The mailing list. The list was then sold before the thief was discovered. The

---

Confidentiality and accuracy should be essential control functions.

---

fraud went undetected for some time because the computer log was not reviewed on a timely basis.[5]

The periodical literature documents many similar examples. A management control computer security process is designed to control the security problem.

The computer security process

The management accounting process has been thoroughly examined in current literature as generally approximating a dynamic continuous flow:[6]

✓ Goal setting
✓ Planning
✓ Decision making
✓ Budgeting
✓ Implementation
✓ Measurement
✓ Evaluation
✓ Repeat the process.

This process is fueled by external input and internal feedback. In much the same manner, the computer security process can be thought of as a continuous process encompassing the following steps:[7]

(1) Security risk analysis evaluation

(2) Evaluation of all security measures extant

(3) Selection of those measures that maximize at a minimum cost

(4) Implementation of feasible and optimal measures

(5) Evaluation of effectiveness relative to cost

(6) Begin the process again.

This process has been defined in slightly a different manner which the authors term "The Security Management Cycle."[8] It is also a continuous process.

I Planning
  (a) Assign responsibility
    1) Define security policy

2) Assess security risk

II Implementation
  (a) Contingency plans
  (b) Security evaluations
  (c) Define access standards
    1) Security systems implementation
    2) Security administration
    3) Security training.

III Measurement
  (a) Security monitor
  (b) Management reporting

IV Evaluation

V Repetition

Another approach to establishing a management computer security control system is to use a check list. The following list provides a typical example.[9] Check for the existence and adequacy of the following items:

✓ An umbrella security policy

✓ Production and machine security controls

✓ Definition of control inputs, outputs and errors

✓ A quality control unit

✓ Control over program changes

✓ Adequately tested systems

✓ Conversion controls

✓ Administrative separation of responsibilities

✓ Physical computer center controls

✓ Disaster procedures for data, programs and hardware

✓ Adequate insurance

✓ Capable of internal or external audit.

Data base security

Data base and information security are used interchangeably here. The terms used in data base security current literature vary widely. The concern is with protecting corporate information that can be compromised through theft, disclosure to unauthorized individuals, alteration or destruction. This information is stored in a data base.

Elements of the access issue

One common method of protect-ing data is to require identification to gain access to sensitive files of the data base. This usually requires assigning identification numbers or access codes. These are usually numbers, letters or alphanumeric characters. They can be created so that they are unique based on a mathematical function, a special sequence, an attribute or particular knowledge. Passwords or access codes can be assigned to files as well as to users. They may have a time element attached so that access is denied or other action taken (e.g., permanent denial enforced and the

---

Passwords are one of many control techniques.

---

source and time recorded for presentation to the security officer) based on a predetermined time within which the identification must be completed or a maximum number of attempts allowed.[10]

Multilevel identification usually assigns a password or code to identify the user account number and to gain access to a terminal. A second access code allows entry to the operating system and data. Management control considerations include:

1) Password secrecy

2) Frequency of changing codes at fixed or random intervals

3) Policies regarding canceling access permission and readmission due to multiple unsuccessful access attempts

4) Password master vault storage

5) Determination of whether the passwords should be printed on the terminal, partially printed, or not printed at all

6) Length of passwords.

Passwords are one of many control techniques. The main disadvantage is that they can be compromised just as the vault combination can be broken.

When many terminals access a single computer for multiple discreet purposes, the possibility exists that data could be compromised. This issue is the object of the operating system and data base security design. These are technical issues, but it is useful to have a feeling for the broad issues. Security can be the function of both the operating system and the data base system. Operating system models typically delineate to the operating system; those items that must be access controlled (e.g., storage devices, files, memory locations, etc.); commands that request access (e.g., read, list, run, etc.); and a set of rules controlling the two. The problem with relying on the operating system security alone to control access is the complexity required. A data base usually has many more objects to be protected; data life expectancy is longer; the architectural levels require security of a different nature; and those items requiring access control can be complex logical structures. Therefore, data base security is usually the responsibility of the data base management system.[11]

Physical security refers to protecting the area in which the various components of a computer system are located. The subject is characteristically classified into: Natural disaster; accidental damage; or intentional intrusion.

Natural disaster

Natural disasters include fire, flood, earthquake and other catastrophic occurrences. Fire is the most common disaster. It is also particularly troublesome because of the concentration of expensive equipment and that water, used to extinguish fire, can be as damaging. It's the same problem the New York City Fire Department experienced when it extinguished a ship fire by filling it with enough water to sink it. Fire control methods include location, design and maintenance of the computer location, detection and extinguishing mechanisms. Water is delivered to a fire primarily through hose and automatic sprinklers. Chemical delivery is available via hand extinguishers and other delivery mechanisms. Finally, gas is also an extinguishing agent, carbon dioxide and monobromotrifluoromethane (Halon). Computers should not be located in low areas susceptible to flood or water seepage and other natural red flags, such as known fault line areas.[12]

Accidental damage

Accidental damage includes a wide variety of potential threats including blackouts, brownouts, operator error, electrical noise, hardware error, software error and magnetic destruction. Electrical power adequate for conventional electrical equipment can be unacceptable for computer utilization. Computers can be damaged by power irregularities of only a fraction of a second in duration, and unfortunately such disturbances are so common that many computer manufacturers do not warrant damage traced to power line sources. Fluctuating voltage is the most common problem and it can be very difficult to trace its origin. Blackouts account for 5 percent of power line problems. A brownout is a utility's way of handling excessive demands by reducing voltage uniformly, usually from 5 to 15 percent. Most electronic equipment is designed to handle a 10 percent voltage variance. Voltage transients (e.g., spikes and faults)

Programming errors are a common source of damage.

---

are also common causing 20 percent of all line distrubances. The majority of line problems however, are caused by electrical noise, which comes from a variety of sources including the computer itself. Solutions to these problems are line conditioning and secondary power sources.[13]

Improper storage handling, alternating magnetic fields from such devices as transformers, high temperature and humidity can cause errors on magnetic storage devices. Programming errors are probably the most common accidental source of damage. It is not always economically possible to test programs against all possible contingencies. New programs can cause loss of data, the compromise of sensitive data and creation of erroneous data.

Intentional intrusion

Intentional intrusion is becoming more common as more information is stored in a single computer and access sophistication and computer knowledge increases dramatically.[14] Further, large volumns of data are transmitted using wireless technology such as microwave and satellite links. For example, there is a 70 percent probability that a dialed long distance telephone call will not be transmitted entirely by cable. Intentional intrusion is possible by tapping into the "peripheral lobes" of energy which escapes as a message is transmitted for several miles surrounding a transmitter. Focusing eavesdropping devices can tap into this stream of corporate data flying through the air. Also, downlink satellite communications transmit signals over an area thousands of miles that are widely termed a "footprint." The information can be intercepted anywhere in the footprint with proper equipment, so that data sent from California to New York via satellite could be stolen in Florida. Corporate data is more vulnerable than many executives think, available to competitors, dissatisfied employees, researchers, governments and others with the appropriate equipment. Encrypting data is the most effective solution, making the data still available, but useless. Encrypting can be expensive, however.

Another solution is the use of sheilded computer space. They generally are of three types. Magnetic shielding is simply storing magnetic

storage devices in a metal vault or iron mine so that the magnetic memory cannot be damaged. Electronic sweeping is designed to detect signals from bugs. It must be repeated at periodic intervals. Finally, permanent radio frequency shields are available. They usually must be included in original site design; retrofitting is expensive and usually involves taking the computer off-line for several months.[15]

Administrative security

Adequate solutions to computer security require an appropriate mix of the subjects discussed in this review. The nature of the mix depends on the sensitive nature of the data; the potentials of compromise;

Intentional intrusion is becoming more common.

---

attitudes of management; and the available budget. Administrative security is probably the single measure most understood and effective for many corporate data security requirements. Organization of duties and audits are familiar topics.

Job separation should be designed to minimize the possibility of single person reliance. Theft, embezzlement, damage by incompetent employees and loss of expertise should require that more than one employee be involved; the notion of required collusion. The classical organization is to separate employees by duties. This may not be adquate for computer security. In many cases it may be advisable to think in terms of computer function. Some suggestions found in current literature include authorization, recordkeeping and custodial; registration, processing, distribution and utilization; and data files, program library, computer and assets.[18]

IBM has suggested the following program:[19]

1) Define those applications that

could be fraudulently manipulated and the programs that go with them.

2) Review new programs as well as changes to old programs.

3) Establish procedures that eliminate avoiding the review policy.

4) Maintain an audit trail of program changes.

Audit procedures include sampling, surprise audits, comparing equal files, separate programs to audit computations; audit retrieval systems; and running fictitious transactions through the system.

Operating system and hardware security

The operating system is software that controls computer hardware resources as distinct from other software which requests use of resources. It identifies resources such as devices, program entry points and file names as well as the user, and the user's authorization to use specific resources. Thus it has an important security function.

The operating system can identify an authorized user through the logging process in which entry is allowed to those devices, programs and data authorized. It maintains a system log recording starting and ending time; processing status; and identification of system data and software used (threat monitoring).

Modularity segregates the operating system into separate levels.

Thus the operating system is a form of access security controlling entry and use of memory, file requests and programs. Multiple isolation methods are used to separate hardware and software so that many tasks are performed in isolation, thus minimizing security violations.

Some general design concepts used include kernals, supervisors and modularity. The kernal concept attempts to reduce or isolate the very large and complex operating system where verification requires long proofs into smaller representative essentials to the security of the operating system. Even though the entire system is not verified, its essential security is hopefully protected; the key is in defining a kernal of an operating system leveled by supervisors. Modularity segregates the operating system into separate levels or layers, each of which are supervised.

Hardware security deals with protecting information in the main components of a computer: The central processing unit; primary and secondary memory; and peripheral devices. Techniques include using bound registers in which protection attributes are assigned to memory areas via CPU registers; locks and keys where identification numbers are tagged to real memory areas for security; and multiple states in which privileged and nonprivileged users are identified so that they may execute privileged instructions.[16,17]

■

About the author

Dr. Collins is professor of accounting, California State University, Los Angeles, CA.—Ed.

References

1. *Computer Security: What can be done.* Business Week, pp. 126-130, Sept. 26, 1983.
2. *Computer Security: What can be done.* Business Week, p. 126, Sept. 26, 1983.
3. *Halper, S., How to thwart computer criminals.* Nations Business 71:61-2 Aug. 1983.
4. *Ibid.*
5. *Ibid.*
6. *Anthony, Robert N. and Dearden, John. Management Control Systems, pp. 1-20.*
7. *Orceyre, Michel J. and Courtney, Robert H., Jr., Computer Science and Technology: Considerations in the Selection of Security Measures for Automatic Data Processing Systems, p. iii.*
8. *The importance of management input in the development of information systems security.* Management Review, pp. 26-41, Aug. 1983.
9. *Kuong, Javier F., Computer Security, Auditing and Controls, pp. 1-11.*
10. *Fernandez, Eduardo B., Summers, Rita C., and Wood, Christopher. Database Security and Integrity, pp 65-81.*
11. *Hsiao, David K., Kerr, Douglas S., and Madnick, Stuart E. Computer Security, pp. 221-275.*
12. *Ibid, pp. 93-105.*
13. *Kemp, D., Security and Electricity.* DATA MANAGEMENT 20:10-14, March 1982.
14. *Seaman, John. Beware the wireless "datanapper."* Computer Decisions 15:54-8, July 1983.
15. *Kesney, Ed., Shielded DP rooms combat industrial espionage.* DATA MANAGEMENT 19:22+ July 1981.
16. *Walker, Bruce J. and Blake, Ian F., Computer Security and Protection Structures, pp. 35-51.*
17. *Hsiao, David K., Kerr, Douglas S., and Madnick, Stuart E., Computer Security, pp. 165-81.*
18. *Halper, S., How to thwart computer criminals,* Nations Business 71:61-2 Aug. 1983, et al.
19. *Walker, Bruce J. and Blake, Ian F., Computer Security and Protection Structures, p. 33.*

Beware of security risks when implementing micro-mainframe links

by Harris Landgarten

Increasing use of micro-mainframe links creates a greater security risk.

When microcomputers are attached to mainframes, there's a huge potential for confidential data to be available to people on diskette and in various other forms.

A diskette is a wonderful device. You can take 1.2 megabytes on the IBM AT, put it on diskette and carry off a lot of confidential data in your pocket!

All kidding aside, there are many kinds of confidential programs and files.

For example, companies will spend a lot of money on custom spreadsheets for analysis that they wouldn't like their competitors to get. A broker may have customer lists on diskette that his or her current employer doesn't want him to take to his next job. There are custom programs companies develop to analyze competitive situations in making marketing decisions. All of these can be stored on diskettes that "walk away" very easily.

Damage can be inflicted by a number of different forces—disgruntled employees, workers about to leave for another job as well as amateur or professional hackers who break into computers to do damage or to steal money.

A classic security horror story involves one manufacturer who developed software that gave him a substantial edge over the competition. He held a meeting to present the program to the sales staff, and the following day one of the sales people moved—with the software— to the competitor.

Companies concerned about people stealing their software can encrypt disks they purchase so that they only run on machines in the company. And they can do it without having access to source code. Five years ago a disgruntled em-

Damage can be inflicted by a number of forces.

ployee wanting to get even would have been found in a file room at midnight loading files into a briefcase. Today, that same employee slips a disk with the equivalent of a roomful of filing cabinets into a briefcase.

And then there's computer theft of hard cash.

No one accurately knows how much is stolen from financial insti-tutions—not even the banks know the amount of money being taken on a regular basis. Most of it never hits the press. In fact, it never even gets to the police because it's cheaper to cover the $25,000 than to disrupt the public's confidence in automatic teller machines.

Approximately 1 percent of all computer crimes are ever known outside of the small group involved in finding the problems and dealing with them. One of the "big eight" accounting firms did a study noting that the average computer crime is $300,000. In contrast, the average traditional bank robbery nets $3,000; and there are numbers floating around that indicate a high of $5 billion dollars a year in computer crime.

The potential for theft in the data security environment has been around for awhile. However, one of the key problems has been that companies don't really budget for security. They talk about it a great deal and they may have a data security officer, but the data security officer's job traditionally has been to prevent people from getting any data at all.

This can be counterproductive. The idea behind giving people personal computers on their desk has been to allow them to be more productive, and make use of the information they should have access to. Preventing them from accessing this information simply stymies one of the productivity aids that's coming into its own.

Partial solutions

There are solutions to this problem. Some are partial. A few that have been promised are still on the drawing board. And there is one that should work quite nicely. If you're considering the partial solutions or the vaporware, *caveat emptor!*

All of us understand quite well that products don't really happen unless there's a marketplace that's willing to pay for them. In the last few years DP professionals have

---

Many companies don't budget for security.

---

seen a lot of products come out that don't have markets simply because venture capitalists have invested on the strength of an idea, not really understanding where the idea was going to lead.

Companies were formed to develop the idea and produce a product using venture capital. And when the product had no appeal in the marketplace, these venture capital companies went out of business.

The economic climate today is quite different and DP departments of major corporations are thinking long and hard about committing to technology before the products are developed.

Data security is one area where the commitments are coming hard and fast—and for good reasons. The first is a directive from the US Department of the Treasury stating that by 1988 "message authentication" must be used in all funds transfers having to do with the treasury. This mandate involves National Bureau of Standards-type data

encryption, so the Federal Reserve banks in particular are in a flurry to implement encryption technology. As a result, there's money to pay for the technology, and there are many types of interim security products currently being installed in the Federal Reserve System.

Information processing managers should steer clear of the vaporware for obvious reasons, be wary of partial solutions and be aware that long-term solutions exist right now.

Two other reasons for the rapid growth of the data security industry are the Right to Privacy Laws of 1967 and 1976. In essence, these laws require companies to guarantee the security of files containing private information about any individual. People who have this information must take all prudent and proper means to keep it confidential. That would include medical records and records stored in credit bureaus.

The point is, there are economic reasons for people to protect data on diskettes and also protect communications between micros and mainframes.

Federal standards

Information processing managers serious about maintaining data access and security can use the National Bureau of Standards data encryption standard developed by the Federal government. It's a standard intensely reviewed every five years, and it's believed to be secure. If anyone finds a way to break it, that information must be published by Federal law. The NBS standard is a method that companies can use, knowing that if theft occurs, they can ultimately fall back on the explanation that they followed the government standard. The standard has been in effect since 1971 when a congressional mandate ordered security standards be implemented for computers. The National Bureau of Standards said it would take responsibility and sponsored a contest in 1975 to provide an encryption

standard that would be relatively inexpensive and easy to maintain and verify. A number of people submitted proposals but all were rejected. A second contest was held in 1976. IBM submitted its patented data encryption algorithm as a potential standard and agreed to make it free. In 1977 it was accepted and blessed as the standard. Every five years the standard is reviewed, and in 1982 it passed again with flying colors.

And it does work. In a communications environment it allows you to conclusively identify not only the person who's using your normal password but the actual PC or terminal being connected to the mainframe. That's crucial, particularly if you only want a specific computer in a specific location to access the mainframe. Using IBM standard data encryption on mainframes and on PCs allows this to be accomplished.

Historically, there has been quite a bit of argument over security in dialup v. leased line networks. Ironically, because dialup networks are quite flexible, and in many cases, quite economical, many companies have corporate policies forbidding dial-in to mainframes because they fear they will not be able to control it. Interestingly enough, if you use

---

There are economic reasons to protect micro-mainframe links.

IBM standard data encryption on your mainframe and your dial-in terminals or PCs have the ability to interact with these mainframes, then dial-in communications is actually more secure than nonencrypted leased-line communications.

Why? Because you can conclusively identify the machine you're talking to, yet a potential data thief can never identify the switched network that phone call is coming through. Hence, the information couldn't really be accessed without it being destroyed. In the case of an unencrypted leased line, all leased lines go through known points—through telephone company central offices. That's how multidrop is accomplished. It's not inconceivable for someone to get into a telephone central office, trace lease lines, tap into them and simply bleed the data

---

It's necessary to have more than password security.

---

off them. This is especially plausible since those leased lines are going to be in place for a long time, and they're going to known locations.

Dial-in security

Dial-in security products are going to open up dial-in networks, making it quite feasible from a security as well as economic standpoint for companies to implement dial-in.

And it's starting to happen already. As a result of the Right to Privacy Laws, one of the biggest applications is the insurance industry where the big carriers are giving agents and physicians access to the mainframe through remote terminals and PCs.

Because much of this information is confidential and the insurance carriers don't want to be in violation of anyone's rights, they are requiring that data be encrypted. Right now that entails the use of data encrypting modems that cost $2,500 each and have no flexibility for downloading information to PCs for manipulation. With dial-in security, the physician uses the PC already in his or her office to access the mainframe and still meets NBS security standards. Another sensitive area involves the insurance applicant who is required to divulge pesonal information that shouldn't fall into other people's hands.

In addition, under current Right to Privacy Laws in the US, corporations have fiduciary responsibility to protect—with all due diligence—personal data on their employees. A person who suffers damage because personal data is stolen from a company can bring a lawsuit against the company and its individual board members.

What are corporations using to protect their client and personnel data files?

Let's use an IBM example for conformity's sake. In the corporate communications environment where there is multiple access to the mainframe, you'd have PCs or terminals on one end. At the other, you'd have a normal mainframe front-end—a 3704 that is programmed at the communication end of the mainframe and eventually gets down to the application layer. On an IBM mainframe you have an option of doing either a hardware or software program called PCF. The hardware feature basically goes in between the communications front-end and the application, and automatically allows encryption and decryption to happen. That's meant to communicate with a 3274 controller that has an option installed in it called the IBM 3680 feature which directs all terminals connected to the 3270 controller to automatically implement the data encryption standard. In micro-to-mainframe communications, the dial-in product allows a PC to emulate a 3270 terminal that has this 3680 feature in it so it can communicate with an IBM mainframe that has a standard IBM data security feature.

With the same dial-in device you can transparently encrypt and decrypt diskettes and files on a user's PC, allowing the user to have diskettes that can be read *only on his or her machine*. This is particularly useful among large companies that want to give an employee a diskette with important data for use on his or her machine. It is important the disk

be very transparent at that level, but you may not want the information to leave that environment and products like the IBM-compatible hardware/software combination accomplishes that. Used in a standalone environment such as a physician's or lawyer's office, the product achieves the same purpose.

Corporations must protect all personal data.

What are the typical physical characters of the product used in a standalone environment? It is a small five-inch board for IBM AT and XT PCs with some circuitry on it and a data encryption chip, all housed in a metal box, soldered together and filled with epoxy. It's absolutely impossible to get into without destroying the board.

When the board is plugged into a PC, the user enters a key. Even if power is removed, the board remembers the key because of a lithium battery that lasts for 10 years.

If the board is taken out of the PC, the key immediately dissipates. However a user with PCs at work and at home can re-enter the key at home and work with the protected data on both machines.

Armed with communications and data security board in a PC, the user can encrypt hard disk or floppy disk, and talk to the mainframe with the IBM standard encryption feature. ∎

About the author

Landgarten is president, Techland Systems Inc., New York, NY.—Ed.

Authors present a phased approach to applying cost/benefit analysis.

Cost/Benefit Analysis of MIS

BY DR. ROBERT T. KEIM and DR. RALPH JANARO

■ In the early stages of a complex MIS design, the lack of specific requirements, the uncertainty of needed manpower requirements, and the inability to estimate intangibles results in very poor attempts at cost-benefit analysis for information systems. The lack of confidence in these estimates on the part of management has led to suspicion, even outright distrust, of information systems development. This article presents a definition of the design process in such a way as to encourage cost-benefit estimation at each step along the way. This phased approach will result in better estimates, closer user control, and more understanding of the process.

The systems designer is often charged with the task of generating alternative system specifications addressing a spectrum of support levels at the outset of the design process. In the relatively short periods of time allocated for such system specification, if CB analysis is included at all, the result is crude and often inaccurate estimates result.

The problem of developing a cost-benefit analysis methodology to be applied to the design and implementation of information systems must be considered in the context of both the system design activity and the cost-benefit analysis activity. This article will address each context along with a recommendation for a view of cost-benefit analysis, different from the traditional, that can be applied to the design and implementation of information systems.

Cost-Benefit Analysis

The design of an information system to support management has not been adequately addressed with cost-benefit methodology. "Part of the reason may be the considerable confusion that exists as to how cost-benefit analysis is applicable to the MIS. Opinion ranges from that of advocating profit and loss (P&L) evaluations to those that would not attempt any cost-benefit analysis."[1]

A cost-benefit analysis is composed of five principal steps[2]:

(1) *Identification of pertinent measures of effectiveness i.e., benefits.* Selection of alternatives must be based on quantifiable selection criteria. This is necessary to avoid selections based upon inadequate criteria.

(2) *Description of alternatives.* Each alternative system design must be examined in sufficient detail to permit identification of its major characteristics which affect over-all system performance and generate costs. All components of the system which are necessary to perform the desired mission should be included in the analysis.

(3) *Expression of performance and cost as functions of the characteristics of each alternative.* A mathematical model is developed to reflect the major relationships. The model will consist of both cost and performance analysis relationships. The primary cost and performance tradeoffs should be obtainable from the model.

(4) *Estimation of appropriate values for the equation parameters.* Generate dollar estimates to incorporate in the analysis.

(5) *Computation, analysis and presentation of results.* As defined by Hatry, the basis for a cost-benefit analysis is the quantification of a selection criterion for the benefits of the various alternatives. This basic premise is most difficult to address in the proposed information system designs as is the exact description of each alternative.

Unlike a weapon system or a public works project, e.g., a flood protection dam, all major characteristics of an information system cannot be specified in sufficient detail until the actual design is under way. Otherwise, it would mean that all possible alternative information system designs would be completely specified before a decision could be made with respect to the alternative with the most desirable cost-to-benefit ratio.

Any attempt at developing appropriate evaluative criteria for the selection of an information system design requires a redefinition of the traditional cost-benefit model. This redefinition will include the specific characteristics of information systems design which by the nature of its complexity defy detailed specifications at the proposal stage.

Information Systems Definition and Design

According to Tomeski[3], management information systems are "planned and organized approaches to supplying executives with intelligence aids that facilitate the managerial process." In an attempt to further define this concept, the managerial process can be viewed in terms of the major activities faced by organizations as defined by Anthony[4]:

1. Strategic Planning—the process of deciding on the objectives of the organization, on changes in these objectives, and the resources used to attain these objectives, and on the policies that are to govern the acquisition, use and disposition of these resources.
2. Management Control—the process by which managers assure that resources are obtained and used effectively and efficiently in the accomplishment of the organization's objectives.
3. Operational Control—the process of assuring that specific tasks are carried out efficiently and effectively.

The early definitions of MIS tended to focus on the information to support the strategic and tactical planning activities. However, through application, this concept has come to be used to refer to information systems that primarily support the managerial control activities that focus on the use and review of information generated by the data processing of transaction activities of an organization.

The original concept of MIS to support the planning activity has been further defined and is now often referred to as Decision Support Systems (DSS). The distinctions drawn between the Data Processing System (DPS) on one extreme and DSS at the other are well defined. Figure 1 contrasts these two concepts on a number of characteristics.

Data Processing Systems (DPS) versus Decision Support Systems (DSS)

Characteristics	DPS	DSS
Problem-solving Structure	Programmable	Non-Programmable
Orientation	Clerical Transactions	Intelligence
Time-focus	Historical	Futuristic
Scope	Internal	External and Internal
Design Criteria	Mechanistic	Behavioristic
Computational Focus	Basic	Complex
Output Orientation	Managerial Control	Planning, Forecasting

Figure 1

Since both extremes of this spectrum can be referred to under the general heading of information systems, it is not an easy task to specify a cost-benefit methodology to evaluate all possible alternatives that a systems designer can be asked to propose. Fundamental to the philosophy of information systems is that information is the catalyst of management, and is the unifying ingredient of the management functions of planning, operating, decision-making, and controlling. Therefore, a fundamental consideration in the design and development of an information system is determining which is the vital information needed for maintaining and extending the organization at desired levels of stability and growth. Lyles[7] presented a framework of planning for MIS that provides a structured and systematic approach that addressed many of the organizational issues.

An important consideration in the design of a system is cost-effectiveness. High quality data, large quantities of data, and rapidly available data involve higher costs for the management information system. However, the cost of the information must be balanced against the resulting reduction of uncertainty, increased predictability of events, and more responsive managerial decision-making[8].

The selection of a particular level of information system for an organization is not always specified by management. The decision is often made as a result of a systems design study undertaken by the organization and managed by the systems analysts. The study is often charged with the specification of alternative system configurations as well as the evaluation of the costs and benefits to be associated with each alternative.

ROBERT T. KEIM, PH.D

Dr. Keim is a member of the faculty of the Department of Quantitative Systems, College of Business Administration, Arizona State University and a Research Associate in the College's Bureau of Business and Economic Research. A member of ASM, Dr. Keim is actively involved with the Phoenix, Arizona Chapter. Dr. Keim has made numerous presentations and published articles and chapters in books as well as authoring a number of research reports on the topics relating to Information Systems and their use in organizations.

DR. RALPH JANARO

Dr. Janaro is an Assistant Professor of Management for the School of Management at Clarkson College of Technology. He has published two texts in the data processing area and currently serves as U.S. Contributing Editor for *International Abstracts in OR*. Mr. Janaro received his DBA from Florida State University.

The design of information systems follows a life-cycle pattern that includes: definition, physical design, implementation, and evaluation. Each phase of this life-cycle pattern has associated costs and benefits.

Costs of the Information System

Information can be considered to be a resource in modern organizations, and there are costs associated with its use that must be taken into account in the design of a system. The costs of the acquisition, processing, storage, retention, and transmission of information are most apparent in those parts of the information system which have become formalized. For example, the formal descriptions of information processing operations in a completely specified system such as a basic data processing system would allow precise estimates to be made of the cost of these systems in normal everyday use. By computing forms cost, data preparation, records retention, output requirements and distribution costs, a well specified accounting process, like payroll, can be accurately costed.

In many organizations, tne cost of a completely specified system is taken as the total cost of the information system. The other elements of the system such as the common data base, the management re-

porting system, and the strategic planning modules are much less developed. The costs of the embryonic versions of these elements that do exist are often included in other budgets. Development of more formal versions of these elements is sometimes taken as an additional cost to the information system. The greatest proportion of the cost of operating a completely-specified system is that of the computer support and the associated personnel.

Benefits of an Information System

The objective of some systems is cost reduction, while in other cases the aim is to replace a labor-intensive operation with a capital-intensive one[9]. The benefits of the capital-intensive projects are clearly measurable in terms of the cost reductions achieved or the services maintained per unit of human effort expended. The benefits to be obtained from implementation of a completely-specified system are similarly easy to assess. However, the benefits that may be obtained from other parts of the organizational information system are less tangible and much more difficult to measure.

The parts of the information system other than a completely-specified system serve managerial decision-making in management control and the strategic direction of the organization. The benefits from the decision support portion of the information system are in terms of a greater awareness and alertness on the part of the members of the organization to both external and internal environments in which they are working. Therefore, the major benefit of the information system is the value of the information it makes available. But, how can we measure that value—how can we quantify it for our cost-benefit analysis?

Value of Information

According to Hirsch[10], any item of information is needed if without it a decision would be different; leading to the conclusion that an item of information has no value if it cannot at least potentially influence a decision. Since perfect information would allow us to foretell or control the future, and since this obviously does not happen, then it is safe to assume that we make decisions with imperfect information. Reasons for using imperfect information:
(1) The needed information is unavailable.
(2) The effort to get the information may be unrealistically great or costly.
(3) There is no knowledge of the availability of the information.

(4) The information is not available in the form needed.

Following Hirsch's reasoning, decisions are made with imperfect information for all of these reasons. Therefore, additional or different information always has value, which must be analyzed to determine whether the costs of providing it are justified.

Value Justification With Calculable Benefits

According to Hirsch, the justification yardstick for information can be stated as follows: If its cost is less than its contribution to profit or reduction of other costs, the information is justified. This yardstick is useful in cases where the information has a concrete measurable objective, and although these cases are probably in the minority, many of them do exist.

One conventional instance of measurable information value would be changes in accounting systems permitting earlier billings and hence earlier payments. Calculation of how much faster payments are then received and of the resulting interest implications is an easy matter. Value justification of information is an easy matter in cases such as this, where objectives are clear-cut and the extent to which they are achieved can be determined. Unfortunately, this holds true in only a minority of cases.

Value Justification Without Calculable Benefits

Most cases of information value determination are less clear-cut than the previous example. Typically, improvements in information systems are designed to bring benefits such as faster order processing. Changes such as this are intended to be beneficial and usually are, but it is difficult and in most cases impossible to make a firm calculation of their dollar impact. An example of this noted by Hirsch would be the major airlines at the time of his article, most of which had or were about to install computer-based reservation systems. Though costly, no attempt was made to profit-justify them. Their justification was instead that they would enable the airlines (1) to continue operating in the face of rapidly increasing passenger volumes, and (2) to prevent competing airlines from gaining a competitive advantage.

The problem in these cases is that the estimation of benefits obtained cannot be a concrete matter, and thus contain an element of risk. Since it takes a long time to determine whether or not the expected benefits are being obtained, an information system may be operated for a long time before it can be decided to discontinue it.

Andrus[11], and Feltham[12], and Mock[13] all discuss methods for determining the value of information. These methods range from theoretical utility approaches to Bayesian (expected value) approaches. The models are logically sound, based on the limiting assumptions, but the assumptions are not realistic. At this point, we are faced with the question: Can we quantify an intangible?

Can an Intangible Benefit be Quantified?

Although models for determining the value of information have been developed, the complexity of the various designs of information systems preclude their application. It is not possible to accurately determine or quantify the value of all information system design alternatives. To even begin building a cost-benefit model for this type of analysis for information systems design requires situation specific models that depend upon many unrealistic assumptions. Many of these assumptions rely upon subjective probability (guesses) distributions.

Information is an intangible resource for which a value cannot be accurately nor reliably determined. But, this does not mean that cost-benefit analysis cannot be used in determining which system to develop. It can be a useful tool, but from a slightly different perspective. Litecky[14] suggested that the systems study team use an estimation or "guesswork" basis that must be fully explained to the management who will evaluate the proposal.

A Phased Approach for Applying Cost-Benefit Analysis to Information Systems Design

In order to assist the system developers and the management decision-makers, cost-benefit analysis can be a useful tool if evaluated within the context of the design process. We will now present a system design methodology that includes a CB technique that becomes more specific as the system design is more concretely specified.

The initial design stages of an effort to specify information systems for the management of an organization will by the nature of systems design specify a range of alternatives. For each alternative the basic components of the system are specified at a level that is appropriate for cost analysis. The initial estimates will be very general. As the system is more definitely specified, the cost analysis becomes more accurate. The components of cost include hardware, software and operating expenses.

Addressing the benefits of the various system alternatives requires a different perspective. Instead of computing reduction of personnel, forms savings, etc. the benefits might be considered relative to the level of decision support provided by the individual alternative. The estimates will be the responsibility of the management to be served by the system. They will be asked to assign a dollar figure to the benefits for each system alternative.

If management learns to evaluate the various information system alternatives relative to the level of output or decision support provided by each alternative, the choice can be made without artificially quantifying intangible concepts. This method of evaluation can be operationalized by an evolutionary concept for system specification that would have a form of cost-benefit analysis embedded in its life cycle.

Such a systems design life cycle would include the following steps:

1. Definition—the range of alternative system descriptions would be defined in general terms with associated gross costs estimates. PERT/CPM cost techniques as applied to a decision analysis could be used at this level.

2. Specification—given the desired output level the management would select a particular cost range along with a system alternative.

3. Detailed definition—at this point since more procedures and requirements will be specified, additional cost estimates and benefits can be determined. At this point the number of alternatives should be limited to a manageable number for the systems analyst to specify. A more detailed, formal cost-benefit analysis can then be carried out. However, the application of traditional cost-benefit analysis will be lengthy and expensive even with a small range of alternatives.

4. Selection—given the alternatives and some best estimates of costs and relative benefits the management, along with the systems analysts, can select the alternative best meeting the planning, controlling and decision making requirements for the organization within a reasonably estimated cost.

5. Detailed design—proceeds along with the detailed design using some form of budget or project management controls to apprise the system sponsors of increasing or decreasing cost and benefit trade-offs.

6. Implementation—the actual installation, training and initial input activities to cut over to the new system.

The Phased Approach to Cost-Benefit Analysis

System Design Step	Nature of CB Analysis	Management Action
1. Definition	Identify relative cost and benefits of a range of alternative system configurations.	Select an alternative or limit range of alternatives for further specification.
2. Specification	At this step, the associated time estimates should be more clear. Identify hardware cost ranges for each alternative and estimate manpower requirements for associated support levels. Benefits will be descriptively identified.	Since costs are more specific, management can begin to budget for further development. Target a specific alternative to meet desired support level. Iterate through this step until a single alternative is agreed upon.
3. Detailed Definition	The level of system specification is complete enough to provide detailed cost estimates and many quantifiable benefits can be specified.	At this point, the CB analysis should be complete enough to determine if the system specification meets management requirements within available resources. If it does not, iterate back to Step 2 and select another alternative.
4. Selection	Specify cost-benefit tradeoffs within the alternative and present figures.	Select actual configuration for detailed design. Prepare project tracking techniques to maintain cost control.
5. Detailed Design	Throughout this step, project progress reports to management should include detailed tracking against project schedule.	This level of reporting should apprise management of potential cost overruns or delays that will impact later design steps.
6. Implementation	When the system is ready for installation, management will have complete cost information along with a clear understanding of the benefits.	Formal acceptance and checkoff as each module or portion of the system is installed.
7. Evaluation	Throughout the stages of the design process, the accuracy and specificity of the CB should increase. At this time, operating costs and realized benefits should be available.	The evaluation of the overall project at this time will provide a more effective CB methodology for future projects.

Figure 2

7. Evaluation—the planned audit and performance criteria applied to the system to foresee the need for system modification or redesign.

The last two life cycle activities mentioned are really the basis of this entire methodology. The activity of implementation is not merely installing a set of computer programs on a computer and giving the users a set of instructions on how to use it. Rather, it is the ongoing activity of keeping the users and sponsors of the system apprised of its impact throughout the life cycle. This is both a behavioral and mechanical process that makes users aware of what is going on and the sponsors are kept up to date on cost estimates.

The system design process is described along with the cost benefit analysis output and management action in Figure 2.

Form of Cost-Benefit Analysis

The traditional cost-benefit analysis methodology can and has been applied to information systems analysis and design. However, due to the evolutionary nature of the final system configuration the original estimates are often grossly distorted. The only way to make evaluations reasonable is to compare relative cost-benefit scenarios for the range of alternatives under consideration.

As with systems design, the approaches to making relative estimates vary. This approach calls for assumptions that distort the actual figures but will come up with adequate relative cost estimates. Since there exist no acceptable unit costs for development, design and operation, the method will have to accept some arbitrary standard and factor it into the analysis.

The top-down approach would start with the product or desired output of the system and factor it into units of programming and operations based upon the experience of the organization and the systems analysts. By applying units to the accepted standard costs a relative system cost can be estimated.

The overall benefits of the system will be estimated by the system sponsor prior to making an action decision at each stage in the life cycle. The costs will necessarily be evaluated in this stage as an impact or negative benefit as it relates to the output of the system and impact on the rest of the organization. Another benefit from using this approach is to involve management in the design at every stage of development. However, this approach will add time and cost to the design process, but the resulting system will meet management expectations that have been revised throughout the process.

Conclusions

The reduction of uncertainty about the impact of a major project upon an organization in terms of cost and benefit is a desirable factor in decision-making. In many instances cost-benefit analysis has provided this reduction of uncertainty to decision makers in the private and public areas. However, as projects become more complex the long term results of cost-benefit analysis have not been very accurate.

The design, development and implementation of an information system is a very complex activity characterized by a large number of alternatives. This activity has also been notorious for cost overruns and reduced levels of projected design capabilities.

This article has presented a phased design methodology whose application can make the use of cost-benefit analysis an effective tool even for complex information system projects. This approach takes account of the system design life cycle and applies a flexible and evolutionary cost-benefit analysis throughout the life cycle. As each stage in the system design defines a more specific system configuration, the updated CB analysis is completed using increasingly specific and quantifiable information and evaluation. Such a phased approach will avoid the traditional, unrealistic and inaccurate CB analyses that rely on a single application at a very early stage of the MIS design.   •jsm

References

1 D. V. Mathusz, "The Value of Information Concept Applied to Data Systems," *OMEGA*, Vol. 5, No. 5, 1977, p. 594.
2 H. P. Hatry, op. cit.
3 E. A. Tomeski, "Management Information Systems," *The Encyclopedia of Management*, Carl Heyel (ed.), New York: Van Nostrand Reinhold Co., 1972, pp. 496-498.
4 R. N. Anthony, *Planning and Control Systems: A Framework for Analysis*, Boston, MA: Howard Business School, 1965.
5 G. B. Davis, *Management Information Systems: Conceptual Foundations, Structure and Development*, New York: McGraw-Hill, 1974.
6 P. G. W. Keen and M. S. Morton, *Decision Support Systems: An Organizational Perspective*, Reading, MA: Addison-Wesley, 1978.
7 M. A. Lyles, "Making Operational Long-Range Planning for Information Systems," *MIS Quarterly*, Vol. 3, No. 2, 1979, pp. 9-19.
8 E. A. Tomeski, op. cit.
9 K. J. Radford, *Information Systems for Strategic Decisions*, Reston, VA: Reston Publishing Co., Inc., 1978.
10 R. E. Hirsch, "The Value of Information," *The Journal of Accountancy*, 1968, pp. 41-45.
11 R. R. Andrus, "Approaches to Information Evaluation," *MSU Business Topics*, Vol. 19, pp. 40-46.
12 G. A. Feltham, "The Value of Information," *The Accounting Review*, Vol. 43, pp. 684-696.
13 T. J. Mock, "Concepts of Information Value and Accounting," *The Accounting Review*, Vol. 96, pp. 765-778.
14 C. P. Litecky, "Intangibles in Cost Benefit Analysis, *Journal of Systems Management*, Vol. 32, No. 2, 1981, pp. 15-17.

MIS often falls short of expectations because of unrealistic goals.

BY JOHN C. CARTER AND FRED N. SILVERMAN

Establishing a MIS

No doubt much has yet to be said about why management information systems fail to live up to the
expectations of both managers and systems' designers. Certainly much has already been said in the past
decade (see references). Disenchantment has been
attributed to causes such as a mismatch between
users and their management information systems,[1]
failure to adopt a top-down approach to management
information system design,[9, 10] and provision by the
management information system of data which are
too general and too late to be useful.[6]

Perhaps there is an even more fundamental reason
why the potential of management information systems is seldom achieved; managers are often not at
all clear about what a management information system is and what they can reasonably expect of it.
Even one who follows the journal literature is torn
between viewing a management information system
as a computer data base[7] or a mirage![2]

It is the purpose of this article to attempt to clarify
the meaning of information and its role in management, and to provide a systematic approach to guide
the executive in establishing a management information system which is relevant to his firm's needs. If
managers have a more focused picture of management information systems and their potential for improving decision-making, perhaps improved communications between users and designers will result.
This could well lead to improved responsiveness of
management information systems to managers'
needs.

What is Information?

Information is a concept whose meaning most
people assume to be obvious. It is commonly thought
of as simply messages we receive from reading and
listening. But many messages we receive are not
relevant to our interests; they are isolated facts
which have no connotations in our frame of reference.
For example, if we are in the catfood business, a news
item about border clashes in Asia is probably not
relevant to managing our business. To distinguish
pertinent from irrelevant messages, we'll refer to the
total set of messages we receive as data rather than
information. By the term "information" we mean
only those data which actively inform us about the
status of some phenomenon of interest to us, like
sales in the Eastern region or the terms of a recent act
of Congress affecting our industry.

Often data become information only when viewed
as part of a pattern. For example, the number of
rejects coming off a production line in a particular
week takes on the quality of information only when
considered in its proper context. Similar data from
the past or total production volume would give meaning to such a number.

Management's Reliance on Information

Managers are paid to make good decisions. In order to be able to intelligently generate alternative courses of action, the manager must have information about his department's or firm's resources. He also needs information on external conditions, such as competitors' actions and government regulations, which can have an effect on the outcomes of his actions. Furthermore, forecasts of the likelihood of these external conditions constitute additional valuable information to be used in developing possible strategies for the decision making process.

The manager also has to evaluate the effectiveness of each of his alternative actions under of the relevant possible external conditions. Usually a large volume of information will be needed for this evaluation. Information about profitability, budgetary requirements and market share are typical examples. With all of this information in hand, the manager is in a sound position to decide which course of action to follow.

Once the manager has implemented a strategy, he has to monitor progress to determine whether corrective action is needed. This requires that performance data provide the necessary information for controlling the implementation of the strategy. It is clear, then, that the availability of accurate, timely information is a resource fundamental to the management function.

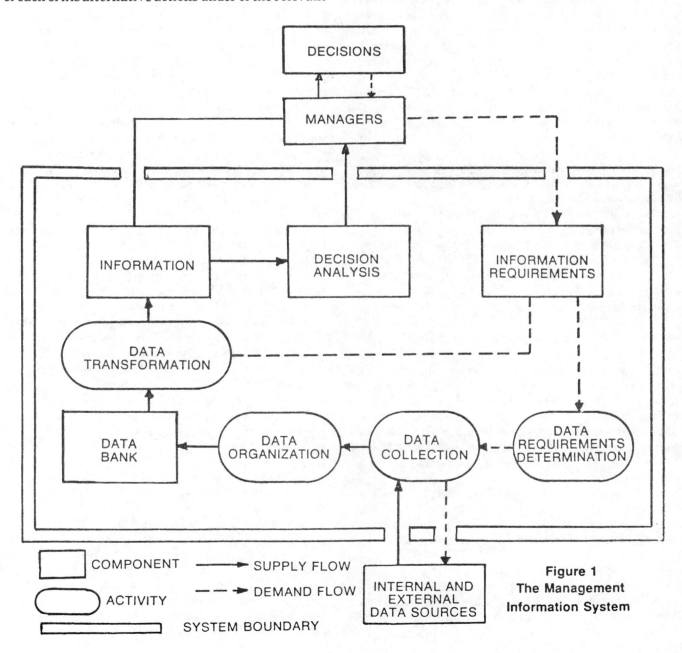

Figure 1
The Management
Information System

47

Providing Information for Decisions

We have all had the experience of having to make a report or solve a problem in a hurry. Doing either requires being able to put our hands on specific information. Unfortunately, sometimes it is not readily available. In such cases, we have the choice of doing without, obtaining a quick (and possibly inaccurate) subjective approximation, or waiting until the relevant data have been obtained. The latter approach often takes more time than we have available and even if it can be followed, delays the task at hand. Indubitably, such an ad hoc approach can be very costly, as most managers are aware.

In contrast to the ad hoc approach to the provision of information, a systems approach would suggest trying to foresee information needs and actively planning for information to be available when required. A management information system provides the means of doing this.

The meaning of the term "management information system" is suggested by the words themselves, although misunderstanding is widespread. Management involves planning and controlling the use of physical and human resources in pursuit of objectives. Information is the very substance of which planning and controlling decisions are made. The system whose function is to provide appropriate information for management decisions is a management information system.

We can add precision to the above description by identifying the components of a management information system and how the components are interrelated.

The management information system is illustrated in Figure 1. The need to make a decision triggers a demand for information. If the information can be obtained from the existing data bank, the information requirements determine how the data must be transformed in order to satisfy the demand. If not, new data requirements are determined and data are collected from the appropriate data sources. These data are organized for storage in the data bank prior to being transformed into the desired information. The manager can either use the information as a direct input to his decision making or he can request a decision analysis by the system in the event that it has analytical capabilities.

Establishing Information Requirements

In taking a systematic approach to solving managerial problems, the first stage is the determination of the manager's goals and objectives. Since we know how important accurate and timely information is for effective decision making, the establishment of the

organizational needs for information enables us to design a system which will efficiently meet these requirements. High start-up costs for system design, equipment purchase, software development, data collection and storage, and personnel training make it important to carefully determine the firm's needs and objectives before deciding what kind of information system to develop.

Information requirements depend on the purpose for which the information is needed. We utilize information for generating reports, monitoring performance, forecasting, planning, decision making.

Generating reports. Many figures are used in the daily operation of an organization. In order to digest the important information necessary for making intelligent decisions, some method of distilling and summarizing the relevant information is needed. One such method is the generation of regular and special summary reports. The regular reports are received by the manager on a weekly, monthly or some other regular basis and special reports are generated at his request when additional or more specific information is required. For example, the Eastern regional sales manager might receive a monthly summary of sales volume by representative. However, if the volume was far below target, he could request a detailed listing of all sales made for particular sales representatives in order to pinpoint the specific problem area.

Monitoring performance. The generation of reports is only the first step in the control function of management. The next step is the monitoring and evaluation of performance. In doing this, we insure that actual performance complies with established plans and forecasts. When variance from these plans is detected, an evaluation of the causal factors enables the proper corrective measures to be taken. While it may be relatively easy to obtain information for comparing performance with expectations, determining the causal factors behind any discrepancies can require analysis of data not normally considered.

To illustrate, the sales manager can readily see when one of his representatives is below quota for the period. However, he may require information from rarely used external sources, such as general economic statistics, to determine the reason why.

The ability of the information system to aid the manager in decision making is dependent on the extent to which these requirements can be foreseen.

Forecasting. Whether we are talking about sales, production, finance or personnel, timely and accurate forecasts are important for good decision making. To plan effectively, most firms have to make forecasts of demand for products or services, the state of the economy, availability and cost of raw materials, interest rates and availability of financing.

DR. JOHN C. CARTER
John C. Carter is Assistant Professor of Management at Bernard M. Baruch College of The City University of New York, where he teaches in the areas of management science, operations management and systems analysis. He holds a PH.D., in management science from Columbia University Graduate School of Business. He has served as a consultant to several corporations.

DR. FRED N. SILVERMAN
Fred N. Silverman is Associate Professor of Management Science at Pace University Graduate School of Business. His teaching and research interests include management information systems, production and operations management and management science. He received his PH.D in management science from Columbia University Graduate School of Business and has authored several articles in the field of management science.

The information required to make forecasts depends on the accuracy desired, the length of time into the future of the forecast and the complexity of the situation. For instance, the many complex relationships governing weather systems seem to give the National Weather Service a great deal of difficulty in forecasting the weather several days in advance despite having large amounts of historical data, sophisticated monitoring devices (satellites, radar, etc.), very large computer systems and expert analysts. On the other hand, a small manufacturing firm may be able to forecast next year's sales very accurately just by extrapolating its sales trend over the past several years.

Planning. The information requirements for short and long term planning are even more complex than for forecasting. Forecasting is only concerned with estimating the likelihood of future events, while planning considers the interactions between these events and current decisions.

In short term planning, we want to efficiently accomplish our objectives in the immediate future. Since the planning horizon is short, we should be able to make reasonably good estimates of the future events which affect our decisions. However, planning also requires information concerning the impact of these forecasts on the results of decisions. For example, in developing a plan for the acquisition of raw materials, we will need information about the quantities of materials used per item and the costs of storage and purchasing in addition to forecasts of demand for our products and raw material prices. An effective information system would be able to recall or compute this information from stored data.

Long-range planning places even more demands on the information system. As the planning horizon increases, it becomes more difficult to make meaningful predictions. Also, long term can be so long that we can be dealing with an enterprise or environment unrecognizable by today's standards. Even so, experience and judgement combined with sufficient relevant information and a systematic approach toward planning can yield acceptable long range plans. While it may be impossible to have all relevant information on all possible ventures a firm may enter in the long term, the information system should be able to summarize and categorize existing information that may be related to a particular future operation and make long term predictions (with confidence levels) on the basis of existing information.

Decision analysis. We have discussed the information requirements of information systems as they are generally used. A next logical step in the development of these systems is to include a procedure for the evaluation and even the determination of the optimal decision. Such a system would incorporate models of specific types of routine decisions. The manager would indicate which standardized problem he wanted solved with appropriate parameter values. The computerized decision making system would be able to collect the relevant data from the information system, apply them to the appropriate model and propose solutions. At the present time, this may only be feasible for standard and routine problems. However, even in this limited scope, such an integrated information and decision analysis system would be able to enhance the effectiveness of managers by freeing them to concentrate on the substantive portion of their work.

For example, the information system used to store inventory data could be programmed with an appropriate inventory model. The model would calculate the optimal inventory policy and could routinely set the purchase manager order quantity and purchase date information for standard items. The system would also issue purchase orders for review by the manager. The manager would thus be saved the clerical chores of computing inventory information for each standard item and could allocate his time to more creative work.

The information requirements of such a system are not substantially greater than those required for planning needs. However, this type of integrated decision system would require more sophisticated computer resources (both hardware and software) and better understanding of its benefits and limitations than would a straight-forward information system.

Building the Data Base

Data are the raw materials of information. T

comprehensiveness and utility of information thus depend on our having an appropriate library of data available when we need it. The first steps in building a useful data base are to determine data requirements, suitable data sources and collection procedures. The data are collected, placed into storage, and provision is made for future updating.

Data requirements are dictated by information requirements. To illustrate, if our marketing planning calls for information about our major competitor's current and potential marketing strategy, we will want such data as past and present prices by product in each of the sales territories, the volume and type of advertisements appearing in the various media, and promotional activities and expenditures, to suggest just a few. Generally, the more pertinent data we can assemble about a problem or phenomenon of interest, the greater will be the potential information value.

Of course, there is a limit to how much data we should collect. Time and cost are the two factors which constrain us. The more complete the data, the more time it will take to assemble and the more will be the costs of collection, storage and maintenance. As with any decision problem, we must be careful to weigh the expected total costs associated with building a data base against the expected benefits. Estimating the costs is usually easier than estimating benefits since data often have greater information value in the future under contingencies which cannot be clearly seen at the time the data are collected. This points up the importance of attempting to foresee future information requirements.

Data are generated by a vast array of sources. Some the firm has ready access to while others are less accessible. The sources to which the firm has the most ready access are internal to the firm itself, making available information vital for planning and monitoring of performance. Sources outside the firm include government agencies, research organizations and special interest groups. The firm can also directly collect data from the marketplace.

Some types of data are available, perhaps in different form, from two or more sources. For example, we could obtain data on consumers' product preferences by either directly questioning a representative sample of consumers or by purchasing data collected by a market research company. Choice of a source in such a case would depend on the appropriateness of the resulting data as well as the relative costs.

Regardless of where the data originated they will have to be stored in some form of data file. Filing systems range from the simplest manual type (like a filing cabinet) to sophisticated electronic files accessible only by computer. All organizations make use of manual systems for storing some classes of data. As the volume of data required to be stored increases and

as more sophisticated information is asked of the data, manual systems rapidly become restrictive. Microform and electronic systems then take on a comparative advantage. We hasten to point out that only when a more sophisticated (and expensive) system can be shown to provide a *net* total benefit relative to the existing system should the change be made.

Organizing Data for Efficient Utilizations

By now we should know what our information requirements are and what data should be collected and stored. The utility of these data to managers will depend on how effectively they are organized in storage. How this will be accomplished depends on the way the management information system will be used and the importance of various performance criteria.

Some of the more important considerations in organizing data files are ease of use, speed of access, security, reliability, ease of file maintenance, storage requirements and costs.

Ease of use. Data can be organized and indexed to make retrieval of specific information as simple as asking a question, or it can be structured so that only a systems analyst can recover the required information. As the system is made easier to access, it becomes more useful by making accurate information readily available to more people, thus enhancing decision making capabilities. On the other hand, such a system entails a more sophisticated data organization with the concomitant requirements of large storage capabilities, sophisticated programming, complex file indexing and difficult file maintenance.

Speed of access. Depending on the capabilities of the system and of the file structure, it is possible to retrieve information almost instantaneously. Less sophisticated systems can require days to retrieve information. An on-line system with rapid turnaround will require enough system capacity to handle peak demands, random access data files, and appropriate computer hardware and software. However, rapid access to information allows it to be used in many situations where delay would render it unusable. If time is not of the essence, a batch retrieval system can be designed at much lower cost and can utilize highly efficient storage devices such as magnetic tape and microform. In these systems the data organization is serial in nature and information retrieval requires the user to know how the data are stored.

Security. A problem which is becoming increasingly important is that of maintaining the security of the data base. Data files and their indexes can be scrambled in the computer so that retrieval is only possible with the use of a secret key. This can be changed frequently and disseminated only to those that have a need to know. Unfortunately, the easier we make access to the system to enhance our information usage, the harder it is to protect the data from unauthorized use. An additional problem can be protecting the data from unauthorized tampering to insure its integrity. Serial data stored on magnetic tape are usually more difficult to tamper with than random access data because they require someone to physically mount the tape which can be stored in a protected area.

Reliability. In certain applications it is extremely important to have as high a degree of reliability as possible in the storage and retrieval of information. In applications requiring a higher degree of reliability than usual, data organization and file maintenance routines can deliberately add redundancy to the system. Thus, if a malfunction destroys one set of files, they can be recreated from other sets. Files containing common data stored in various forms for different applications can be used to verify or recreate potentially damaged files. While redundant information can enhance reliability and more closely accommodate the needs of various users, it adds to storage and file maintenance requirements.

Ease of file maintenance. Any information system must be periodically updated with current data. This can be amplished in several ways depending on the data organization and the design of the system. Sophisticated on-line systems that have rapid and easy retrieval capabilities generally will also require sophisticated file maintenance programs. This is due to the necessity for updating indexes and cross references in addition to the data themselves.

Usually, file maintenance is done by technical staff on a periodic batch basis. This can help prevent the input of inaccurate or erroneous data. It is possible, however, to have the files updated on-line from remote locations; for example, the deduction of units sold from inventory on hand using a point of sale terminal. File maintenance requirements will therefore affect the complexity of the system and the organization of information files.

Storage requirements. The organization of the data files also influences the amount of space required to store the information. This is applicable to any method of storage from filing cabinets to microfilm to high speed computers. Unless raw data are inherently well structured, the organization required to make storage and retrieval easier will increase the requirements for storage space. To illustrate, we could save space in a filing cabinet by pasting two half page documents onto a single page. However, this is seldom done because the costs of matching and retrieving halves are greater than the benefits derived.

Cost. The capabilities of a management information system will depend largely on the budget for designing, implementing, operating and maintaining the system. A larger budget permits greater capability which will generally require a more highly structured data base.

Utilizing the Management Information System

We hanow talked about all the components of a management information system except the process by which data become information. In this section we want to breathe life into the system by describing how the manager utilizes the management information system.

Management information systems can be classified on the basis of how directly they serve users' needs. At the lowest level, we have systems which only supply raw data about a phenomenon of interest. In order to utilize the information content of these data, the user has to select the pertinent data and process them, looking for patterns or otherwise relating them to the problem context. In this case the management information system is simply performing the function of data storage. The user requests a specific data file and it is provided. A manual management information system is often suitable at this level of utilization.

To give an example, a personnel manager may face the task of determining which employees are to receive year-end bonuses and of how much. The determination is to be based on productivity level. Daily throughput records are kept for each worker and stored in a file classified by workers' names. The raw data for the personnel manager are the file contents for the past year. The data themselves constitute quite rudimentary information. To convert them into a directly usable form, the manager has to calculate for each worker some index of productivity and compare this year's index with last year's.

A higher level management information system allows for selective data retrieval. Some elementary processing (screening) of raw data is carried out by the system before the data are delivered to the user. Relative to the lowest level, such a management information system requires a more complex organization of the data base. The user is then able to call for only those data which meet certain specified conditions. For example, sales data might be classified by sales territory, size of account, client's name and transaction date. If a manager faces a promotional policy decision and requires information about sales trends for major clients in a particular territory, the appropriate data can be assembled and reported by the system. While manual systems can sometimes be adequate at this level, a computer-based system is usually more appropriate.

At the third level of sophistication, the management information system has an elementary computational capability; namely, an ability to aggregate. The ability of a management information system to aggregate data is a big step forward from the user's viewpoint, making many kinds of data more directly useful by producing information of a higher order. At this level and higher we are necessarily talking about computer-based information systems.

"Totals" are important summary measures of many phenomena. It is easy to see in our above two illustrations how valuable aggregate information can be. In the first instance total yearly throughput of each worker may well constitute a suitable index for the personnel manager. In the second case total quarterly sales figures provide a useful basis for comparing the relative value of clients or salespeople.

At the fourth level of sophistication the management information system can perform more advanced computations. While totals constitute valuable information in many contexts, measures like averages, medians, ranges and standard deviations are more directly useful for many monitoring and planning activities. Such measures succinctly summarize the information inherent in sets of data. For example, we commonly think in terms of the average price or range of prices of raw materials or product lines. These and other statistics help the executive by giving a summary "picture" of pertinent phenomena. A management information system having the capability of generating relevant statistics draws more heavily on the processing ability of the computer than lower-level system. However, all business computers can be programmed to perform these calculations and many proprietary software packages are readily available.

The greatest potential of a management information system is reached by integrating it with management science models. In such systems mathematical models are stored in the same way as data and can be called into play as needed. The beauty of having a library of models available is that the manager can use the system to process data into highly refined and directly usable information. Descriptive models, like breakeven, PERT and queuing models, are used primarily to answer "what if" questions. They describe and explain relationships among variables of interest and serve as an efficient way for the manager to test alternative ideas. Prescriptive models such as linear programming and inventory models actually tell the manager which action he should take. The extent to which the model's prescription needs further weighing before implementation depends on how comprehensively the model incorporates all relevant factors.

It should be clear that a manager who has a management information system with these capabilities is able to make better decisions more quickly and thus has released time for other important activities.

Conclusion

We have indicated that managers need relevant, timely and accurate information in order to make good decisions. Information is used for a variety of purposes, including forecasting future events, determining alternative courses of action, evaluating the effectiveness of decisions and controlling the operations of the firm.

While management information systems should be able to provide managers with much of the information they need, there is growing concern that these systems are not being utilized to their full potential. There are several reasons for this. One is that data bases have inappropriate content or organization for providing information that is needed by managers for decision making purposes. Another is that managers often have inadequate access to the system. Furthermore, sometimes the system is not designed to provide information in a form that is needed by decision makers. Finally, potential users are not always conversant with the benefits and limitations of the system, even when it meets all appropriate design criteria.

It is our contention that if managers become more involved in the establishment of their management information systems, the above problems will be alleviated. Specifically, the direct involvement of potential users in system design will produce systems more responsive to their needs. Consequently, managers will better understand the capabilities as well as the limitations of their systems and how they can be used to maximum advantage. ●jsm

References

1. Richard L. Daft, and Norman B. MacIntosh, "A New Approach to Design and Use of Management Information," *California Management Review*, (Fall 1978), pp. 82-92.
2. John Dearden, "MIS is a Mirage," *Harvard Business Review* (January-February, 1972), pp. 90-99.
3. Phillip Ein-Dor, and Eli Segev, "Organizational Context and the Success of Management Information Systems," *Management Science* (June 1978), pp. 1064-77.
4. Michael J. Ginzberg, "Steps Toward More Effective Implementation of MS and MIS," *Interfaces* (May 1978), pp. 57-63.
5. Charles W. Hofer, "Emerging EDP Pattern," *Harvard Business Review* (March-April 1970) pp. 16-170.
6. Henry Mintzberg, "The Myths of MIS," *California Management Review* (Fall 1972), pp. 92-97.
7. Richard L. Nolan, "Computer Data Bases: The Future is Now," *Harvard Business Review* (September-October 1973), pp. 98-114.
8. Martin J. Shio, "New Look at MIS," *Journal of Systems Management* (May 1977), pp. 38-40.
9. Burton E. Swanson, "Management Information Systems: Appreciation and Involvement," *Management Science* (October 1974), pp. 178-188.
10. William M. Zani, "Blueprint for MIS," *Harvard Business Review* (November-December 1970), pp. 95-100.

PART III

DEVELOPMENT AND IMPLEMENTATION OF A CBMIS

LEARNING OBJECTIVES:

- Be able to discuss the basic steps in information system development.

- Appreciate the various methods available for systems analysis.

- Recognize the information needs and impact of MIS technology on the chief executive of an organization.

- Recognize the impact of computer graphics in helping managers make better decisions.

- Be able to discuss the basic principles for successful CBMIS evaluation and implementation.

INTRODUCTION

In this section, the narratives serve to introduce additional elements to be considered in the life cycle of an information system, namely, the methodology of systems theory as a logical approach for design and implementation of CBMIS is introduced. Systems theory is a method for dealing with complex systems and in most cases, information systems would most certainly qualify. The use of systems theory allows the investigator to partition the proposed system into subsystems or modules and from this partitioning, develop a hierarchical structure of modules. By identifying the appropriate modules, one can identify the inputs and outputs as they flow from one module to another. In essence, systems theory provides a logical framework for analysis and design of information systems.

In the development process there are two interrelated components, namely, the managerial and technical sides of a computer based information system. On the managerial side, the information system must provide the user/decision maker with information they want. This information must be commensurate with the mission of the organization and presented in a form that the decision maker can identify and use effectively in exercising their responsibilities. In most instances, decision makers are accustomed to receiving information in a specific form and resistant to change. Since the system will be designed to provide information to the manager for decision making, it is incumbent on the part of the manager/user to be involved in the analysis, design, and implementaton of the information system.

On the technical side, it is the systems analyst responsibility to act as a catalyst in bringing together the needs for decision making information and the technical capability of the physical system to produce this information. The systems analyst must develop an understanding of the physical system that presently exists or may be developed to accommodate the information system. The analyst must also secure enough information about the decision makers' needs to design an information system. The design of the system follows a planning phase whereby subsystems relating to functional areas are identified. The analyst must know what each subsystem will produce in terms of the overall decision makers' needs. From this understanding, the analyst considers alternative designs for the proposed system. The output from the design phase will be detailed documentation and may take a number of forms such as narrative, flowchart, and/or pseudocode, which is sufficient in form to be given to the programmer for coding. Inherent in this process is a continual flow of communication between the user and the analyst.

Over the years, a number of techniques have been developed to facilitate the analysis and design of an information system. These developments have evolved from the traditional flowchart which depicts the major components of a system. Basically, this method uses symbols to show the relationship between the flow of data through the system and the steps or processing done at various stages as one progresses from either top-down or bottom-up in analyzing the systems requirements. One drawback of this traditional approach relates to the fact that the flowchart only shows data flows through a physical system - the actual system that presently exists or will exit after the information system has been designed in terms of hardware, software and the physical manipulation of data throughout the system.

One of the difficulties with this approach to analysis and design is that the methodology employed may or may not relate to the users defined needs. It may only relate to a system which is perceived to meet the decision makers information needs. From this traditional approach, the concept of structured analysis emerged. Structured analysis is basically an itrative process whereby data flow diagrams are used to represent how data move from level which may include a high degree of aggregation, to another level which may be less aggregated. The data flow diagram is a top-down concept, where diagrams, narratives, and a data dictionary are incorporated in the partitioning of system at various levels of details. A number of methods have been developed for structural analysis. The second article in this chapter entitled "Evaluating Alternative Methods of System Analysis" by Jeffery L. Shevlin describes some of the methods employed in systems analysis. In summary, systems analysis is based upon a detailed study of user needs. This process allows the system to be partitioned into modules as they relate to a logical flow of data and information through the system. The classical approach in terms of flowcharting focused physical aspects of system hardware and operating procedures. By focusing on the logical aspects of data flows and how the data are to be converted into information, the analyst can better identify the essential information flows and transformation processes required in the new system.

The design phase of the life cycle uses structured analysis to produce data flow diagrams, data structure diagrams, data dictionary, and identification of the transformation processes. These outputs are in turn used by the programmer to code the system.

As the system analyst proceeds through the analysis and design phase of the systems development, there are a number of considerations that must be identified and addressed. Some of these factors are related to the technology of the work place. Is the information system to be designed for a decision making environment where the work place technology is well defined and information requirements are well understood, or a work place where the technology is not well defined and information requirements ambiguous? The analyst, in designing the system, must broaden the investigative scope to look beyond the specific users request and commercially available information processing technology to consideration of the technology currently being employed in producing the organizations product or service.

The analyst must also understand the relationship between the technical information processing environment that exists within the organization and the degree of user sophistication in understanding this environment. The reverse is also true in terms of the data processing side understanding the users needs and requirements. If the analyst provides good liaison betwen the user and that data processing department, chances are improved for enhanced productivity by both parties.

In examining system design alternatives, the analyst again must understand the relationship between a specific request and other needs within the organization. That is, the scope of the analysis must go beyond a single user's need to a cognitive recognization of needs by many users within the organization which may be compatible with the scope of the current information system project. For example, the computer has invaded the executives' domain and executives are now beginning to understand and use this technology as an end-user to analyze rapidly changing conditions faced by the firm. This in turn requires that systems be available for this kind of personal analysis by executives in making strategic decisions.

The concept of end-user personal analysis has led some companies to set up information centers. An information center is an entity within the data processing department which provides end-users with software tools which they, in turn, can use to develop their own application programs or models. This concept allows the data processing department to maintain control of the organization's data resources but at the same time help eliminate pressure on the data processing resources for developing end-user systems. That is, it may help in reducing the backlog of requests for system development faced by the data processing department.

The analyst in designing the system must also be cognizant of the form used to present the information to the decision maker. The kinds of reports, graphs, etc., must be designed to provide the decision maker with information which they can interpret as usable in their decision making role. The analyst needs to tailor the output to meet the users requirements. With advances in graphic technology, computer graphics can enhance the value of information provided by the system.

Implementation and post-implementation of the system is the final area covered in this section. Once the system has been designed and coded, the next phase in the development cycle, implementation, begins. Implementation requires the planning and coordination of a number of activities which are spelled out in detail in the implementation phase. During the implementation phase, it is vital that management and the appropriate end-users be heavily involved. Education of management and end-users is one of the most important element in the implementation plan because not only must physical facilities be brought on line, the end-users must know how to access the system. Making the system operational is the goal of the implementation plan.

Once the system has been implemented and made operational, the development process does not stop. Post-implementation of the system, a major consideration in all systems development, must begin. Post-implementation involves an evaluation of the system to insure it is performing in an efficient and effective manner. In other words, does the system do what it was intended to do? Techniques must be devised for evaluating the system along with a mechanism for reporting the results of the evaluation. Productivity of the entire organization as the over-riding consideration is the prime factor to be considered at this stage of systems development.

DISCUSSION QUESTIONS

1. What is system analysis?

2. What are some of the steps involved in CBMIS deveopments?

3. Who should participate in CBMIS development?

4. How do you evaluate a CBMIS?

5. What is structured systems analysis and design? Why has this method been so common recently?

6. What are some alternative methods of systems analysis?

7. Why users should be involved in all phases of systems analysis and design?

8. What is CEO role in CBMIS implementation?

9. What are some of the characteristics of CBMIS for executives?

10. What is the significance of "exceptional reporting" in CBMIS design?

11. Why format of the information generated by the CBMIS should be different for different levels of the organization?

12. What is "management commitment" in CBMIS design.

13. What is post-implementation audit? Why this step is needed?

14. What is the outcome for post-implementation audit?

Article details the seven basic steps in developing an information system.

Basics of Information Systems

■ Because of the rapidly increasing cost of office labor and the spectacularly decreasing cost of electronic systems, the computer is making an ever-greater impact on business and government. It is certainly true today that most business systems and all major new systems incorporate the use of a computer. This article will present an overview of the development of information systems and will provide a framework within which to function during the development of any specific information system. The framework is structured as seven basic steps, each of which is further broken down into seven sub-steps.

Unfortunately, the development of computer-based systems is always difficult and often disastrous. Most difficulties arise because the system designers are either accountants who know little about the computer or computer people who know little about accounting. Accountants often use the computer to merely automate some mechanical, clerical tasks. However, because the accountant does not appreciate the computer's capabilities, the computer is grossly underutilized, and the major result is increased rigidity in the system. Now the computer must be served instead of a clerk. Additionally, because the accountant knows little of computer technicalities, the system takes far longer to develop and install than anticipated. On the other hand, computer people who know little about accounting try to fully utilize the computer's capabilities, but ignore the legitimate needs of accounting. As a result, the developed system lacks adequate internal controls and possibly even an audit trail because the computer person eliminates checks and redundancies as "inefficient." This inevitably leads to excessive errors, user dissatisfaction, and tremendous difficulty in backing up final figures from source documents. Following is an approach to the development of an information system which is designed to avoid both types of errors.

There are seven basic steps in information system development:

1. **System Analysis.** This step documents the present system, details the system's deficiencies, and provides recommendations for improvement.
2. **Statement of Objectives.** This step gives the goals (general and specific) the new system will try to accomplish.
3. **System Design.** This step describes how we will accomplish those objectives and whether the system will be worth its cost.
4. **System Specification.** This step details exactly how the system will work.
5. **Programming.** This step involves developing the computer programs necessary for the system.
6. **Implementation.** This step gets the new system in operation in place of the old.
7. **Evaluation.** This step analyzes how well the new system is working and what can be learned from the system development process.

System Analysis

In the system analysis stage, the analyst prepares documentation on the present system and how it works. This documentation will describe the firm and picture its information processing flow. The study should then identify any deficiencies and recommend improvements.

The system analysis is critical to the development of new systems. To understand why this is so, however, we must briefly mention the three basic ap-

Development

BY DR. JOHN R. PAGE AND DR. H. PAUL HOOPER

proaches to system development:

   (a) The first approach is to apply a standard package to the problem at hand. This approach has the advantage that the system can work, since it has already worked, but the disadvantage that it may not completely fit the present situation. This approach implies that the present system need not be understood.

   (b) The second approach is to use the computer to automate the present system directly. This approach has the advantage that the new system will be essentially the same as the old, with the computer simply relieving some of the clerical burden. The disadvantage is that the capabilities of the computer are not effectively utilized. This approach implies that the computer need not be understood.

   (c) The third approach is to understand both the present system and the objectives it is to accomplish and then to utilize the computer to meet those objectives more efficiently and effectively. The computer's advantages cannot be used properly unless the entire system is rethought. Thus, this approach has the greatest potential benefits, but the disadvantage is that it requires more time *initially*.

Notice that only in the third approach is the system analysis required. In this case, the system analysis should contain:

1.1 General Background This is a description of the organization, its place in the market, and its future prospects. This section should set the context of the system under analysis.

1.2 Organization Structure This is a chart and written description of the lines of authority and division of responsibility for the firm.

1.3 Job Descriptions This gives each of the job positions in the firm, with a discussion of the duties and responsibilities of each.

1.4 Documents This is an inventory of the forms and reports used by the firm in the system under study.

1.5 Procedures This describes the steps followed by the firm, both in the form of written descriptions and system flowcharts of the relevant system.

1.6 Deficiencies This is a list of those areas in need of improvement, either because of inefficiency or weak internal control.

1.7 Recommendations This is a detailed list of the changes necessary to correct the deficiencies in the present system.

Statement of Objectives

The Statement of Objectives lays out (in management terms) the goals the new system will be designed to accomplish. This report will then be reviewed by management and signed if they approve. One of the major reasons for system development disasters is a lack of top management involvement. The Statement of Objectives helps to solve this problem by requiring an early review and approval of the system by management. Of course, even after this signature (approval), management must be additionally involved in the remainder of the system development process.

The breakdown of the Statement of Objectives step is:

2.1 Overall Purpose This is the basic reason for the system and what the system will try to accomplish.

2.2 Specific Objectives This details the specific tasks and goals necessary to accomplish the given overall purpose.

DR. JOHN R. PAGE

Dr Page is Assistant Professor of Accounting at the University of New Orleans and is a CPA in Louisiana. He has had consulting experience in the development of computer-based information systems with his own firm and with an international public accounting firm.

DR. H. PAUL HOOPER

Dr. Hooper is Assistant Professor of Commerce at the McIntire School of Commerce of the University of Virginia. He has taught extensively in courses and seminars on computers and information systems at many levels. Dr. Page and Dr. Hooper are co-authors of a recently published book, *Accounting and Information Systems* (Reston Publishing Company, Inc., 1979).

2.3 Required Output This describes the reports and information that management needs to accomplish the above objectives.

2.4 Required Data This gives the data necessary to produce those reports, but also details where the system will obtain that data.

2.5 Necessary Controls This lays out the controls the system needs to ensure the accuracy and reliability of its data.

2.6 New Policies or Procedures This describes any changes to organization policies and procedures which will be required by the new system.

2.7 Management's Signature Agreement This represents an agreement by affected management that the given system objectives are desired by them.

System Design

The next major step is to create the system conceptually. The System Design will show how and where the system collects data, the flow of data, and the disposition of system outputs.

Designing the system is the most creative part of system development. The analyst must understand the present status and future prospects of the company, understand the goals of the new system, and then create a system which is appropriate for that situation. This design is a general look at the different approaches we can take (direct access vs. batch, multiple small computers vs. one large computer, etc.). It discusses the costs and benefits of each approach and then selects one approach which the system should take.

Again, the System Design is broken down into seven steps. These steps are:

3.1 Scope and Boundaries This is a description both of what the system will do and what the system will not do.

3.2 Specific Requirements This gives the reports, files and data necessary for the system.

3.3 Conceptual Design This describes how the system (both manual operations and computer programs) will fit together into an overall functional design.

3.4 Resource Requirements This estimates the amount of money, manpower, and contracted services necessary to develop the system.

3.5 Tangible Benefits This estimates the "hard dollar" savings from reduction of direct operating expenses.

3.6 Intangible Benefits This describes the important but hard to quantify results of improved service or better information.

3.7 Cost/Benefit Analysis This is a comparison of anticipated costs and benefits to determine whether the system will be worth what it costs.

System Specification

Once the conceptual design is selected, the next step is to detail the exact components of the design and how it will work. The System Specification is the most important and difficult technical step in the entire system development process. Prior to this step, everything has been somewhat conceptual, even vague. After this step, the computer programming should be a fairly mechanical step if the specifications are done properly.

System Specification is broken down into seven component steps:

4.1 Control Section This secures approval of the report by users and management and describes areas of authorized later changes.

4.2 System Description This is a narrative in management terms of what the system will do and how the system will do it.

4.3 System Flowchart This gives a picture of how the system will fit together and interact with other systems.

4.4 Computer System Requirements This describes the hardware and necessary software packages necessary for the system to function.

4.5 Data Management Summary This details the exact descriptions of the input data, the files to be maintained by the system, and the system output.

4.6 Individual Module Design This is a narrative and flowchart of each manual operation and computer program utilized by the system.

4.7 Implementation Schedule This lays out the timetable describing how the system will be developed and implemented.

Programming

Writing the computer programs necessary for system operation may begin after the system specifications are made and approved. Despite the temptation to start programming early, the details of system specification must be first spelled out. Spelling out the systems specifications before programming begins will avoid large amounts of programming efforts being wasted.

There is, however, not one best way to develop computer programs. Some companies have a staff of in-house computer programmers. Other organizations (even large ones) have found greater success by contracting with software houses to develop programs to meet given System Specifications for a fixed fee. Smaller companies utilize independent EDP consultants to write the programs. Finally, many companies utilize software packages to be integrated into the system.

Programming breaks down into seven basic steps:

5.1 Narrative Description This explains the purpose and uses of each individual program.

5.2 User Instructions This gives a step-by-step description of exactly how to use each program.

5.3 Sample Input This is a concrete example of the type of input desired by each program.

5.4 Sample Output This is a concrete example of the printouts generated by each program.

5.5 Test Data This gives data with known results which check the proper operation of each program.

5.6 Operator Instructions This details any separate instructions necessary for the computer operator.

5.7 Program Listing This is a printout of each program's statements.

Implementation

System Implementation is the difficult and time-consuming task of replacing the old system with the new system. Certainly, the central problem is the people problem, since all systems must work through people, not around or to the exclusion of people. However, the employees will be familiar with the operation of the old system and thus will be likely to resent or at least dislike the traumas of changing to a new system and learning new procedures. Additionally, most people do not have a strong ability to conceptualize and thus cannot understand the fundamental ideas of a new system until it is actually in operation. As a result, a good sense of humor and an ability to get along with others are more critical in this phase than is technical knowledge.

Implementation breaks down into seven steps:

6.1 Hardware Installation This involves getting any new equipment in place and properly operating.

6.2 Procedure Writing This is the developing of step-by-step instructions for each job position which is part of the new system.

6.3 Personnel Orientations This introduces employees to the computer and the positive impact of the new system on them.

6.4 Training This instructs employees in the new procedures and operations they must perform in the new system.

6.5 Testing This puts the new system to work and checks that the results generated are correct.

6.6 File Conversion This changes the data in the files of the old system to the format of the new system and introduces new data.

6.7 Parallel Operation This is the use of the new system at the same time as the old system so that the results can be compared and the new system verified.

Evaluation

The final step in the process of system development is Evaluation. This step requires stepping back from the system after it has been implemented and has operated for a reasonable time, say six months. The analyst should try to take an objective overview and: (a) analyze the system in operation to determine if anything can be improved, and (b) analyze the system development process to see if any lessons can be learned from the company's experience. This process is in fact very difficult to do successfully, especially if it is done by those who originally designed or are currently operating the system. As a result, evaluation of the implemented system should usually be done by independent reviewers.

Evaluation breaks down into seven steps:

7.1 Documentation Review This is an analysis of the system documentation, its completeness, accuracy and adequacy.

7.2 Cost Analysis This compares the costs anticipated in the System Design to the actual costs incurred.

7.3 Benefit Analysis This compares the benefits anticipated in the System Design to the actual benefits obtained.

7.4 Acceptance of Users This reviews the degree of enthusiasm with which the users have reacted to the system.

7.5 Internal Controls This is a review of the internal controls of the new system to determine whether they are actually in use and are adequate.

7.6 Deficiencies This details the weaknesses and omissions of both the new system and the system development process.

7.7 Recommendations This gives specific steps to be taken to improve the new system and/or the system development process.

Summary

System development is thus a process of systematically refining our conceptions of a problem and its solution, making them more and more specific until we finally have a completed, implemented system. The process is similar to that of painting: the artist begins by sketching the overall conception of the painting; then, gradually adds more and more detail to the painting until it is complete.

Figure 1 gives a schematic of this overall information system development process. It brings all of the ideas presented in this article together in one place.
●jsm

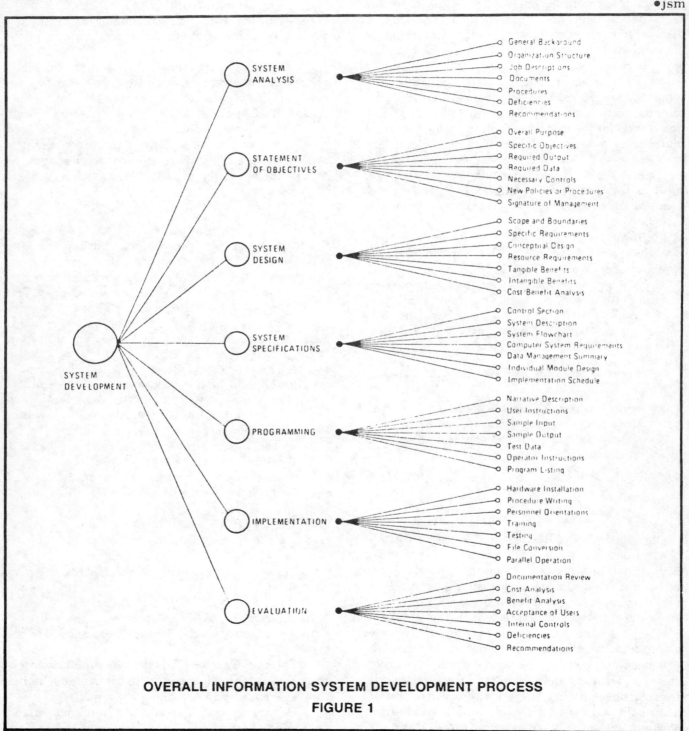

OVERALL INFORMATION SYSTEM DEVELOPMENT PROCESS

FIGURE 1

Evaluating alternative methods of systems analysis

by Jeffrey L. Shevlin

The best method of systems analysis? You have your believers on numerous methods:

- Traditional
- Yourdon
- Warnier-Orr
- HIPO
- Logic charts

Claiming that one method of systems analysis is best is like claiming that one computer is best.

The best systems analysis methodology depends on the type of system that's developed.

Many new methods of systems analysis have emerged in the past 10 years. And, the developers of each method claim their's is the best.

The type of system—distributed, centralized, online, batch, large system or small—and other factors such as the level of user involvement, degree of difficulty and reporting requirements (IFBs, FSRs, RFPs, government, fiscal and auditing) will determine what is needed from a systems analysis methodology.

Traditional

The first methods used, traditional systems analysis techniques, were developed from the 1960s through the early 1970s, and have many basic similarities. A hierarchical chart identifies the major compo-

nents of the system in a top-down fashion. Usually included in the analysis are systems flowcharts and functional narratives, down to program flowcharts or program hierarchical charts, record layouts, print layouts and even pseudo code. Systems are broken down to programs, which are broken down into modules.

One of the setbacks of the traditional method was that systems were developed that did not meet users needs. User requirements were often neglected.

Traditional methods interwoven with some newer systems analysis techniques are still widely used to-

day, but many of the newer methods are quickly becoming popular. The older methods are best suited for what they were designed to do—the development of batch centralized systems, where the problem is well defined and does not require much user involvement.

Yourdon

Yourdon, a popular method used today, was formalized in 1978 by Tom DeMarco in his book *Structured Analysis and Systems Specifications*. The final product of Yourdon-structured analysis—the structured specification—consists of three related components: Data flow diagrams

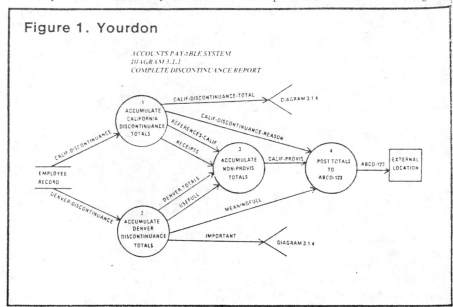

Figure 1. Yourdon

ACCOUNTS PAYABLE SYSTEM
DIAGRAM 3.1.1
COMPLETE DISCONTINUANCE REPORT

(see Figure 1), process narratives and a data dictionary.

A data flow diagram shows each line representing a data element or group of data elements and each circle representing the processing of data. As data flows, elements and groups of elements are defined in the data dictionary. Data element definitions usually include the data element name, a narrative description, values and size. Process descriptions, the final component of the specification, are structured English narratives explaining how the data is manipulated in each bubble.

According to Ed Yourdon, "All of this is intended to make the requirements document—the functional specification—considerably more rigorous, considerably more precise than it typically is now, so that the design programming can eventually be done by somebody else."

The Yourdon technique is different from traditional methods in that it concentrates on the data, following it through processes, making this technique suitable for online

---

Claiming that one analysis method is best is like claiming that one computer is best.

---

systems development. Yourdon-structured analysis does not lead directly into programming—the analysis phase is followed by Yourdon's structured design phase; the program coding follows.

One of the advantages of using Yourdon is that it is a formalized methodology: It is well documented and defined. One of the drawbacks of traditional methods for larger organizations, where there may be several concurrent projects, is that the particular techniques used, the products developed and the level of detail could all vary considerably from project to project.

Utilizing a Yourdon methodology would enable someone working on one project to readily understand the analysis phase of a different project. The design and implementation phases would become more consistent, and therefore somewhat simplified.

As a result of the top-down approach and leveling of data flow diagrams, more levels of user staff are involved in evaluating the correctness of the analysis product. There is a considerably greater amount of user involvement.

Systems analysis is an iterative process; the first analysis usually isn't the correct one. With Yourdon, the majority of small refinements and improvements are made to the data flow diagrams, and it's easier to modify diagrams than narrative text.

The Yourdon methodology is well suited for large projects and is used in government, as well as private industry. Data flow diagrams, process narratives and the data dictionary have been documented in feasibility study reports to identify the type of analysis to be used.

Using Yourdon, however, can significantly increase the amount of time spent in the analysis phase of a project because it is more iterative than traditional methods, and the user is more involved. In fact, it is not unusual to have the users identifying corrections and making modifications to the data flow diagrams themselves.

Warnier-Orr

Like most systems analysis methodologies, Warnier-Orr has its roots in the traditional methods. "As we progressed from one level of understanding systems to another, we evolved a new structured documentation tool called the Warnier-Orr diagram, which is aimed at the documentation of systems, programs and data," says Langston Kitch and Associates, Inc, proprietor of the method.

Warnier-Orr diagrams are similar to other top-down or tree diagrams

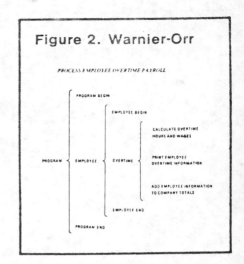

Figure 2. Warnier-Orr

PROCESS EMPLOYEE OVERTIME PAYROLL

in that they are hierarchical, yet they proceed from left to right, rather than from top to bottom. From the programming point of view, coding can be accomplished directly from the diagrams, which encourage structured programming techniques.

Different types of Warnier-Orr diagrams exist. The basic data structure diagram identifies the relationships among data in defining repeating or alternative groups of data. Program diagrams (Figure 2) provide a method of defining the logic of a process. In-out diagrams and assembly line diagrams are also used with the Warnier-Orr method.

According to Langston Kitch, structured design begins at the end—the output. Design does not begin until it is determined what the user wants for output. The problem of systems analysis and design is attacked from the output backward.

Unlike some other systems analysis methodologies, Warnier-Orr does not neglect the programming stage. They have clear rules and procedures for translating the systems design programming code, particularly COBOL.

Warnier-Orr is well suited for complex data base applications, and is more geared toward the data processing technician than the users. The method has been documented in a variety of books and is a widely accepted systems analysis methodology.

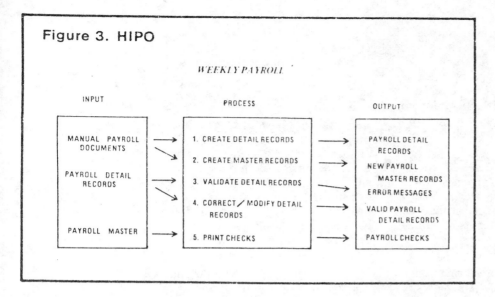

Figure 3. HIPO

WEEKLY PAYROLL

INPUT

MANUAL PAYROLL DOCUMENTS

PAYROLL DETAIL RECORDS

PAYROLL MASTER

PROCESS

1. CREATE DETAIL RECORDS
2. CREATE MASTER RECORDS
3. VALIDATE DETAIL RECORDS
4. CORRECT / MODIFY DETAIL RECORDS
5. PRINT CHECKS

OUTPUT

PAYROLL DETAIL RECORDS
NEW PAYROLL MASTER RECORDS
ERROR MESSAGES
VALID PAYROLL DETAIL RECORDS
PAYROLL CHECKS

HIPO

HIPO stands for "Hierarchical plus Input-Process-Output," and consists of two components. A hierarchical chart shows how each function is broken down into subfunctions; for each function or subfunction identified on the hierarchical chart, there is an input-process-output chart (see Figure 3).

The input-process-output chart shows the inputs and outputs to each function, and the processes each function performs with those inputs and outputs. The HIPO design process is an iterative top-down activity in which the hierarchical chart and the input-process-output charts are developed concurrently. Program design can be made more efficient by applying HIPO techniques at each level of the analysis and design phase.

The HIPO chart is structured so as to be understood and validated by the user; it is iterative in that each level of design is validated against the level above it. For each component of the system, different levels of design exist, from a high level to a detailed level. During development, frequent reviews should be performed to insure that a given design meets its objectives.

The first step of the design should contain display screen formats, report layouts and up to a two-level

hierarchical chart with HIPO charts. The analyst should walk through these charts with the user and be sure this level of design meets the user's requirements.

As the system is divided into functions, and each function is broken down, the hierarchy evolves toward greater detail. Each upper-level HIPO chart should be validated and revised before continuing with the design process.

Each process that is broken down has clearly defined inputs and outputs; this allows modules to be delegated to developers. At the module level of the hierarchy, the design is sufficiently detailed, and program code can usually be written directly from the design.

Logic charts

Logic charts were first developed in 1973-74 and are more tied into traditional methods than HIPO charts. Introduced as a modeling Continued on page 25

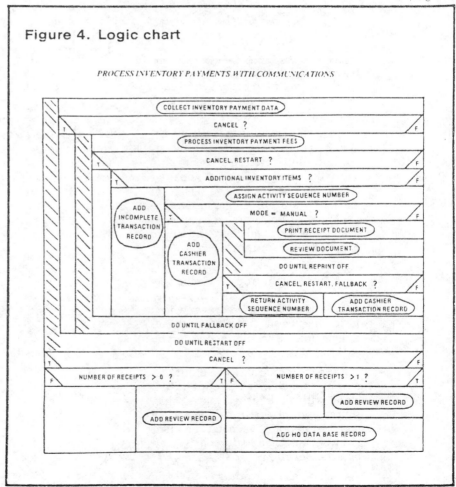

Figure 4. Logic chart

PROCESS INVENTORY PAYMENTS WITH COMMUNICATIONS

COLLECT INVENTORY PAYMENT DATA

CANCEL ?

PROCESS INVENTORY PAYMENT FEES

CANCEL, RESTART ?

ADDITIONAL INVENTORY ITEMS ?

ADD INCOMPLETE TRANSACTION RECORD

ASSIGN ACTIVITY SEQUENCE NUMBER

MODE = MANUAL ?

ADD CASHIER TRANSACTION RECORD

PRINT RECEIPT DOCUMENT

REVIEW DOCUMENT

DO UNTIL REPRINT OFF

CANCEL, RESTART, FALLBACK ?

RETURN ACTIVITY SEQUENCE NUMBER

ADD CASHIER TRANSACTION RECORD

DO UNTIL FALLBACK OFF

DO UNTIL RESTART OFF

CANCEL ?

NUMBER OF RECEIPTS > 0 ?

NUMBER OF RECEIPTS > 1 ?

ADD REVIEW RECORD

ADD REVIEW RECORD

ADD HQ DATA BASE RECORD

tool to aid in the development of structured programs, logic charts prevent unrestricted transfer of control. With logic charts, there is no representation for the branch instruction, so the developer is forced to design programs in a structured manner, free from branch instructions.

Since no more than 15 to 20 symbols can be drawn on a single sheet of paper, and there are no off-page connectors, the final structured flowchart or logic chart is modularized.

Also known as Chapin charts, they usually include rectangles whose top edge is a single entry point and whose bottom edge is a

With Warnier-Orr, analysis and design are attacked from the output backward.

single exit point. The flow of logic is always from top to bottom, and each rectangle determines which path the logic will follow next.

A DP department that is currently using traditional systems analysis methods but intending to develop an online system should consider using logic charts for the design of their new system. Logic charts are generally used with a traditional system hierarchical chart and a data element input/output chart.

The hierarchical chart is leveled—each box on the top level chart is broken down and defined in greater detail—until it can be drawn with a logic chart. One complete transaction or process would be defined by each logic chart.

For each logic chart, the input and output data elements are identified along with their usage, class, size, source and destination. The source and destination of each data element is either another logic chart or an external location.

One of the advantages of logic charts for the development of online systems, is that the logic paths executed as a result of a control decision are mapped out (see Figure 4).

Logic charts are ideally suited for the design of event-driven or transaction-driven systems. The translation of a logic chart into a structured program is relatively easy. The use of logic charts, however, does not make the designer's job any easier, and in fact, more forethought may be required. Users could also have a problem with logic charts at first, because they are not as readily understood as some of the other systems analysis techniques.

There's a variety of systems analysis methods to chose from. For some of the techniques, adequate training is readily available—from consultants or other sources—but the availability of adequate training may preclude the use of one technique rather than another. The best method to use depends on the type of DP shop and the types of systems that will be developed in the future.

About the author

Shevlin is a systems analyst for the State of California. He has held programmer/analyst positions in private industry, county government and with the State of California. He holds a BS degree from California State University, Sacramento.—Ed.

After Implementation What's Next? Evaluation

BY DR. GARY I. GREEN and DR. ROBERT T. KEIM

DR. GARY I. GREEN

Dr. Green is an Assistant Professor of Computer Information Systems at Arizona State University. His current research projects include the evaluation of the computer information system and the determination of behavioral skills for systems analysts. He holds a Ph.D. from the University of Washington and has published in several journals.

DR. ROBERT T. KEIM

Dr Keim, a member of the faculty of the Department of Quantitative Systems in the College of Business Administration at Arizona State University, is interested in the analysis, design, implementation, and evaluation of Information Systems. He is the author of a forthcoming book on computer information systems for smaller organizations. He is an active member of the Phoenix, Arizona Chapter of ASM and has been a member of the International Membership Committee.

■ Systems development generally proceeds with a life cycle starting with problem awareness and definition stages followed by varying levels of design culminating with implementation. The end products of the process are operational programs, defined procedures and trained personnel. Throughout this life cycle the need for effective planning coupled with follow-up evaluation is of concern to top management, users, and systems design personnel.

Increasing backlogs, technical staff turnover and lack of qualified replacements have resulted in most projects being over budget and delivered late. Evaluation of the systems development process and its resulting products, can be formalized to hopefully improve the overall performance. Unfortunately, due to competition for resources and initial systems success, the evaluation activity is usually not considered until problems hit the critical list.

A Change in Emphasis

The initial emphasis for systems evaluation was centered on hardware utilization. This emphasis was justified due to the relatively high cost of early computer systems. Systems analysts and programmers were very much concerned with evaluating throughput and capacity as long as the job was accomplished. In fact, most evaluation procedures were used for cost justification or were oriented toward the installation of new hardware.

A change in emphasis for evaluation is taking place. In the near future, the productivity of the system and its development will be of paramount importance. Evaluation will focus on how well the planning function was carried out; on user involvement; on attitudinal assessments about systems usage; on control of organizational resources; and on the process of development. Although it will remain an important consideration for computer design and engineering, hardware utilization is receiving much less attention. The causes for this change of emphasis are: the high cost of human resources and the growing organizational dependencies on the information systems function.

When Should Evaluation Take Place?

Typically evaluation takes place at the conclusion of the implementation stage. Certainly a system should be evaluated during implementation as well as follow-up through operations and maintenance. Furthermore, evaluation should take place at all stages of systems development: project definition, design, development, implementation and operations. There are several justifiable reasons for considering evaluation at all stages of development:

- Evaluation may aid in project management and control throughout the duration of a project.[2]
- Evaluation could help to ensure compliance with user community objectives before implementation.[9]
- The process of systems design may be evaluated at all stages to aid in improving the effectiveness of the design team.[7]
- Cost savings may be realized by modifying systems through evaluation before, rather than after, implementation.[4]
- Evaluation could help to ensure that proper design procedures and policies were being carried out.[10]

These evaluations should be conducted when and where they are appropriately required. In order to facilitate evaluation, a framework for evaluation must be developed. This framework should focus upon the salient processes and should utilize measurable variables so that adjustments may be made to enhance the particular system.

What Should be Evaluated?

Table 1 presents the major processes for evaluation as well as those variables in the systems function that are measures of the process. The processes that should be evaluated include: performance, interface, and change. It is important to understand and evaluate how well a system is performing to stated goals. Performance may be operationally defined as the level of goal achievement. Second, it is increasingly necessary to evaluate the interface process, i.e. interactions between a system and other units. Specifically, interface is the extent of linkage between resource units, including both those designing and using systems. The third major process that should be the focus of evaluation is the overall change process. The change process must be monitored and managed to help insure proper systems performance.

Table 1
What Do You Evaluate?

Variables	Process		
	Per-formance	Interface	Change
Control	Time Errors	Access Redundancy	Cost Compliance
Usage	Frequency Ease of Use	Shared Data Decision Support	Resistance Disruption
Environ-mental	Market Response Service	Structure Satisfaction	Documentation Training

The processes of performance, interface and change should be evaluated by a set of well defined variables. These variables may be classified into the three general categories: control, usage, and environmental.

1. *Control variables* — Control variables are those most often associated with error detection, security procedures, and compliance. Perhaps more effort has been devoted to the development of control variables due to the increasing attention given to evaluating performance. However, other uses of control variables are represented in Table 1. Interface and change may also be subject to evaluation. Certainly management would desire to assess the control aspects of communication access, or unit record redundancy. Any change could be evaluated for its cost and compliance to policy or budget. These change items should be planned so that appropriate control variables could be developed.

2. *Usage Variables* — Usage variables have historically been associated with assessing frequency of a variety of hardware performance parameters (e.g., number of times a disk file was accessed, frequency of entry from a terminal, CPU utilization). This particular area of evaluation of performance is the most often utilized for monitoring the efficiency of equipment. The results of performance could be used to evaluate equipment/program maintenance or repair.

Usage variables may also be applied to help evaluate the "ease of use" of systems or the behavioral dimension. For example, performance in a data entry device may be relatively easy or hard to use depending upon screen format design. It could be most helpful to identify "the ease of use" by collecting usage statistics and interviewing users. Performance might improve if some systems (such as word processing, text editing, query facilities, data entry screens, user friendly prompts, and interactive applications) were easier to use.

Interface is playing an increasingly more important functional role in information systems usage. Two variables that are closely associated with interface are shared data and decision support. The shared data concept may be measured for evaluation purposes by capturing who and for what purpose the data is being utilized. Data Base Administration is an important means of implementing this concept. As an example, an accounts payable system may share vendor authorization codes with contract administration. Usage evaluation of the interface of decision support systems with data bases on any other application programs should be an important consideration. Indeed, many decision support systems facilitate access to statistical packages, plotting routines, or other applications (such as data merging). The assessment of this interface could lead to a determination of the financial success of a further investment in DSS interface. Conversely, usage statistics in a low range might indicate limited benefits from enhancement. Also, low range usage could indicate a need for greater training so that more users could take advantage of the interface.

Change processes may be measured based on usage variables. Table 1 suggests that any resistance or disruption resulting from change could be observed through usage. Resistance may occur after an implementation by individuals refusing to utilize the new system. Determination of resistance may be inferred by the difference between expected usage and actual usage. Disruption, on the other hand, may be more difficult to measure but certainly could be observed. With improper consideration for conversion, a new applications program could receive little usage due to the disruption of the change process.

3. *Environmental Variables* — Evaluation of the operational functions (performance, interface, change) based upon environmental variables is essential in order to measure implementation success. Performance of a product could be partially determined by how well the product was able to provide an acceptable response to the user market. Another variable might be the capability of providing the level of service necessary for the user community. Customer inquiry systems should provide a certain level of service in order to meet performance specifications.

The interface of an application program with other programs as well as decision support for the user could be measured with environmental variables. The structure, or linkage of the application with other applications or systems may be assessed by a study of: information and control data that are coupled to other systems; the degree or strength of coupling; and the extent of coupling (number of connections). In addition to structure, the intangible user satisfaction with the decision support

or processing functions of a program is important to assess. The user group's satisfaction with the program's capability for interfacing decision support requests should be addressed in the evaluation process.

Change should be planned. The impact of implementing a new program could be observed through environmental variables, such as documentation and training. Documentation certainly incorporates a wide range of materials. Nonetheless, proper documentation for the implementation process could result in substantial productivity savings over the life of the product. User manuals, data dictionaries, structured charts, pseudo code may be included in determining the degree of success in implementation. The obvious difficulty lies in the qualification of success. This qualification must be rather subjective in the assessment of quality, but the major issue will be whether the documentation (or type of documentation) even exists. Lastly, an environmental variable that should be included to account for change is training. In some cases, implementation plans ignore user training. Quality (and even quantity) of training is difficult to plan for, but nonetheless must be part of implementation for most circumstances.

How to Evaluate

There is no one best way to evaluate a system. Evaluation techniques range from those that have high reliability and objectivity, such as monitors, to those with questionable reliability and high subjectivity, such as surveys. Nonetheless, evaluation should take place. At issue is how to evaluate a system.

Evaluation, as a process, should attempt to determine whether or not a system has performed to expectations based on a set of criteria. As suggested in the previous section, this task may require the selection of several techniques with the results all supporting a given purpose for evaluation. Evaluation should progress as follows:

(1) Determine the purpose for evaluation;
(2) Recognize what should be evaluated;
(3) Select appropriate techniques for assessing the system; and,
(4) Combine the results of the evaluation by appropriate criteria.

Methodologically, the task of evaluation is difficult. One must recognize that there has been a lack of effort in developing a unified approach for assessment. Each organizational situation is different. A systems development project that was successful in one context may not be successful in another. Also, organizations are dynamic and assessment of a system design with static measures may not be very appropriate. Evaluation does take time and could be costly. Results of evaluation should be interpreted with caution. With these difficulties in mind the following discussion describes some of the major techniques used in evaluation.

Monitors—Monitors are primarily software products that collect information on processing. One example of a monitor is the IBM product SMF (Systems Management Facility) that is under the auspices of the IBM operating systems. SMF collects a variety of information for each process used. Typically a monitor will record the time and length of processing, records and files used, user identification and authorization, system program statements used, CPU time, disk access time, appropriate dollar charges for the entire process, and many other details.

Statistical analysis of sets of information collected by monitors may be valuable in identifying performance difficulties in using the data set in the auditing process to test for compliance, improper access and/or usage, and systems performance. Results of such an analysis need to be formalized with report procedures. Monitors are relatively easy to implement and are beneficial in evaluating performance interface and change functions for control variables.

Costing—Traditional accounting functions of comparing actual expenditures to budgeted amounts (on standard costs) is a most helpful evaluation method, particularly in assessing stages of project development. Project management and control necessitates some form of evaluation. Accountability for time spent on steering committee assignments, analysis, design, documentation, implementation, testing, training, installation and follow-up review should be facilitated by formalized evaluation.

Specifications play an important role in identifying areas for data collection on expenditures. Evaluation of standard costs and variances is widely practiced and has been incorporated in a numbers of formalized development processes. The specifications that are utilized for performance of the design team are in turn the basis for evaluating project expenditures. These budget or cost control techniques are particularly helpful in evaluating progress. Once a project has been completed the costing techniques may be useful in determining the viability of maintenance, modification or even redevelopment.

Surveys—Questionnaires might be desirable for collecting information about users' perceptions and attitudes of project success and resulting problems. Also included in this category would be interviews. Surveys may be vigorously controlled and provide an abundance of statistical information but caution is urged in designing them and interpreting their results. If the user community is dissatisfied with the performance of an application program that source of dissatisfaction should be identified. This general technique may be applied at all stages of project development.

Evaluation should serve the purpose of providing a mechanism for feedback. Survey type of techniques offer the best opportunity to formalize the feedback process. Questionnaires can allow the user community to freely comment on relevant issues such as: reported usage of the system; attitudes about the system; areas of concern about the project; suggestions for improvements; and critique of data entry and reports. This information may be aggregated and analyzed to provide insight as to how the user community views interface and change functions for usage and environmental variables. This technique also provides for an outlet of expression and a concensus may be evaluated as a potential problem.

Surveys serve another valuable function by allowing the analyst to assess the need for training. More training, or better training, may be the solution to users who do not avail themselves of the opportunities provided by the systems.

Debriefing—A seldom used technique by the analyst is the process of debriefing. Most military missions require debriefing for the obvious reason of learning from past experience how to improve. The benefits to debriefing are: a review of procedures that could have been enhanced; discussion of communication difficulties; assessment of how to better productivity of staff; critique of documentation; and an overall evaluation of project scheduling and control. Debriefing should take place at the conclusion of each phase of system development.

Debriefing should be held under the auspices of the senior analyst and in a non-threatening environment. Preferably the debriefing process should be held off-site in a retreat context. The technique is primarily concerned with determining potential productivity enhancements of the development process. Those who participated in design should have an opportunity to share their insights and observations on how to improve the process. After implementation, the project team (or individual analyst for that matter) should debrief as a matter of course rather than an afterthought. A debriefing manual should be kept to document the content of a debriefing session.

Post Implementation Review (PIR)—There has been an attempt at developing an encompassing set of procedures known as a Post Implementation Review (or Post Implementation Audit). This methodology focuses on the success of implementation as judged by users, analysts, internal auditors, and management. Major issues such as whether systems objectives were fulfilled and what needs to be done to achieve the objectives are addressed by PIR. In fact this method incorporates what some of the other methods attempt to accomplish.

The difference between PIR and the other techniques mentioned is that PIR occurs only after implementation. Also PIR is an attempt to synthesize the various techniques so that a combination of criteria might by employed to evaluate systems effectiveness. Some of the criteria include cost effectiveness, technical quality, budget compliance, and user's satisfaction. Usually a PIR would be the responsibility of a commmittee, whereas the other methods could be undertaken by individuals (i.e., internal auditor using costing and systems staff using monitors).

Purpose of Evaluation

There are many different purposes for evaluation. A particular methodology or technique should be selected depending upon the purpose. One purpose for evaluation might be to determine compliance with started performance objectives. This purpose would necessitate an entirely different method for evaluation than the purpose of evaluating the subjective user's satisfaction with the performance of the product. Yet both evaluation techniques may be employed to help assess a given application program.

Quite obviously there are a number of different reasons for evaluation as well as a number of different evaluation techniques. Table 2 suggests that a combination of techniques might be applied depending upon the purpose for evaluation. As an example, compliance with stated performance objectives may be assessed using such techniques as performance monitors, budget performance and post implementation review. There may exist other techniques taken singularly or in combination that might also help in the evaluation of compliance. Compliance would require evaluation techniques that could objectively capture and assess information related to performance.

Table 2
Selection of Evaluation Techniques

	Techniques				
Purpose for Evaluation	Moni-tors	Cost-ing	Survey	De-Brief-ing	Post-Imple-menta-tion Review
Compliance	X	X			X
Usage Deter-mination	X		X		X
Maintenance Require-ments	X		X		X
Productivity Enhance-ments	X	X		X	X
User Feedback			X		X

There are many other requirements for evaluation as suggested in Table 2. Usage determination refers to whether or not a system or systems feature is being em-

ployed and to what extent that system is being used. The issue of usage could be extremely important in justifying project development costs, or conversely, in deleting a system with poor usage and high maintenance costs. Maintenance requirements is another reason for evaluating a system. After implementation there should be an effort to determine when maintenance is warranted. The techniques to help identify maintenance requirements vary from monitoring to user surveys. Similarly, productivity enhancements to a particular system may be determined by several different techniques. The purpose for evaluating a system's capability for improving productivity is, of course, a primary concern. How well a system has been able to increase productivity of information processing, control, and managerial decision making should be answered. Lastly, it is rather important to have a mechanism for users to report their satisfaction or dissatisfaction with a particular system.

Reported Results of Evaluation

Even though evaluation is deemed to be important there are in fact very few reported results of using evaluation techniques. The only exception might be the reported results of using monitors; but even so, monitors are not being fully utilized to support internal auditing and program development. What few results that have appeared in the literature generally conclude that the process of evaluation is fraught with difficulty and that few organizations are conducting evaluations. One other important issue should be considered: each organizational situation is different and it is risky to generalize from specific case analysis. Nonetheless, there appears to be some consensus in comparing research results as well as instructive suggestions:

- User satisfaction and involvement are important factors in successful implementations;[5,6,8]
- There is a need to assess characteristics of information and use;[6,8]
- Post implementation review has been attempted by several companies;[1]
- It is necessary to relate performance to strategic plans for the information system;[5] and
- A committee involving internal auditing, the comptroller, systems, and users should conduct the evaluation.[5]

Framework for Evaluation

Evaluation centers on the concept of how productive the information systems function (ISF) is relative to the organization's needs. ISF should be assessed with the resultant evaluation used to enhance systems development and systems usage. This paper has focused thus far on reasons and methods for evaluation. A general framework for evaluation is presented in Figure 1.

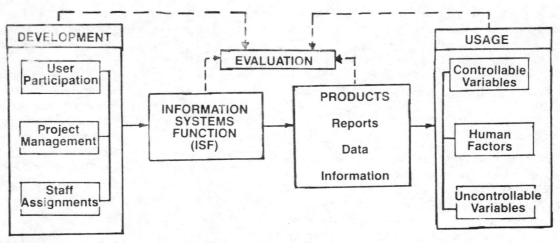

Note: --▶ represents feedback for control or enhancement
--▶ represents a direct linkage

Figure 1
Productivity Assessment of the Information Systems Function

The Information Systems Function (ISF) represents any system and its associated resources that are used to support organizational data processing and decision making requirements. The ISF should involve the systems analyst both in terms of design and usage as shown in Figure 1. Evaluation should take place at all stages of systems development and should focus on user specifications, project control, and productivity of the staff. Likewise, evaluation should take place after implementation and should include the identification of controllable and uncontrollable variables as well as those human factors related to ISF (i.e., decision making processes, training, usage).

Products of ISF are reports, data, and information. These products and ISF may be subject to evaluation based upon their productivity. The assessment of performance could serve as feedback to control (or enhance) systems development and/or usage. This framework would suggest that the process of evaluation is essential if a change were desired. In fact, the evaluation process should identify what needs to be achieved to meet the objectives of ISF. A great deal could be accomplished by combining the defined variables (control, usage, environmental) with appropriate evaluation techniques within the framework proposed in Figure 1. This task is the subject of a great deal more research effort.[3]

Conclusions

Clearly there is a recognized need for evaluation of the performance of information systems. Perhaps the evaluation process could center on the information systems function. Unfortunately, there has not been an adequate effort in identification of criteria for evaluation or for that matter, what should be evaluated. Indeed, there really has not been a well developed set of evaluation procedures that has been empirically validated or widely used. Cer-

tainly there is a pressing need for the development of better methods for evaluation notwithstanding the fact that different situations may require different evaluation strategies. The systems analyst simply cannot afford to ignore the basic task of assessing performance especially after implementation.

At issue is the assessment of productivity. A great deal of concern exists with respect to how organizations can best deploy their systems and programming staff. High turnover, stress, and tremendous demand for maintenance and new systems pose serious problems. Productivity enhancement of not only the professional systems staff but also the end users offers the promise of beneficial results stemming from evaluation. The question is not whether to evaluate, but when and how was evaluation conducted.   ●jsm

References
1. Cerullo, Michael J., "Determining Post-Implementation Audit Success," *Journal of Systems Management*, Vol. 30, No. 3 (March 1979), pp. 27-31.
2. Cleland, David I. and William R. King, *Systems Analysis and Project Management*, 2nd Edition, 1975, McGraw-Hill: New York.
3. Green, Gary I. and Robert T. Keim, "Information Systems Productivity Factors," Paper presented to ORSA/TIMS Annual Meeting, San Diego, October 27, 1982.
4. Keim, Robert T. and Ralph Janero, "Cost/Benefit Analysis of MIS," *Journal of Systems Management*, Vol. 33, No. 9 (Sept. 1982), pp. 20-25.
5. King, William R., and Jaime I. Rodriquez, "Evaluating Management Information Systems," *MIS Quarterly*, Vol. 2, No. 3 (September 1978), pp. 43-51.
6. Neumann, Seev and Eli Segev, "Evaluate Your Information System." *Journal of Systems Management*, Vol. 31, No. 3 (March 1980), pp. 34-41.
7. Nolan, Richard L., "Managing the Crises in Data Processing," *Harvard Business Review*, Vol. 56, No. 2, (March-April 1979), pp. 115-126.
8. Senn, James A., "Management's Assessment of Computer Information System," *Journal of Systems Management*, Vol. 31, No. 9 (September 1980), pp. 6-11.
9. Schultz, Randall L. and Dennis P. Slevin, editors, *Implementing Operations Research/Management Science*, American Elsevier: New York, 1975.
10. Yourdon, Edward and L. L. Constantine, *Structured Design: Fundamentals of a Discipline of Computer Programs and Systems Design*, 2nd edition. New York: Yourdon Press, 1978.

PART IV

DATABASE: A CRUCIAL COMPONENT OF CBMIS

LEARNING OBJECTIVES:

- Be able to understand the evolution of database and DBMS.

- Be able to understand the functions of database.

- Be familiar with different types of database models including hierarchical, network and relational.

- Have an understanding of costs and benefits of database utilization.

- Be able to recognize the relational database model as a prominent database model.

- Be able to establish a conceptual model for a "user-friendly" database system.

- Be able to understand some of the problems facing database design.

INTRODUCTION

In the evolution of computer based information systems, the problem of sharing data and data management among programs and end-users has been identified and addressed. Since data is a very valuable resource to an organization, accessability is an important attribute to be built into the system. In the traditional transaction processing system (EDP) and simple CBMIS, sets of data were devoted to individual programs where one or more data files were used to produce a single report. These files were generally designed for a specific application and when the firm designed many application programs, some of the same data items were included in many of the application files. As the demand for application programs and end-user access to data files grew, the problem of data sharing became a major issue. In particular, end-user applications generally involve one or more of the following functions: file creations, searches, sorts, reports, and screen displays. All of these functions involve access to data which may be conceptually located in many files, records or physical locations. Hence, the problem of data redundancy became a major problem to be addressed in terms of efficient utilization of the data resources. More specifically, a data file requires physical storage capacity and if the same data items were incorporated into a number of files, efficient use of the storage capacity, minimization of storage costs, data file maintenance were negated. Also, since the files were initially designed to support specific programs, a change in format of one file could affect many application programs. As the application programs became more complex and end-user needs emerged, there arose a need to remove the problem of data redundancy and to make application programs and data independent. This problem relates to the management of data which, itself, is a primary requisite to a successful management information system. To overcome the problem, the concept of database and database management systems came into being.

A database was conceived and developed as a means for building independence between data and programs. That is, a database is an integrated set of files which contain data relative to the activities of the organization and is used to operate the organization. Databases are generally designed to allow a large number of users to access data and information from the database and use this data and information for a multitude of purposes in many different formats. Typically the database is centralized and by cutting across organizational lines, data and information are made available to all managerial levels. The data in the database should be not only accessible but reliable, accurate, high quality, and easily modified relative to application program require-ments. To bridge the independence of data and programs, an environment needed to be created which would integrate users, data, and systems. In turn, there was a need to develop a system which would allow users to deal with more than one set of data at a time through standardization and integration of data resources.

Basic functions of a database include file creation, file update, file manipulation, sort and search. Also, with the availability of powerful and inexpensive DBMS packages for both the micro and mainframe, database design is becoming a relatively easy task.

Security protection and multi-user access are the other features available in many of DBMS on the market. In a multi-user setting all authorized employees have access to the same common data. At this point, data, the most important resource of a company, may be shared by all key decision makers.

Query language is another powerful feature available in a majority of database management systems (DBMS) products. Query language enables a user to inquire a database in a free format manner. This type of language closely parallels conversational English and they are more forgiving than traditional high-level languages such as FORTRAN, COBOL, etc.

A database is composed of two basic views, namely, the conceptual and physical structure of the data. The physical view relates to how the data are phyically stored. For example, are the data files stored on disk, tape, in main memory, etc. The conceptual view relates to the users view of the data as they are to be retrieved and transformed into information.

Three major types of database models are: heirarchical, network, and relational. The hierarchical structure involves the storing of data in binary form and can be viewed as a tree structure where each branch may be segmented into other branches. In essence, this may be thought of in terms of a parent-child relationship. In this model, the relationships are fixed at the time the database structure is defined. Hence, all access to the database must be made through the links established when the database was constructed. Changes in the structure will require re-entering all the data. The network model (or more specifically, simple network) is like the hierarchical model with the exception that an element may have more than one parent, as long as the parents have different types of records associated with them. In complex network, the parent node may have a number of children associated with it and a child node may have a number of parents associated with it. In fact, there may be clusters associated with each node. Here again, any changes in the structure require a re-entering of the data. In the relational model, the data are stored in two dimensioned tables where each table is a model of the real world data relationships. This structure is based on a conceptual view of the relationship within and between files. The relationship between data items is completely flexible and information can be accessed by defining the desired relationships. This structure is simple to use and understand. It also has the property of allowing new information to be added by simply adding a new table. In the relational database, data are represneted strictly by data values without structure or connecting information. Secondly, the database is more user oriented (friendly) because the user can query the data by asking virtually any question and the database management system, which uses a high level language, performs the necessary operations without algorithmic or procedural specification. Many consider the relational database model to be the best way to make data available to users.

The database management system (DBMS) is the software which supports the database. It is designed to manage and maintain the database resources. In general, the DBMS is application independent, can be used in any environment where data has to be managed, is not dependent on specific applicaton programs or files, and has the capability of making data available to many application programs. The DBMS deals only with the manipulation of the data, retrieval, and data organization. It is differentiated from a CBMIS in that the DBMS does not involve itself with the meaning of data but only with the data management functions.

Associated with a DBMS is an individual who is responsible for database maintenance. That is, responsible for maintaining the accuracy and completeness of data within the database. This individual carries the title of database administrator (DBA).

Some of the steps involved in establishing a database include:

1. The involvement of senior management.
2. User education.
3. A thorough cost/benefit analysis.
4. A thorough data analysis.
5. A thorough function analysis.

6. The establishment of data standards.
7. The selection of software.
8. Defining the database administrator's functions.

In summary, the implementation of a database and database management system includes many benefits in the form of the ability to access data from many files without the functional boudaries inhibiting the retrieval process. A second major benefit involves the ability to support new and changing user requirements and a third relates to increased data reliability. All three are factors which must be included in any successful design and implementation of a CBMIS.

Database is an absolute requirement for a successful CBMIS design and implementation. In the process for designing a database, users must be directly involved because the database must closely relate to users needs and requirements. A database must present a model of the organization and its content must change with the growth of the organization.

DISCUSSION QUESTIONS

1. What are some of the features of a non-database environment?

2. Why must data be treated as a common resource?

3. What is a database?

4. How has database evolved to its current form?

5. How do you compare a database with so-called "flat files"?

6. What are some of the functions of database management?

7. What are some of the costs and benefits of a database?

8. Identify some database types (or models)?

9. Why have relational databases become so popular?

10. What is logical design in database development?

11. Why must users be involved in database design?

12. What is data integrity and how is this related to a database?

13. What are some of the important factors to be considered when you are looking for a database product?

14. What are some of the problems involved in database design?

15. What is DBMS and how do you compare it with database itself?

16. Is security higher or lower in a database environment?

Let's Talk DBMS

Just like the weather, everybody talks about data base management systems, but are we doing more than just chat?

By Jan Snyders, Senior Editor Software

You cannot discuss data base management systems (DBMS) without a good working definition of a data base, according to George Fadok, area manager of Honeywell's Information Systems Div. Field Technical Services in Phoenix. A data base is a representation or model of the things, descriptions and relationships that define the business and the environment in which that business operates. It is the raw material that supports the production of information. The data base therefore becomes a resource that belongs to the entire company as opposed to any one specific functional area or application.

A DBMS then, according to Shaku Atre, president of Atre International Consultants of Rye, NY, integrates data files into a data base and provides different views to different users. Therefore, the software, hardware, firmware and the procedures that manage that data base make up the DBMS.

Ronald G. Ross, editor of the *Data Base Newsletter,* published by the Data Base Research Group, Houston, stresses three vital points.

• Data are defined independently of any of the application programs; so there is a layer of insulation between programs and the data itself. This is so you won't be able to change the data without affecting the program.

• The DBMS should increase accessibility. That is, it provides access to data without programs procedurally having to look through larger volumes of data in order to find the specific data wanted.

• The DBMS needs to provide for sharing of data. It must support multiple users who need to get at the same data simultaneously.

It all depends on whom you're speaking with when you discuss the various DBMS types. Fadok speaks of three: hierarchical, codasyl network and relational. Atre, on the other hand, discusses four types based on data models: relational, hierarchical, network and inverted files.

In reality, though, Atre contends there are really two distinct data models: relational and network. Hierarchical is a special kind of network, she says, and inverted files is more of an implementation issue. Since there are successful data base management systems that use hierarchical and inverted files, some differentiate between four models. But these systems were not really planned; they evolved.

In the early 1960s, no one tried to come up with different data models and then build a DBMS. In the case of hierarchical and network, there was no systematic approach to developing data models before DBMS. The inverted file then was developed because developers

77

Reprint from INFOSYSTEMS, December 1984, Copyright Hitchock Publishing Company

DBMS

"Don't try to convert your existing applications as a first try."

Shaku Atre, President
Atre International Consultants
Rye, NY

wanted to have something that would make it easier for people to access the data base records as well as to have different views of the same data.

Relational DBMS took an opposite tack. The relational data model was developed and then the relational DBMS.

Of the first three, none is completely 100 percent what its name implies. According to Atre, hierarchical is anything that has about 80 percent of the structure based on hierarchical and 20 percent is picked up from other data models. Therefore, none of the systems is 100 percent hierarchical, network or inverted file since they have features from other data models.

Of course, relational, the latest entrant into the DBMS arena, does have some definite properties that distinguish it from the others. For instance, Dr. E.F. Codd, an independent consultant in San Jose, CA, states that a relational DBMS provides automatic navigation through the data base. That means that you specify what you want, but not how it should be obtained.

A second important property is high-level language capability. A relational system provides a form of retrieval, update, insert and delete. In addition, one can be authorized to do things with various parts of the data base that are defined by means of the high-level language. This means you can protect both application programs and terminal activities.

Fadok points to three major DBMS components or subsystems. First are languages for data definition and manipulation. Second is space management. This part stores a record in a specific area in a certain manner. This is comparable to storing parts in a warehouse on different shelves in specific areas. Third is the data organization itself; the organization and structuring capabilities provided by the system.

As far as Atre is concerned, "The major components of a DBMS reside in an area very few people go into." The major components, according to her, are data manipulation language, data description language, query and report generators, applications programming language (a part of the data manipulation language) and data communications interface. She also mentions physical implementation and utilities.

The data description language ex-

Selecting the Right DBMS

Since it is so important to select the right data base management system (DBMS), extreme caution should be taken at the onset. Shaku Atre, who has gone through the process of evaluating various DBMSs for clients, has a systematic approach. Atre is president of Atre International Consultants in Rye, NY.

• Identify the application, function and parts of the business that will be using the DBMS. This is the needs identification.

• Based on the needs identification, eliminate the DBMS products that cannot even be considered in the evaluation process.

• The DBMS must be compatible with your hardware and operating system. It must also be compatible with your teleprocessing monitors if you already have applications running on them. The DBMS also has to be compatible with the programming language being used and with any prepackaged applications software that has been purchased.

• The DBMS also should have an easy-to-use integrated data dictionary. If you don't have an integrated data dictionary, you could have problems because you might be moving into a segregated data base environment using a mainframe and microcomputers.

• Once the needs and specifications have been outlined, prepare the request for proposal from several vendors. This should not be voluminous but should list all of your requirements.

• On receipt of responses from the vendors, again it is time to eliminate the vendors that do not meet your standards.

• When you have made the selection of several potential suppliers, ask each of them to arrange meetings for you with their users. Preferably, these should be users with installations similar to yours. That is, comparable in hardware, operating system and language.

• After visiting users, you should go one step further and visit the vendor's headquarters. Of course, if it is a vendor like IBM, it is senseless to visit the headquarters to find out more about the financial situation of the vendor. But in others, it is important to know if the DBMS vendor will be around five years from now.

• The final step is writing the recommendations for management. This should not only include the reasons for selection of this particular vendor but reasons for not selecting those eliminated. (IN)

DBMS

"Today people are paying less attention to processing and concentrating more on data."

George Fadok, Area Manager
Field Technical Services
Honeywell Information Systems
Phoenix

plains the structure of the DBMS and how it will look. The data manipulation language is used to write applications. This involves calls imbedded in the host language such as Cobol, PL1, Fortran or Assembler.

Another type of language—usually called fourth-generation languages (4 GLs)—has created confusion as to whether these are actually 4 GLs or DBMSs. As Ross said, "All DBMSs have some kind of special language. You need something beyond Cobol if you're going to work in a data base environment. How friendly that is and how easily learned by relatively unsophisti-

cated users is a different question."

According to Ross, DBMSs have a language that is difficult to use, even by professionals. He cites, for example, IBM's IMS as difficult, and Model 204 from Computer Corp. of America in Cambridge, MA, and Adabas from Software AG of North America in Reston, VA, as less difficult.

The 4 GL types were built to provide accessibility basically for retrieval in a different environment. They are oriented toward a private workstation concept and not toward a high volume of shareable data with concurrent updating.

The data dictionary also is becoming a

vital DBMS adjunct. While the DBMS has a specific function to provide languages, space management and data organization, above that is a larger umbrella: the data dictionary. "Today people are paying less attention to processing and concentrating more on data," said Fadok. Since the DBMS stores so much data, it is almost vital to have a data dictionary to help in the running of the business. The data dictionary is useful in the operation and control of the information system and in the design of new applications where the user has to have access to the available data.

Depending on how you define an installation of a DBMS, it can take anywhere from a few days to years. Basically, the initial installation should take about four days. That is, when trying to install the DBMS you are probably still running the rest of the company business in your data center. Therefore, the actual installation must be performed at night or on weekends. The actual installation of the software from the vendor should take no more than four days with the DBMS vendor's help.

Putting the data in the DBMS takes weeks, months or even years. Again, Atre suggests a planned approach. Her advice is, "Don't try to convert your existing applications as a first try." It is better to select one or two new applications and install those. Phasing in or converting existing systems can take place once new applications have been installed.

One organizational element that has arisen since the introduction of DBMS is a new job description for your employees. According to Ross, "To be effective with a large-scale DBMS requires a new perspective on the management, design and planning of data resources. It requires moving away from an application-by-application focus and thinking more strategically in terms of what the information architecture needs to be and how we can achieve that in some kind of evolutionary manner."

DBMS Removes Bottleneck

Wickland Oil's data collection, recording, processing and reporting have all been computerized for some time. But in mid-1982, it became clear that the company was outgrowing the capacity of the existing data processing resources. Response time was slowing down; disk space was filling up. Wickland was having so much difficulty keeping pace with current needs that future development tasks were getting pushed further and further away. In September 1982, Bob Irvine, director of MIS (management information systems) proposed and implemented a three-part solution to Wickland's problem: an IBM 4331 L2 mainframe, IBM's DOS/VSE/SSX operating system, and Software AG of North America's products (Adabas, Natural, Complete and Predict) to enable the company to implement its new systems.

While the hardware and software were being installed, Irvine began training his staff in the Software AG products, and laid down the design criteria for a proposed new daily sales system. On Oct. 1, 1983, programming began using Natural, Adabas and Predict running under Complete. Four months later, with an average of three people working on the project, the new system was coded, parallel-tested and brought up for use in production. Over 95 major on-line and batch functions, supported by 417 program modules, were involved.

"From a development standpoint, Adabas, Natural and the other Software AG products have given my group a tremendous boost in productivity, in terms of speed, quantity and capability—arising out of a specific, controlled expense, namely software, instead of an uncontrolled expense, namely, additional personnel," said Irvine. "And from a management perspective, the company now has much greater ability to manage and control data. We can handle more of it, access it faster and more flexibly, and make more use of it. And this is precisely what was needed to let the company keep growing." (IN)

DBMS

"To be effective with a large-scale DBMS requires a new perspective on the management, design and planning of data resources."

Ronald G. Ross, Editor
Data Base Newsletter
Data Base Research Group
Houston

Once you take the position that data is a resource and that it is separate from the applications portfolio, it needs to be planned and administered. Now, there are various functions that need to be involved in that management administration at various levels.

The most technical of these administrative functions is the data base administrator. The data base administrator is someone who is proficient in the technology of the DBMS such as reorganization, recovery, restart, programming type standards, and basically anything required to implement the DBMS as a software package and keep it operating. This job will require someone's full attention along with a full range of expertise.

The second type of job requires less of a technician in the sense of being proficient with the system. But this position requires being able to coordinate data and systems standards, develop data element standards and procedures for turning systems over to operations from the design stage. This person should be primarily concerned with the data dictionary and be able to establish that as a viable resource for the company.

Third is the model administrator who is over the information resource management group. This group, or person, is not involved with the technology of the DBMS or with the procedures and coordination of standards, but rather the business information and planning. This model administrator should be reporting to somebody outside of the Data Processing/Management Information Systems department, since planning for business information systems means establishing priorities for work.

Above and beyond knowing what constitutes a DBMS, how to select one, how to install one and how to staff the department, there are still other questions. These include the importance of integration, the status of distributed DBMS, DBMS on a micro and what we may see in the future.

Tough Times Ahead

The data base management system (DBMS) market is thriving, and is expected to continue to grow at a 30 percent per year rate through 1988. But most of this prosperity will fall to the larger DBMS vendors, while smaller companies face a shakeout. So says an industry expert at Predicasts, a Cleveland-based research firm.

"Smaller outfits with limited product offerings and small customer bases will be hurt the most," warns analyst Edward Hester. "With DBMSs becoming increasingly sophisticated, it's getting more difficult to stay on top of the technology."

In addition, says Hester, customers are coming to rely on vendor reputation for their software. "A few years ago there was a mishmash of software companies, but now a number of companies are moving to the forefront," he explains. "People want a name."

Hester says that more established vendors such as Applied Data Research, Cullinet and On-Line Software International will continue to expand in the competitive DBMS market, partially at the expense of the smaller companies, many of whom will be bought out by their well-heeled competitors. The biggest player of them all will continue to be IBM, which Hester expects to hold on to a one-quarter share of the market for at least another five years, despite its unimpressive DBMS offerings.

By then, IBM's aggressive competition could begin to chip away at its DBMS customer base. Hester notes, though, that IBM is not going to give up without a fight.

Hester, who co-wrote a recent report on the industry with Predicasts analyst Robert McLean, cites several trends he expects to emerge in DBMS over the next five years. Among these trends:

• DBMSs will become better integrated with applications and will become easier to use, relying more heavily on fourth-generation languages.

• Relational techniques will not catch on heavily among mainframe DBMS users for some time because of high conversion costs and performance problems. By the mid-1990s, about one-quarter of the market will be relational.

• Personal computer DBMSs will be the fastest growing segment of the market, as products grow in sophistication beyond file-handling capabilities. Relational DBMSs are more likely to catch on at the PC end.

• Growth among minicomputer DBMSs will be flat, as most users turn to either mainframe-based corporate data bases or PC-based personal data bases.

McLean says DBMS users can also expect to benefit from technological improvements such as chip-resident programs and intelligent peripherals—but not right away. "It's a growing area," he notes, "but it may be 10 years before the new technology has a big impact." —DHF

DBMS

"Sooner or later, people are going to realize—even the users with a million or two million dollars worth of data in other DBMSs—that it's not futuristic to go relational."

Dr. E.F. Codd
Consultant
San Jose, CA

Although the trend seems to be toward less integration, Fadok said, "I feel integration of data is still very important." The solution to problems in most businesses cuts across functional lines. It is rare that any function within a business is self-contained and independent of others. Problems and solutions cut across functional areas of the business and therefore, data cuts across functional lines and must be shared. It is important then that data be standardized, consistent and stored in one repository.

There has been much written about the subject of a DBMS on a micro in connection with the micro/mainframe. There are even vendors talking about their DBMS running on a personal computer. As Ross said, however, "If you take the position that data base means shareability of data by many people performing different functions, then a data management system on a personal computer providing access simply to one person who established the data base is not really a data base management system in the true sense."

But, in the area of distributed DBMS, Ross was more emphatic. According to him, we do have large-scale DBMS areas that support transaction switching: routing transactions across a network to other places where data resides. By definition, where the distribution of the data is independent and transparent to all users and all programs, there is no such thing today.

On the other hand, Codd is just as emphatic that there *is* distributed DBMS. If not exactly in user hands yet, it is close. This is in the relational DBMS area. According to Codd, two companies have a DBMS where the user and application programs do not need to know where the data is in the network. Relational Technology in Berkeley, CA, is coming out with a distributed version of Ingress and IBM. Although it has not announced any products, it has a prototype called R*.

Looking a bit into the future, relational DBMS, as the latest entrant, appears to have the features most users would like to see. Cobb thinks DBMS will take over from the existing approaches. "But I am never of the view that some development is the last we'll ever see," he said. He asserted, however, the relational approach will last a long time before some improvement comes along.

With relational DBMS, there will be a standardization, Cobb predicted. The standardization will result in one high-level language. Since all of the information in a relational data base has to be represented explicitly by values and tables, it makes for a simple language. Once there is standardization, software houses will build on top of that idea. This is not to say that all of the other DBMSs will suddenly disappear from companies. But "sooner or later, people are going to realize—even the users with a million or two million dollars worth of data in other DBMSs—that it's not futuristic to go relational," he said.

One thing is certain: it is important to keep on improving. The word is that the Japanese have come up with a fifth-generation approach which relies on relational data bases as the foundation. (IN)

For a list of vendors, their packages and the equipment they run on, enter No. 2 on the Reader Information Card.

For an extra copy of this article, please enter No. 13 on the Reader Information Card.

Maintenance Costs Reduced

Take one company in Texas and one in New York and give them similar problems. They will not only come up with similar solutions but also similar savings. Phillips Hay, data processing manager at Tracor Instruments Div. of Tracor Inc. in Austin, TX, and Edward Erickson, project manager at AMF Bowling Products Group in Westbury, TX, were tied into systems at locations off-site. They knew they could do better jobs for the company with an in-house data base management system (DBMS) and subsequently installed System 2000 from Intel Corp. in Austin.

At Tracor, all processing had been performed at the corporate headquarters on a Sperry computer system. Hay installed an IBM 4331 and started converting the systems from the Sperry. At the same time, the decision was made to write all new applications in-house because of the unique business structure. The easiest way to do this was to install a DBMS.

At AMF, one of the major warehouses in Glendale, CA, a minicomputer was installed with a turnkey DBMS. After developing some applications, Erickson brought the idea to the New York office and hereto, because of unique business applications, decided to install the System 2000 because of the ease of use.

The major benefit, according to both, is savings in maintenance. As Hay said, "Previously we had an inventory control system that included six master files. Each of these files contained a repetition of the part number, description, unit of measure, etc. Now, we've located in the data base one field with that information in it and that can be maintained in one spot. We have one program and it changes the description for the part and all information at one time." Maintenance costs are reduced when only one single area is changed. (IN)

Author describes the steps in implementing a comprehensive database system.

BY RORY C. ROBICHAUX

The Database Approach

■ The term database involves more than simply an alternative technique used in the design of automated storage files. Its implications extend beyond the use of generalized software packages, even beyond the design and implementation of the automated information system. It is a concept that can be used to organize and control the information of an entire business enterprise, whether that enterprise is a corporation or a government agency. A comprehensive database system is one that controls the storage and operations of all information of a business, whether the information is processed in an automated or manual procedure or some combination of the two.

In the database approach, information is regarded as a vital resource of the business. This approach provides an efficient and effective means for controlling this resource.

In order to fully realize the benefits of the database approach, the way in which the business currently processes its data may have to be completely altered. This would entail undertaking a lengthy analysis, design, development and implementation process. This article provides a broad background for those who may be considering undertaking the task of implementing the database approach. This background includes a definition of terminology and functions, criteria that can be used to evaluate the feasibility of implementing the database approach and a methodology that can be followed from the analysis through installation of a comprehensive data base system.

Evolution of the Database Approach

In order to understand and appreciate the use of a business-wide database system, one must first understand the design of earlier automated systems. The use of the database, and finally the database management system (DBMS), came about in a fashion similar to many technological advancements: through the design, redesign and enhancement of earlier systems. It is those earlier systems that will be discussed.

In the early days of automated data processing, systems design rarely extended beyond the design of an individual program. A single program used one or more files to produce a single file or report. There was virtually no sharing of data between programs. This situation is graphically displayed in Figure I under the heading of "Conventional Systems". This caused not only redundancy in stored data, but also redundancy in updating similar information on separate files. The resulting inefficiency was in part due to the limited technology that programmers had at their disposal at that time. Thus, this limited nature of systems design would continue until a further advancement in technology occurred (e.g., indexed and random access files).

The next advancement in systems design came in the form of the integrated management information system (IMIS). This is displayed in the middle of Figure I. The IMIS was made possibile in part by operating systems that supported indexed and random files. Capabilities such as these afforded the user greater control of the data required by the program. Systems were being designed such that there was a high degree of integration between the data and the programs. In many cases, the input to a program was the output of one or more previous programs. In designs such as these, data utilization was much more efficient than in the conventional systems approach described above. However, the data and programs in such systems often became so dependent upon one another that if any given file or program failed, the entire system failed. This was a high price to pay in order to make the utilization of data more efficient.

The concept of integrating a system eventually evolved into the database management system (DBMS), as displayed at the bottom of Figure I. The basic design of a DBMS points out the general change in the emphasis of systems design: from the individual program, to the overall system, and finally to the point where the data is the focal point of the system. In the DBMS environment, the user communicates with the DBMS software either through programs or special commands. It is this software that then performs the necessary operations (e.g., store, retrieve, delete, etc.) on the data in the file(s). In many cases, the user need not concern himself with

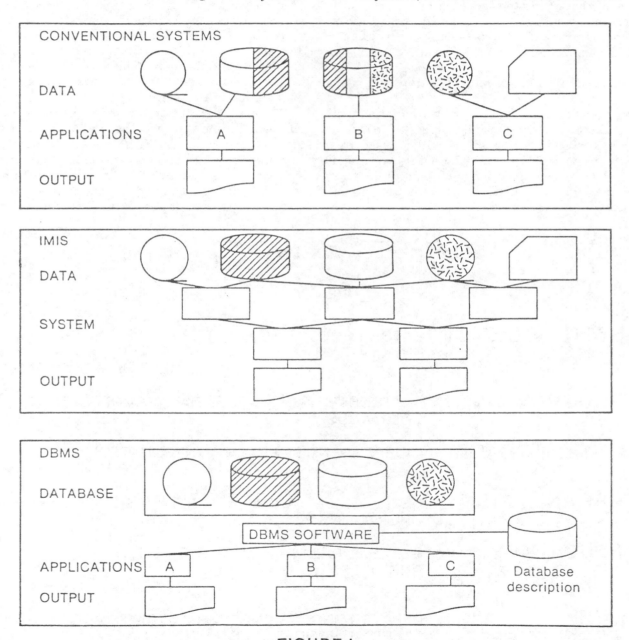

FIGURE I
Evolution of Information Management Approaches
(Reprinted from, *Database Systems: A Practical Reference* by Ian Palmer)

the physical organization of the data on the file(s) as was required in the previous approaches to the systems design. Thus, the use of a DBMS allows the user to logically share data with other users, while not having to be concerned directly with the operations of other programs or the physical structuring of the data.

Upon close examination, using a DBMS as part of the overall database is a feasible approach. The DBMS allows the data processing personnel to use a technique that makes the data used by the programs the focal point of the system. In this way, the DBMS is analogous (in a data processing sense) to the overall database approach taken by the business.

Database: Terminology and Functions

Before embarking on a study of various aspects of the database approach, it is first necessary to define some basic terms. These terms will be used frequently throughout the remainder of this paper, and it is necessary to eliminate any ambiguity that the terms may relate. It should be noted, however, that the definitions given and discussed below are not the only viable definitions of the terms. Because the various terms can often be used in a number of contexts, other definitions may be more appropriate in other cases. The following definitions are provided as a source of reference for these terms in the context in which they are used in this paper.

A definition of a "database" is a set of files on which an organization's activities are based, and upon which high reliance is placed for availability and accuracy. A definition of a "database environment" is that environment resulting from the integration of users, data, and systems—both manual and automated—by implementing the database approach. To carry this defining process to the highest level, the definition of the "database objective" is the full utilization of data resources through standardization and integration.

Several important points should be noted in the above definitions. In each, the focal point of the definition was information. This illustrates the fact that the usage of information is of primary importance to the database approach. Also, the phrase "both manual and automated", explicitly stated in the second definition, is implicit in both the first and third defi-

ASPECTS OF DATABASE

	CONVENTIONAL	DATABASE
SYSTEMS DESIGN	BATCH PROCESSING BULK OUTPUT	TRANSACTION PROCESSING EXCEPTION REPORTING
PROGRAMMING	INPUT/OUTPUT COMMANDS	DATA MANIPULATION LANGUAGE
DATA STORAGE	INDEPENDENT FILES	INTEGRATED STRUCTURES
ORGANIZATION	DEVELOPMENT AND OPERATIONS SECTIONS	DATABASE ADMINISTRATION SECTION
EDUCATION	SYSTEMS, PROGRAMMING AND OPERATIONS	REVISED ATTITUDES AND RESPONSIBILITIES
USER PROCEDURES	DELAYED PROCESSING CLERICAL PROCEDURES	IMMEDIATE ACCESS TERMINAL CONVERSATIONS

FIGURE II
Alternative Functions in Using the Conventional and Database Approaches

nitions. This concept is very important and should be kept in mind throughout the discussions of the use as well as the design and implementation of a database system. Finally, a third important point is the idea of integration. As indicated in the second and third definitions, integration is necessary on a number of levels: between "users, data and systems."

Conventional vs Database Approach

To begin the analysis of the database approach, it will be useful to once again contrast the methods used to accomplish various system functions using the conventional and database approaches. Figure II outlines many of the major functional differences between the two approaches.

In several of the functions, the requirement to utilize data in a more direct, straight-forward manner is evident. In System Design, the emphasis has shifted from processing large amounts of data at once to processing a single piece of data, or transaction, at a time. In Data Storage, instead of having to physically manipulate a number of distinct, mutually exclusive files, the user need only handle a single, logically integrated structure/In User Procedures, access to data has been speeded up from an environment of delayed processing to one in which immediate access to data is possible. These aspects illustrate the point made in the definition of database: "high reliance is placed (on) . . . availability."

An important point to consider in the overall database approach is that which is made with respect to education. When implementing a comprehensive database system, the attitudes and responsibilities of those who must deal with the data must often be revised. Without a thorough understanding of this concept, the benefits available through the use of a database system can never be fully realized. This point will be discussed in more detail later.

Database Functions

Having defined the terms basic to the database approach and compared the database system with a conventional system, the functions of a database can now be discussed. These functions include:

- Administration and Control
- Data Base Definition
- Maintenance and Reporting
- Privacy/Security
- Integrity
- Operation

Each of these functions can best be described by outlining the various facilities available for performing each of them.

There are a number of facilities to aid in the administration and control of a database. One is the use of a data dictionary. This helps ensure conformity in the naming and defining of all data elements. Another is the implementation of standards. These standards are in regards to operations, programming, development, testing, design and revisions. Also, the use of performance, data usage and system resource monitors can aid in the control of the database. The final two facilities to aid in the administration and control can be seen as administrative requirements. The first is to allocate a department in the organizational structure that contains the staff responsible for the administration and control of the database. This department is under the direct control of a database administrator. The database administrator is responsible for the analysis, design and development of the database, overseeing the implementation of any revisions, insuring the integrity and maintaining the proper security constraints of the database. Finally, to reiterate a point that was made earlier, all persons handling data must be educated to allow the most effective use of the database

The second function, definition of the database, must be handled on three separate levels. Starting at the lowest level, the individual data elements must be defined with respect to format, edit criteria and utilization. Next, the logical structuring of the data must be determined. Finally, the storage media that is to be used to store the data must be determined.

In the areas of maintenance and reporting, many of the facilities relate primarily to the automated portion of a database system. Some common maintenance facilities are loading, updating, purging, reorganization, restructuring, and archiving. Basic reporting facilities include user queries, a report writer and application programs.

In general terms, the privacy/security facilities simply specify who can make what changes to which set(s) of data. This is accomplished through the control of the usage of the data by any number of means. Also, a person(s) must be assigned to enforce these controls. As a means of verification, usage monitors can also be used to keep a log of all uses of the data.

The integrity of the database can be handled in a number of ways. It can be handled through controls built-in to handle system failure. On a lower level, there can also exist user error handling routines. These and other controls can either be physically handled by the person(s) involved or logically handled by an automated procedure.

The final database function listed above is operation. This function relates to the mode under which the database is to operate. These operating modes include interactive, batch and multi-user. Very often, the nature of the uses of data in the database will determine the mode of operation.

RORY C. ROBICHAUX

Mr. Robichaux is Executive Vice President of Information Services, Inc. in New Orleans, specializing in the marketing of turnkey general business computer systems and consulting services. Prior to that he was with CACI, Inc. as a data base analyst. He is a graduate of the University of Southwestern Louisiana.

Implications of the Database Approach

Prior to implementing the database approach there are a number of activities that must be performed. Some of these activities need only be performed once, while others must be performed on a continual basis. The required activities related to the database approach include:

- Involvement of Senior Management
- Widespread Education
- Thorough Data Analysis
- Thorough Function Analysis
- Establishing Data Standards
- Selection of Software
- Database Administration Functions

Although specific database applications may require specialized activities, those listed above can be seen as a core of the required activities for the design and implementation of a database system. Each of these requirements will now be expanded upon.

The need to involve senior management should be seen as a primary requirement when considering the database approach. This is necessary for several reasons. First, it is personnel at the senior level that must provide the necessary authority for the sharing, centralization and controlling of data. They must also be made aware of, and approve, any changes in priorities. Second, it is management personnel who provide adequate funding, staffing and equipment resources throughout the design and implementation of the database system. Finally, such individuals are in a position to communicate with others in various sectors in the business. This is necessary in imposing standards across departments. This includes standardization of such things as data names and definitions, system design and development, testing, revisions and operations.

The requirement for the education of personnel in the use and understanding of the database system is necessary in order to realize the full benefits available through the database approach. This education process must be undertaken on all levels. Management personnel should be educated to the degree that they gain an appreciation of the benefits to be realized from using a database. They should understand the objectives and costs as well as any tradeoff decisions that must be made. The database administrator, who is responsible for the overall maintenance, integrity, and enhancements of the database, should have an in-depth knowledge of many of the facilities related to the database. These facilities include the analysis and control of data, database design and tuning, and procedures to insure the integrity and concurrency of the database. The systems analysts should be made aware of the overall database approach and how it relates to data and functional analysis, database design and the design of transactions. Programmers should learn the data manipulation language, implications of certain procedures on performance, and debugging database programs. Operators should also be afforded an appreciation of the database approach and be instructed as to how to perform the set-up and recovery procedures. Finally, users must be provided with detailed instructions on the use of the systems, with emphasis on transaction procedures and report generation.

The next requirement of this approach is the data analysis. There are a number of reasons for the requirement for an in-depth analysis of the required data and the design of an optimum logical structuring of this data. The reasons include the need to reduce redundancy of data; eliminate ambiguities; determine relationships and dependencies between data elements; ascertain quality and completeness of data; define volatility and timeliness of data; and project possible growth patterns.

Another important requirement is the need for function analysis. The primary purpose of this requirement is to determine the ways in which the data will be utilized. Examples of specific uses of the data would be for display, sorting or computation. In addition, the function analysis should attempt to determine the expected responsiveness of the system and the frequency of use of the various portions of the system.

The need to establish data standards is one that is basic to the overall database approach. Three reasons for the existence of these standards are to ensure reliability of data, to support maintainability and coordinate modifications, extensions and enhancement. These objectives are only possible if data names and their meanings are consistent throughout the database. Other reasons for the standardization of data is to provide privacy and security and to control development and production costs.

Within the overall database system, there will probably exist a portion in which the data is controlled through automation. This requires the selection of one or more software packages to maintain and control the automated data. Types of software packages available to perform these functions include database management systems, data dictionary systems and library management systems.

The final requirement that is discussed with respect to the database approach is the need to install a Database Administrator. This Administrator is charged with the task of coordinating the usage and any enhancements to the database system. This is accomplished through the establishment and enforcement of all standards, coordinating application and design efforts and maintaining the database environment. It is also the function of this Administrator to control privacy and security and provide education and user liaison support.

The set of requirements discussed above is the minimum set of functions required to implement the database approach. It is of vital importance that an organization considering the database approach understand and be willing to accept the imposition of the previously described functions. If the imposition of these functions is not considered prior to the decision to take the database approach, one of several cases may occur. First, the design and/or implementation efforts may be cancelled after an unexpectedly large expenditure of resources (*funding*, personnel, etc.) causing the business to revert to the conventional systems approach. Second, the design and/or implementation phases may be cancelled for the reason stated above, with the business deciding to use the partially developed database. Third, the design and implementation continue to completion, but one or more of the required functions are omitted to limit the amount of resources expended. In any of these cases, the business is left with less than a comprehensive database system as a result of not fully understanding, or not being willing to accept, the implications of the database approach. Thus, to reiterate what was said earlier, before deciding to implement the database approach, be sure that all implications of this approach are understood and acceptable.

Determination of Need

In order to determine whether a business should undertake the task of implementing the database approach, many factors must be considered and many questions must be answered. The process of determining the relative requirement a business has for this approach is known as the feasibility analysis. It is during this analysis that the decision is made to either go or not go with the database approach.

The first step in this analysis process is to answer some of the probing questions regarding how the database will relate to the business. A major question regards the scope of the envisioned system. Will the database contain all information for the entire business, or only for some subset of departments? Of course, a comprehensive database would include all information for the entire business, but this is not always the case. Another major consideration is whether the implementation of database is being considered to solve some immediate, short-term problem or maximize the efficiency of operations over the long-term. If the solution that is required is to a short-term problem, the database approach may not be the most feasible solution. This is because of the amount of lead-time required to implement this approach. Other considerations are the many implications of taking the database approach. Is the business willing to expend the resources necessary to implement the required functions? If the answer to this question is not a definitive *yes*, then it would be best if some other systems approach were analyzed in lieu of the database approach.

Cost/Benefit Analysis

The aspect of the feasibility analysis that is often studied most carefully is the cost/benefit comparative analysis. It is in this way that the business determines the cost effectiveness of implementing the database approach. Thus, the person performing this analysis must be aware of the specific costs as well as the benefits that result from using a database system. Because some of the costs and/or benefits are not immediately evident, they are each discussed in detail below.

There are many costs involved in implementing and using a database system. Many of these costs relate directly to the "implications" discussed earlier. However, these costs, along with several others, will be discussed here to provide a concise description of the costs of this approach.

The cost factors can be grouped into four categories: software, staffing, hardware and education. Within each category the costs can be broken down even further. For software, there may be one or more general purpose packages that would be used. These include a database management system, a data dictionary system and a library management system. In addition to the cost of the actual software, there is the cost of documenting all such systems. In staffing, there are a number of positions that must be filled. These positions include the database administrator, system support personnel, database design analysts and user liaison. In hardware, the CPU *usage*, storage media and terminals comprise the bulk of the costs. In education, the costs relate to teaching personnel at various levels what they must know in order to perform their function in the database environment. This cost for education, particularly with respect to the user, is a continuing one. However, it should be noted that the cost for educating the user, as well as several of the other costs, would be incurred irregardless of which systems approach is chosen, database or non-database.

There are also a number of benefits to be derived from the use of the database approach. In many cases, these benefits outweigh the respective costs. To appreciate this fact, the benefits of the database approach should be carefully studied. Figure III illustrates many of the benefits and expanded functions available through a database system.

A major benefit of a database system is the ability to access data across functional boundaries. This capability tremendously increases the users' ability to utilize a broad cross-section of stored data. The restriction of conventional systems not allowing this sort of access was a major reason for the development of database systems. This capability is made possible through data relationships built-in to the logical structuring of the data.

A second benefit of a database system is the ability to readily support new and changing requirements. This is accomplished through the centralization and standardization of data. Thus, the need for additional files or the synchronization of multiple files is eliminated. This capability is also aided by the fact that there is a separation of the logical and physical views of the data. Also, since the database consists of a single integrated system with one support manager and staff, the cost of making enhancements to the system is reduced.

There are a number of benefits that are realized

BENEFITS OF THE DATABASE APPROACH

FLEXIBILITY	• RESPONSIVE TO CHANGE
SIMPLICITY	• REALISTIC REPRESENTATION OF DATA
USER ORIENTATION	• FEWER RESTRICTIONS ON THE USER
CENTRALIZATION	• CONTROL OF DATA RESOURCES
STANDARDIZATION	• ESTABLISHED DEFINITIONS AND PROCEDURES
GROWTH	• READILY EXTENSIBLE
DEVELOPMENT	• FASTER IMPLEMENTATION OF NEW APPLICATIONS
DATABASE ADMINISTRATION	• REDUCED PROGRAMMER/ ANALYST INVOLVEMENT
DATA INDEPENDENCE	• LOWER PROGRAM MAINTENANCE
GENERALIZED SOFTWARE	• ADDITIONAL FACILITIES — MULTIPLE CONCURRENT USAGE / DATA INTEGRITY / RECOVERY & BACKUP / DATA PRIVACY / USAGE STATISTICS
DATA SHARING	• ENHANCES THE USE OF — MULTIPROGRAMMING / DATA COMMUNICATIONS / MANAGEMENT INFORMATION SYSTEMS

FIGURE III

directly by the programmer. The first is that he can deal with less complex programs since the DMBS now handles most modifications to data through a straight-forward data manipulation language. Also, the programmer is no longer burdened by the physical structuring of the data. Finally, extra facilities such as report generators reduce the complexity of programming required.

The use of a database system also allows increased data reliability. This is made possible through a number of integrity and security controls built into the system. In addition to these controls, the use of a data dictionary increases reliability through standardized definitions. This capability, like accessing data across functional boundaries, is one of the major assets of a database system. The database system also provides the user with an increased throughput of data. The ease of use of the database system makes this aspect possible. Also, increased reliability and concurrent processing serve to enhance this benefit.

The benefits described above, in conjunction with those outlined in Figure III, are in no way meant to be an all inclusive list of benefits to be derived from the database approach. They are a representative sample of the benefits that a comprehensive database system can provide. As such, these benefits can be used in a cost/benefit analysis to judge the cost-effectiveness of the database approach for a specific business.

Potential for Failure

Having considered the implications of the database approach and performed the cost/benefit comparative analysis, there is one more factor that must be considered before deciding whether to take the database approach. It is the potential for failure. It would be a fallacy to expect that simply because one has "followed all of the rules" in designing and implementing the database system, that the production of a totally effective and efficient database system will result. Two of the major reasons for failure are discussed below.

A factor that could contribute to the failure of a database system is the existence of unreliable data. Any information system, database or non-database, automated or manual, is only as good as the information it contains. If, for some reason, the data to be contained in the database is unreliable (i.e., inconsistent, incomplete, invalid, etc.), it will not be possible to design a reliable database system that utilizes this data. In cases where this occurs, the data will either have to be modified prior to its utilization in the database or it would have to be totally disregarded and new, valid data entered into the system.

A second factor that could affect the quality of the database system is the technical expertise of those performing the analysis, design and development of the database. For example, if those responsible for selecting an appropriate DBMS for the specific database application are not knowledgeable in the area of DBMSs, an inappropriate DBMS may be selected. This could force a structuring of the data in a format that is not the most effective or efficient for that application. Thus, it is important that those making the technical decisions concerning the overall database system have an in-depth knowledge of those matters for which they are responsible.

At this point, all major factors relating to the implementation of the database approach have been considered. The decision to either go or not go database must now be made. If the decision is to implement the database approach, certain guidelines have to be followed during the implementation process. The following section discusses an approach that can be followed to implement a database system.

Implementing a Database System

The first function to be performed after deciding to implement the database approach is to establish an organization whose function is to control and maintain the database system. At the head of this organization is the individual having overall responsibility for database maintenance. This responsibility includes coordinating interfaces with other databases systems, maintaining viability within an evolving system, coordinating and implementing enhancements and resolving system problems as they arise. This person is the database administrator (DBA). The DBA must also have an in-depth knowledge of the details of the system as well as its functional capabilities. A second position in this organization is the data administrator. It is the data administrator who is responsible for maintaining the accuracy and completeness of the data within the database. Through the use of various reports, random searches and individual error reports, the data administrator should monitor all data maintained by the information system and take responsibility for its correctness. He should be given authority to make corrections and updates to existing data. Another position in the organization is that of the database analyst. It is the analyst who is responsible for the logical and physical design of all data structures, as well as tuning and maintaining the database. A fourth position in the database organization is the DBMS software programmer who maintains the data and all related software. Finally, a user liaison must be appointed to support and educate end users. This support includes the communication of the requirements of the users to the analysts and support personnel. In the description of each position cited above, the implication was that one person would handle each position. In reality, this is seldom the case. Depending upon the relative size and complexity of the database, there may be more than one position held by a single person, or more than one person per position.

The next function to be performed is the systems analysis. This analysis process is usually divided into three categories: data analysis, functional analysis and administration analysis. In the data analysis, the characteristics of the data are examined. The attributes of all necessary data elements as well as the logical structuring of these elements are determined. An attempt is made to identify and eliminate any data ambiguities. In the functional analysis, each of the functions the database system must perform are examined with respect to their specific processes, their value and cost, and their data requirements. In the administration analysis, all of the administrative functions required to control and maintain the database system are determined.

The third function to be performed in the implementation of a database system is the system design. In this phase, various system alternatives are studied in order to determine which would most effectively and efficiently meet the requirements of the specific database system being designed. Some of the design alternatives include: batch processing vs interactive processing, bulk output vs exception reporting, delayed response vs immediate response, and non-DBMS vs DBMS. In some cases the alternatives cited above are not mutually exclusive. For example, a single database system may in some cases require the use of batch processing while in other cases it may require interactive processing. In such a system, it would be feasible to allow the capability for either type of processing.

The next phase in the implementation process would be the development of the database system. It is in this phase that the actual "building blocks" of the system begin being assembled. The administrative procedures determined earlier begin being implemented at this time. The logical and physical structuring of the data within the database is determined. All required software is also written and tested. This includes procedures to maintain the data on all automated files as well as produce all required reports.

Following the development phase is the conversion/loading process. It is during this process that existing data is integrated into the new database system. It may also be necessary to initiate a procedure to initially capture data required by the database that does not already exist in some file or group of files. Initial load programs have to be written to create those automated files that are required

by the database; a reorganization of certain manual files may have to be done as well. Following the conversion, loading, and reorganization, the data contained in the database has to be validated. This validation process is absolutely necessary, because, to reiterate a point made earlier, a database system is only as good as the data it contains.

Upon completion of the conversion/loading process, the database system should be at a stage where it could be put into production. This is the point at which the system, with all of its capabilities and safeguards, is turned over to the user. It is only at this phase that the system is truly tested as to whether it meets the requirements of the user community. All prior testing was, by definition, performed in an artificial environment. Thus, when the database is initially put into production there are likely to be some extensions and/or modifications to the system that must be made. If all of the steps in each of the phases of analysis, design and development have been carefully followed, these enhancements should be minimal. However, enhancements such as database tuning to increase efficiency and software modification to extend the capabilities are an integral part of the production cycle, and as such, should be anticipated.

Conclusion

The decision to adopt the database approach, and thus implement a comprehensive database system, is a critical one that should be considered very carefully. This decision could affect the operations of diverse sectors of the business in a number of ways. The decision, like the implementation process, should have the involvement of senior management from each sector of the business. Each of them must understand the implications as well as the benefits of this approach. If senior management is not involved in this decision-making process and made aware of the costs, the database that evolves from the analysis-design-development process is unlikely to afford the business the maximum benefits that could otherwise have been realized. However, if senior management is involved in the database decision, and the decision to adopt the database approach is based upon a genuine need for the functions that can be provided by a database system, the first major obstacle in the implementation of this approach has been overcome. If a proven design methodology is carefully followed throughout the implementation process, the business should realize the greatest benefit afforded by this approach: effective management of one of its most valuable resources, information.   •jsm

BIBLIOGRAPHY
Ian R. Palmer. *Database Systems: A Practical Approach* (London, England, C.A.C.I. Inc.-International, 1975)

DATABASE MANAGEMENT
Matching a DBMS to user needs

ANDREW BURLINGAME, Prime Computer, Inc.

*Today's database-management systems offer control,
ease of use and limited redundancy*

No one questions the "why" of a database-management system any longer. Most people now agree that any DBMS is flexible and can reduce redundancy and make changes simply.

What else should a prospective buyer look for? At a minimum, a DBMS should support more than one language and have a standardized database design, a query/report writer and programs that are easy to develop, use and change.

A general DBMS should implement the Conference on Data Systems Languages (CODASYL) advanced recommendations and specifications, and should offer concurrent user protection and backup and full automatic recovery. The net benefits of a good DBMS are its adaptability to change, data integrity, support for many structures and centralized control and standardization.

Changes are easier with data independence

The principal difference between a DBMS and a traditional file system is that a DBMS has data independence, which a file system lacks. Data independence means that data and programs can be changed independently of each other. Users have individual logical data structures and can program regardless of organization. This allows the database to be altered easily to reflect changes in an organization without affecting existing programs and systems.

Much data in an organization exist more than once in a system. A good database removes much of this redundancy. Multiple data should occur only:

● When the same data items occur in many records and documents. Using appropriate software, different records can be assembled from a non-redundant database.

● When the same records and data groupings are used for multiple applications. A database system enables many applications or users to share the data groupings.

● When entire databases contain data that can serve the needs of many operations and organizations. Access to and design of databases should transcend organizational boundaries.

The ability to respond quickly to changing user demands is one of the most important features a DBMS

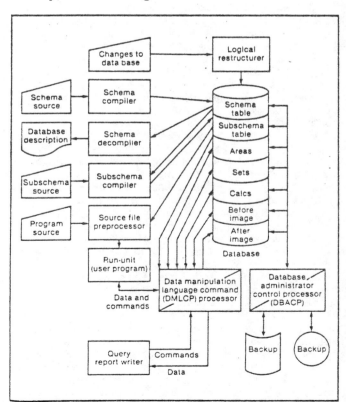

Prime's DBMS: *a functional description*

Because a DBMS supports a variety of data structures, it easily models the operations of virtually any business and lends itself to various access and search strategies.

offers. The ideal system uses existing data for new purposes and programs and easily accommodates changes and additions.

When DBMS data are independent of the application programs, programmers and systems analysts can concentrate on their own logical data structures and applications without regard for how the data are organized and manipulated. Existing programs still function when data organization is changed.

A major benefit of a strong DBMS is that new programs with data-description changes can be run without causing changes in existing programs that use data in original form. Without this capability, new application development requires rewriting existing programs. Programs are easier to write with a DBMS because data are automatically inserted into the program by a data-manipulation language facility.

A database in an organization is no more static than are the contents of the organization's filing cabinets. The ways data are stored and used change continuously. Programming costs have reached substantial proportions, but time spent on new applications has fallen steadily as greater effort has been placed on maintaining and modifying existing programs. As a result, users should be able to modify a DBMS to improve its performance or to meet new application requirements without affecting existing programs. Data independence and database logical-restructuring tools aid in efficient applications development and significantly reduce program maintenance caused by change.

Data integrity is preserved

A strong DBMS guarantees data integrity through before-and-after image-journaling, transaction-oriented updates, interactive facilities to perform database

---

PRIME'S DBMS: A FUNCTIONAL DESCRIPTION

Prime's DBMS is based on CODASYL specifications for defining a standard database language. A data-definition language (DDL) provides a way to separate the layout of files from the definition of data in the applications program, enabling the use of an independent I/O module that understands the database description.

At run time, the I/O module provides services upon commands, in the form of a CODASYL-specified data-manipulation language (DML). Because access to the data is through a central portion of the software, many features can be built into a DBMS that are lacking in a typical file system. The data description defines constraints so that contents of the database are validated by the data-manipulation-language-command processor (DMLCP), and sensitive data are protected from unauthorized use. (Prime claims that its DBMS is the only database product to use the full extent of security defined in the CODASYL specification.)

Because the data description is maintained in a data dictionary for the DMLCP's use, users see the data in consistent but different ways, a feature called data independence. Extensive changes can be made to this database system, and programs that ran correctly before they were made will continue to run correctly afterward. Prime also claims that its DBMS prevents a program from running if it will not run correctly because of database changes.

The DMLCP also allows many different users to update a database concurrently. The Prime system ensures that all users see a logically consistent database, of particular importance when the programmers coding the applications programs are inexperienced. Concurrent update has subtle implications about what data really mean at a given time. Some database systems are difficult to use because they require a series of complicated call statements. Prime has found that a programmer familiar with FORTRAN or COBOL can learn enough in a day to write effective database programs.

Five distinct functional groups comprise Prime's DBMS structure: the database-creation group (shown in red), the host-languages-support group (green), the logical restructurer (blue), the query/report writer (black) and the execute-only module (yellow).

The database creation group consists of:

● The schema compiler, which translates the CODASYL data description into a format to be kept in the data dictionary;

● The DMLCP, which provides run-time support of COBOL and FORTRAN programs and of queries;

● The database administrator control processor (DBACP), which provides an interactive means of saving, restoring, recovering and expanding the database;

● The schema decompiler, which allows legible, up-to-date descriptions to be made from a database description in the data dictionary.

The host-language-support group contains a sub-schema compiler for COBOL and FORTRAN that provides a language-specific view of the database description. A source-file preprocessor inserts the correct data description for the database, checks the DML syntax and inserts calls into the DMLCP to aid the programmer.

The logical restructurer allows extensive changes to be made to the database, including the addition of new data files, relationships between new or existing records and new fields to existing records. This can be done without changing existing programs.

The query/report writer allows users to access information easily in an ad hoc manner through simple non-procedural statements. Navigation through the database via these statements is handled internally and transparently to the user. Retrieved information is formatted using the report writer. Subsystems for various query and reporting tasks include retrieval, formatting, cataloging and HELP functions.

The execute-only module consists of the DMLCP and the DBACP. The former is used for processing COBOL and FORTRAN DMB commands against the database, which is used to define and manage the DBMS environment interactively. This group of facilities allows users with several systems to develop programs on one system and run them on others at reduced cost.

To many executives and managers, the most outstanding benefit of a DBMS is that it provides access to the timely and updated information they need to make accurate business decisions.

"saves" and "restores," on-line recovery from incomplete transactions and protection from being aborted while a user is attempting to access a locked resource. The DBMS—not the application program—should manage all data, such as backup and recovery.

Privacy and security features should be integrated into a DBMS's operating system. DBMS security features, complemented by access-control rings and memory-protection hardware, keep unauthorized users from accessing or modifying the database.

Database-management systems are usually well-suited to transaction-oriented processing, in which each transaction is completely processed, and the relevant files are simultaneously updated. This results in a low transaction-cycle time, unlike that of batch processing, in which a transaction may wait days before it is completed.

DBMS supports many structures

With a CODASYL-compliant structure, a DBMS supports many distinct or related coexisting databases. The only limit to the number or size of databases supported by some systems is the physical restraint of disk storage.

Because a DBMS supports a variety of data structures, it easily models the operations of virtually any business and lends itself to various access and search strategies. Data can be retrieved through direct-, keyed-, calculated- or serial-access strategies. Any number of sort or search keys can be specified within the database to provide more efficient access to data.

A strong DBMS enables users to query the database quickly and easily, as well as to perform relatively complex searches and report-generating functions. A query/report writer allows access to and extraction of information from databases through non-procedural statements. Retrieved information can then be formatted using a report writer. A query/report writer usually comprises retrieval, formatting, cataloging and HELP functions.

Centralized control and standardization

All database users in an organization should operate on identical data. Duplicate or redundant information and the possibility of conflicting data values stored in different files should be minimized or eliminated. Data resources with centralized control serves many purposes and users.

A DBMS provides an overview of data, without design limitations, and facilitates modeling of user organizations and operations. This simplified view leads to better understanding and more efficient use of the data.

A good DBMS allows users to model business conditions regardless of file-system restrictions and future report and inquiry needs. The system allows easy implementation of use standards and supports the use of naming and structuring standards in database design. It should provide backup and recovery, validation of data and data relationships, data security, privacy and use statistics for all standard applications. Standardization reduces program maintenance and the need for familiarity with every application, and makes the organization's information more accurate, consistent and controllable.

Efficiency is the result

An effective DBMS streamlines multiprogramming, data-communications and MIS-related tasks. It greatly increases the scope of multiprogram scheduling by making the same data concurrently available to all authorized users. DBMS also supports the management-information system concept by eliminating many of the bottlenecks found in conventional non-DBMS systems, increasing the availability of data and making retrieval easier.

To many executives and managers, the most outstanding benefit of a database-management system is that it provides access to the timely and updated information they need to make accurate business decisions. The query/report writer of a DBMS allows users to query the database quickly and to extract information easily. The information is formatted and printed—if desired—using the report writer. Default formats can be selected, or users can create a format that specifically fits their needs. As direct user involvement increases, dependence on programmers decreases, eliminating many delays that may have been previously encountered in obtaining information. ∎

Andrew Burlingame is DBMS marketing manager, Prime Computer, Inc., Natick, Mass.

Relational systems meet the real world

by David Wood

Ever since the landmark work of E.F. Codd and C.J. Date in the early 1970s, the concept of relational data base technology has engendered considerable excitement, as well as confusion, in the computer industry.

The excitement revolves around the promise of relational technology: The ability to efficiently access and manipulate data, regardless of the manner in which the data is physically stored.

Where the confusion comes in, however, is the myriad ways in which "relational" has been defined and implemented by hardware and software suppliers.

Most commercial implementations of relational data base management systems (RDBMS) have been criticized for poor performance. However, there are other, more significant problems with many RDBMSs, including:

- The enforcement of data integrity
- Uncontrolled update anomalies
- The lack of automatic maintenance of data redundancy
- The disallowance of, or severe limitations on, an application's ability to directly insert, delete and update derived relations in order to compensate for these above shortcomings.

In fact, most commercially available RDBMSs are not full-capability data base management systems. To shed some light on what is (and what isn't) a true RDBMS, and what this means in the real world of data processing, "relational" must be defined.

What is relational?

Three separate, but related definitions with respect to relational DBMS will be reviewed:

✓ Fully relational

✓ Full capability

✓ Purely relational.

Fully relational

According to C. J. Date, the term "fully relational" refers to two principal components of the relational data base model: The relational data structure, and the relational algebra.

In Date's own words: "A data base system may be called fully relational if it supports: Relational data bases (including the concepts of domain and key and the two integrity rules); and a language that is at least as powerful as the relational algebra (and that would remain so, even if all facilities for loops and recursion were to be deleted)."

Full capability

The term "full-capability" has been defined by author David Kroenke (among others), as follows: "We will consider a rela-

Relational

tional DBMS to be a system that has most of the nine functions of a full-capability DBMS, and which also models and processes data as relations."

The nine functions Kroenke refers to include:

- The ability to store, retrieve, and update data
- The provision of integrity services to enforce data base constraints
- The provision of a user-accessible catalog of data descriptions
- The ability to control concurrent processing
- The support of logical transactions
- The ability to recover from failure
- Provisions for security
- The provision of an interface with communications control programs
- The provision of utility services.

Purely relational

Another term that has been bandied about is "purely relational," focusing primarily on the physical data structure used for implementation. There are at least two problems with this particular term:

✓ At the physical data storage level, nothing has really changed. Those who look "under the hood" of a "purely relational" RDBMS invariably tie together groups of related records, using some type of physical pointer mechanism. To do otherwise is to invite serious performance problems.

✓ Definitions of RDBMSs consistently reinforce the importance of independence from this physical level. Data management and accessing capabilities must be provided, regardless of the underlying physical structures that may be involved.

Author Nicklaus Wirth has defined an application program as being composed of algorithms and

data structures. Therefore, the real power of a full-capability, fully-relational DBMS lies in its ability to enable algorithms to operate directly upon data structures as the algorithms view them, independently of how that data is physically stored within

---

An application program is composed of algorithms and data structures.

---

the data base. A full-capability, fully-relational implementation permits applications (and their users) to take advantage of that power.

Thus, if the two concepts of "fully-relational" and "full-capability" are combined, a basic definition of what an RDBMS actually should be is arrived at: *A system that functions as a full-capability DBMS, and at the same time, supports relational data bases and a powerful procedural language.*

Conceptual models

Data base designs should reflect the integrated needs of all applications. In other words, the data should be organized in accordance with the way business is done. Increasingly, such designs are being modeled around the operations of the organization, rather than the needs of a specific application.

Conceptual data base models are implemented in the real world through data base files, using the physical structure(s) provided by the DBMS. Seldom in today's data base environments is the data physically stored in the same manner in which an application's algorithms view it.

The problems associated with each application having its own files structured specifically for its own needs are what led most

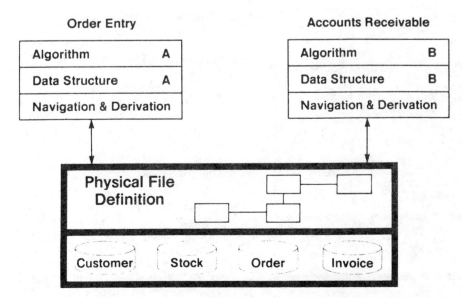

With traditional DBMS, the program is independent of the physical files, but now includes code to navigate the DBMS and to derive the applications data structure.

Relational

organizations to pursue the concept of data base in the first place.

However, many organizations are finding that different parts of their conceptual data model are implemented within different DBMSs, or are not under a DBMS at all. These organizations basically have two choices: They can either ignore the relationships and redundancies that exist between different parts of the data base, or, they can implement and manage these relationships and redundancies completely through application coding.

If the RDBMS is really independent of the physical implementation, then it should be capable of maintaining relationships and redundancies across physical boundaries, including maintaining integrity and security. In this way, the RDBMS can

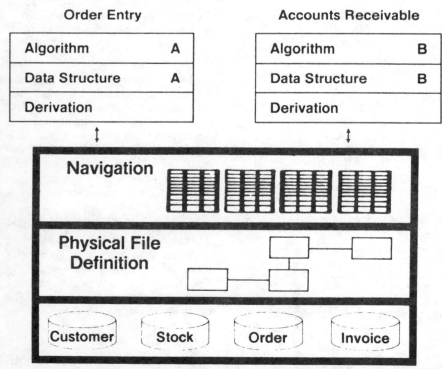

Order Entry

Algorithm	A
Data Structure	A

Accounts Receivable

Algorithm	B
Data Structure	B

Derivation

Navigation

Physical File Definition

Customer · Stock · Order · Invoice

With the full capability, fully relational implementation, the program no longer needs to contain logic to navigate the DBMS or to derive its own view of the data.

Order Entry

Algorithm	A
Data Structure	A
Derivation	

Accounts Receivable

Algorithm	B
Data Structure	B
Derivation	

Navigation

Physical File Definition

Customer · Stock · Order · Invoice

With some implementations of RDBMS, the program no longer needs to contain logic to navigate the DBMS, but it still has to derive its own view of the data.

manage the entire data base, as defined by the conceptual model.

Data, then, must be managed both physically and logically in order to have a full capability, fully-relational DBMS.

Physical data management problems

A point mentioned earlier bears repeating—The real power of a full-capability, fully-relational RDBMS lies in its ability to enable application algorithms to operate directly upon data structures as the algorithms view them, independently of how that data is physically stored within the data base.

Traditional DBMSs have done an excellent job as physical data managers. By this is meant managing such areas as integrity, security, recovery and record format independence for the files over which they have control. However, traditional DBMSs force the applications to take on the task of logical data management as well.

The task involves defining how the application's data structures relate to the actual structure and content of the data base. To the application, this means the addition of logic to navigate the DBMS structures to derive the desired application structures.

Such applications suffer from significant problems:

√ They tend to be larger and more difficult to write

√ The potential for multiple errors is great

√ Development time tends to be expanded

√ Applications therefore require larger resource investments

√ Changes in the data base structure may require reinvestment in applications to enable them to derive the same desired data structures

√ Applications can only depend on the DBMS for management of the files over which it has control.

Similar problems also exist with most implementations of an RDBMS. If the only benefit a RDBMS can provide is the ability to view as relations (base tables) what has been traditionally viewed as files, then only a partial solution to the problems of logical data management is possible.

Applications may be freed of dependence upon the navigation mechanisms of the physical data manager. However, applications are *not* freed from dependence on the structure of the data base. Therefore, they will still have the responsibility for defining how the desired logical structure is to be derived from the physical data base structure. A case in point could be the moving of "price" from the sales base table to the item base table. The applications using price must then be modified because of their dependence on the logical structure.

Derived tables

A full-capability, fully-relational DBMS actually enables the algorithm to operate directly upon derived relational tables. This is in sharp contrast to other relational languages in which the derivation process is specified as part of a query facility, using a relational algebra or calculus.

The algorithm should be free not only to "GET" tuples (record occurences) within the derived relation, but also to "INSERT," "DELETE," and "UPDATE" tuples within the same relation. There should be no need for this relation to be redundantly stored in order to accomplish these operations, and it should be reflected automatically **back onto the base tables of the data base by the RDBMS.**

Full integrity should be maintained during these modifications, just as security should be maintained to assure that only the authorized users perform only the authorized functions on only the authorized tables.

RDBMSs which permit such operations only upon redundantly stored tables, and do not automatically reflect such modifications back onto the base tables, present their users with the same problems a DBMS was acquired to solve: Uncontrolled redundancy, serious integrity problems, and multiple versions of the "truth" being used for decision-making within the organization.

RDBMSs that permit such operations only upon the base tables directly, but not upon derived tables, force users to maintain a dependency on and a sensitivity to the structure of the base tables of the data base. This means that the organization will have to go back and rewrite parts of the applications to enable them to derive the same desired data structure from the new underlying base tables.

The ability to enable algorithms to operate directly upon data structures as the algorithms view them means that the derivation process should not be a part of the application at all in a full-capability, fully-relational DBMS, and must be specified separately.

In order to be independent of the navigation mechanisms of the physical data manager, the derivation process should be specified through relational operators. This specification should only be tied to the application and the physical data manager at execution time. This allows for the most accurate binding possible between an application's desired data structure and the actual structures within the data base.

Relational DBMS benefits

A full-capability, fully-relational RDBMS provides a series of important benefits to the organization implementing it, including:

● The ability to develop smaller applications with relative ease

● Significantly fewer application errors

● Shortened development time

● Smaller resource investments in applications

● Insulation from changes in the data base structure, giving applications a longer life span

● Applications that depend on the RDBMS to manage the entire data base.

How to choose the right RDBMS

Once it is known the advantages a full-capability, fully-relational DBMS can provide, the next step is acquiring a system that can actually provide those advantages. However, don't simply take the vendor's word that the system is, in fact, "relational." To paraphrase George Orwell, some RDBMSs are more relational than others.

The minimum criteria for identifying a full-capability, fully-relational DBMS include the following:

✓ The ability to work directly upon derived relational tables

✓ Freedom from restrictions on retrieval only, regardless of the number of underlying base tables

✓ The capability of reflecting inserts, updates and deletes to derived tables automatically onto the appropriate base tables without update, insert and delete anomalies, and automatically enforcing data base integrity

✓ The capability of managing the entire data base (including redundancy, integrity, security and recovery) even if the physical data involved is stored within different data managers.

Additional factors to consider are the availability of such features as query languages, end user facilities, decision support tools and fourth generation languages for application development.

Software technology has made great strides since the concept of a relational data base was first delineated in the early 1970s. Unfortunately, many systems currently being marketed with a "relational" label are subject to the problems outlined above.

The buyer of an RDBMS should beware of these claims and demand proof of the vendor making such claims. Look carefully at any system purported to be relational to make certain that it not only conforms to the accepted definitions of the term, but also actually functions in the real world of data processing. ■

About the author
Wood is technical product manager for Cincom Systems, Inc., Cincinnati, OH.—Ed.

PART V

TELECOMMUNICATIONS AND DISTRIBUTED DATA PROCESSING

LEARNING OBJECTIVES:

. Understand the responsibility of management in bringing DDP into their organization.

. To identify the building blocks available for the DDP designer to use in designing and implementing DDP.

. Differentiate between centralized and decentralized corporate information resources.

. Differentiate between DDP and local area network.

. Recognize the relationship between office automation and local area network.

. Understand the future of LAN and DDP and their roles in CBMIS design and utilization.

INTRODUCTON

In part IV, the concept of database was discussed and along with the general problem of making data available is the question of the organization of the data resources. Should the information resources of the firm be centralized or decentralized? That is, centralization vs. decentralization in information systems organization. Recently a new organization which probably possesses the nice features of both centralization and decentralization has become very popular. This is called Distributed Data Processing and experts in the field believe DDP will be the standard of the future.

In designing a system in light of the above questions, the following descriptions of the alternatives should be well understood:

(1) Centralized: All processing is done at a single computer center which provides all information services through a large computer system and supporting staff. This design may include input from remote locations but all processing and data storage are done at a single location.

(2) Decentralized: With this design, the firm maintains independent computer systems which do not interact with each other.

(3) Distributed: This system is made possible through recent developments in communication technology and is a system where the physical computer resources are spread throughout the organization and communication links between the different locations is accomplished through the cooperative use of applications software.

Centralization of computer resources is generally justified on the basis of economic rationale. That is, the firm may be able to significantly increase the computing power, through economies of scale, by allocation of financial resources to a single computer system. The single location design would also allow less overhead in the form of reduced staff, administration, etc. With one single location, it may also be possible to develop a highly trained staff of specialists. Since all application programming development and maintenance would be housed in one location, it would be easier to integrate applications for more efficient use of information resources. However, centralization is not without its disadvantages. As with all large organizations, when there is significant resource investment in one facility, the organization may find a lack of synergism between the computer center staff, i.e., systems analysts, systems programmers, etc., and the end-users the center is responsible for serving. This lack of synergism may be manifest in the form of lack of knowledge of end-user needs and response time in reacting to a request for service.

Historically, computer technology and computer resources have generally been associated with a centralized system configuration. However, recent advances in communication technology, particularly in the cost of data communication which has continued to decline, the availability of low cost mini and microcomputers, and more sophisticated knowledgeable end-users have made the concept of distributed data processing a more feasible alternative. Some specific benefits from this organizational design would include better end-user service because the processing of specific end-user application programs takes place at the end-users location, while at the same time, system wide application programs can still be processed at the central facility. There may also be better communication between end-users which could allow a higher degree of integration of application programs. Another primary benefit from this organization of information resources is better servicing of the needs for data and information which is critical to meeting the managers decision making responsibility. Hence, the designers of a DDP must understand both the corporate environment and DDP application software available to design and implement a DDP application. There are multiple alternatives available and they should be studied closely in order to meet the specific needs or requirements of the firm.

With the advent of DDP has come many problems. In general, distributed systems are more complicated and costly to service. In some cases the technology is being stretched in terms of integration of databases, remote site location data processing, data transmission standards, controls, and protocols. Also with distributed processing has come a problem of security. In many cases the direct access via microcomputers has promulgated a situation whereby control over the information system resources, and in particular data, has moved from direct control to almost no control. For example, when a company allows some workers to move their work unit from the office to a work station in their homes without adequate planning, data security can be compromised. The breakdown in security has in many cases contributed to the increase in computer crime. Because of the nature of the relationship between the remote micro setting and mainframe or host computer, catching a person engaged in computer crime is most difficult. Many corporations have finally realized that security must be included as a high priority item when developing a plan for incorporating telecommunications, especially a DDP, into the firms computing resource capability.

Along with DDP as part of the telecommunications network, local area networks, or LAN's, have been developed. A local area network is described as the transmitting of data within a relatively small area such as within a building. The rise in development of LAN's is based on the observation that most business communications takes place between workers who are located relatively close to each other. They have also been tied to the rapid increase in the development of the automated office. A LAN not only will bring the functions of the automated office such as electronic mail, word processing, etc., to other areas within the network, but will also distribute some of the data entry and data processing capabilities of the firm to end users.

Since distributed data processing with its problems still presents some unique advantages, we should see a lot more applications of this type of processing. Some of the existing problems in DDP areas should be resolved by developing tighter security systems and more integration among different hardware and software. Also LAN will become a lot more popular with improvements in the quality of automated offices and will expedite the adoption of applications such as eletronic mail, message transmission and text processing.

DISCUSSION QUESTIONS

1. What is DDP?

2. What is centralization? What is decentralization? What are some of

   the advantages and disadvantages of each policy?

3. What are some of the problems in DDP environment?

4. What is the technology involved in DDP environment?

5. What is telecommunications?

6. What are some of the components of a telecommunications system?

7. What are some of the managerial concerns in DDP environment?

8. What are some of the applications of DDP?

9. What are some of network architectures?

10. What is LAN?

11. Why LAN is important in CBMIS?

12. What is the relationship of LAN and office automation?

13. What are some of the factors which you should consider before establishing a LAN system?

14. What are some of the components for a successful LAN system?

15. Based upon the readings in this part, how do you see the future of LAN?

16. What is going to be the dominant communication channel for the future networks?

17. How do you protect and/or improve security in DDP environment?

18. What is the trend for future development in DDP area?

Network topologies: The ties that bind information systems

by John G. Burch

Burch is professor of accounting and information systems at Northeast Louisiana University, Monroe, LA. The fourth edition of his textbook, Information Systems: Theory and Practice, *has just been published by John Wiley & Sons, Inc.—Ed.*

The recent "Live Aid" rock concert provided a unique glimpse of modern telecommunications technology in action. Live entertainment was broadcast simultaneously from North America and Europe to a worldwide audience.

What does a rock concert have to do with information systems management? Plenty.

The telecommunications technology that enabled Live Aid to "wire the world" and achieve its success is the same technology that will soon change the way information systems are configured. This technology, especially as it relates to network topologies and their application for information systems, is discussed below.

Network components

The basic components of networks are nodes and links. *Nodes* are points that can accept data input into the network, process it or output information. Subnodes act as relay devices that manage information between input, processing and output nodes. They act as front-end or back-end information traffic controllers that provide polling and queuing tasks. *Links* are channels or paths for the flow of information between input/output and relay nodes. A growing number of nodes and links offer the systems analyst a variety of

---

Nodes and links form the basic components of networks.

---

configuration possibilities. Nodes and relay nodes can be anything from a printer to a facsimile device, a PC to a giant mainframe, a modem to a multiplexer or a word processor to a multifunctional workstation. Link media can be terrestrial (e.g., cable, microwave, laser, optical) or extraterrestrial (e.g., satellites). Transmission mode can be either analog or digital.

Nodes may be tightly or loosely coupled, or even decoupled, but the overall system is still integrated and interconnected. The network allows the dynamics of both dependency and autonomy to work in a complementary fashion—a coupling of interdependency while at the same time a decoupling of autonomy. A spare tire in the trunk of a car, for example, is coupled for dependency but decoupled until needed. Some nodes may be singularly linked; others may have multiple relationships. Within networks, some nodes are clustered and more closely linked to each other than they are to the rest of the network. The greater the interdependency of task, the tighter the couplings and the denser the clusters dealing with these tasks. All couplings should be cooperative and collaborative, not competitive.

Network topologies

Topology is the interconnecting arrangement or configuration of nodes in a network. Network topologies can "look" like anything from a string with a knot in one end to a plate of spaghetti. The basic topologies are, however, the star, hierarchical tree, loop, bus, ring and web, all of which are illustrated in Figure 1.

Star. All communications are routed to and handled by a major, central node. Generally, the central node does most of the processing and is responsible for switching all messages between outlying nodes, such as a mainframe to a timesharing VDT. Most, if not all, of the outlying nodes have minimal standalone capabilities, and perform fairly uniform tasks.

Hierarchical (Tree). This topology looks like an upside-down tree, and is characterized by intermediate nodes between communicating nodes, in which the intermediate node operates in a store-and-forward mode. Applications of this topology may have a mainframe at the top of the hierarchy, serving as the coordinator and controller of computing, minicomputers at intermediate levels performing analysis and data management, and microcomputers at the lower levels performing basic input/output functions.

Loop. The loop topology is often used to interconnect a series of similar-sized nodes doing similar work, such as a group of order entry clerks or word processors. Each node in the loop must be capable of all the communications functions of the network. Some network designers also call the loop topology "daisy chaining," because of its one-to-another mode of communication.

Bus. A bus network assigns portions of network processing and management to each node. Hardware nodes can range from small, portable terminals to large computers. This topology is common in local area networks (LANs) serving one site, such as in one building or office complex. Each node has access to a common communications line (the bus), but the individual nodes perform widely varying tasks—from word processing, transactional processing and general accounting to analysis and strategic planning.

Ring. The ring is a combination of loop and bus topologies, but is more similar to a bus. If an individual node on the ring crashes, either no effect, or a small degree of degradation on the total ring network is felt, because unlike the loop topology, the failed node is not directly in the communication path.

Web. A web is the spaghetti topology of networks. Each node in the network is connected to each other by means of a dedicated link. Fully connected nodes possess as many links as there are nodes. A web that has N nodes, Has $N(N-1)/2$ links. Web topologies are used where the network needs to be dense and tightly coupled, such as in a system that controls a space launch.

Note that it is not necessary to hardwire or permanently connect all the nodes of any of the preceding topologies. Indeed, in any network a few of the nodes are usually wireless or loosely coupled. For example, cellular phones and other mobile devices can be used in designing effective networks. Moreover, all kinds of hybrid topologies are possible, using one topology to fit one part of the

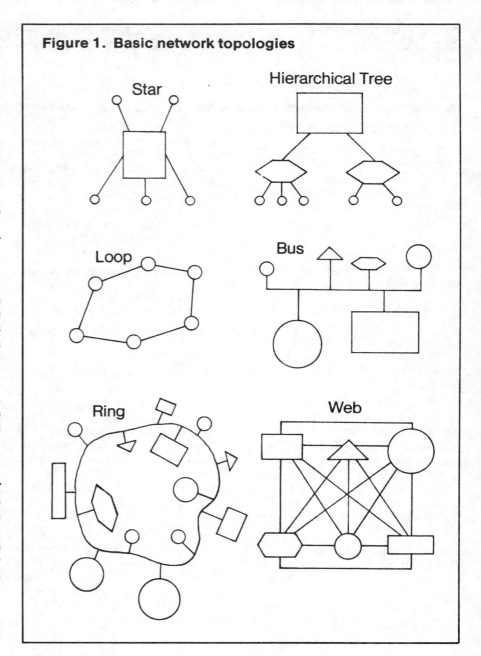

Figure 1. Basic network topologies

Figure 2. Metanetwork example

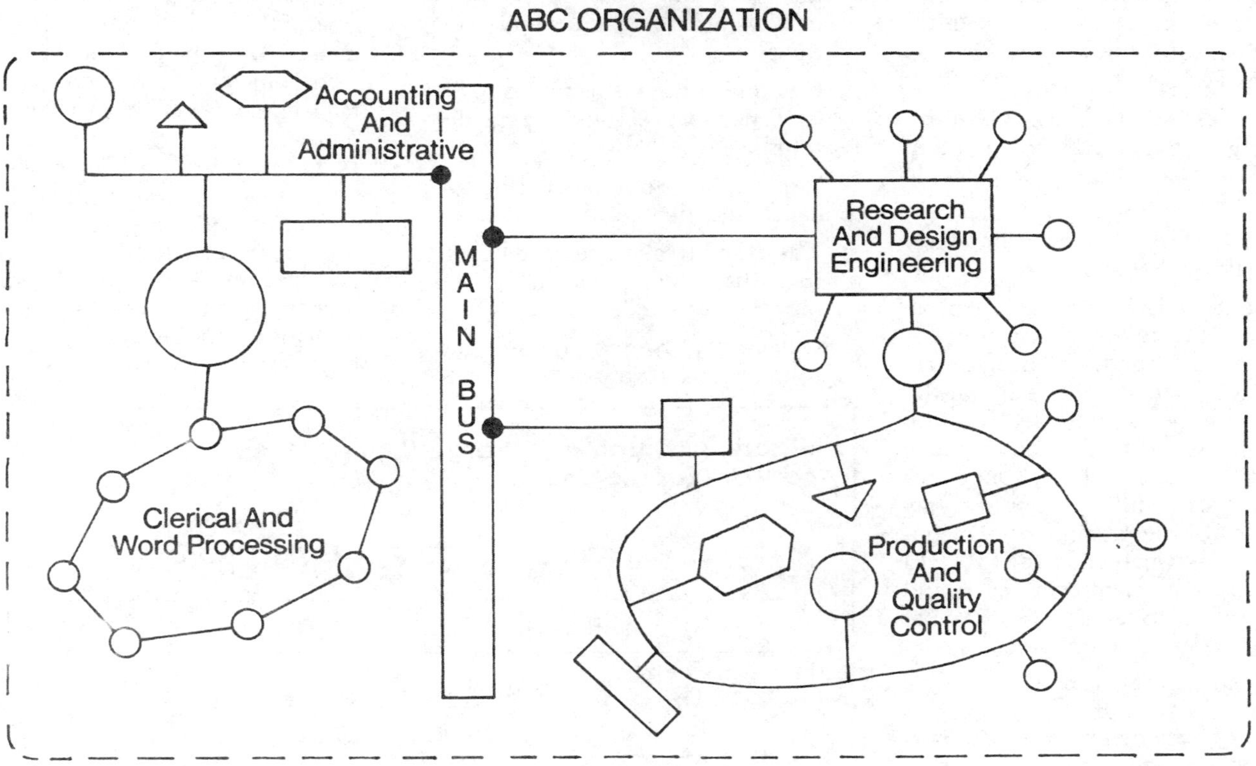

organization, and others for other parts forming a metanetwork. Figure 2 illustrates this point.

The ABC organization is served by an information system metanetwork made up of: The bus that serves accounting and administrative functions, the loop that is for clerical and word processing tasks, the star that supports research and design engineering and the ring that aids production and quality control. All the subtopologies are connected by a bus topology to form the metanetwork.

Topology selection

Deciding what network topology to use promises to be as interesting and controversial a process in the near future as it has been in the recent past. Today's information technology permits the systems analyst to design any topology he or she desires. But as in nearly all cases, the main question is not technological feasibility, but organizational factors and culture. It is, however, somewhat incongruous to design a ring topology with standalone nodes distributed throughout an organiza-

tion if the organization is highly structured, with a centralized, bureaucratic management and an insular culture, and is committed to that style. A highly centralized organization would presumably be better off using some form of star or hierarchical topology that provides it with a centrally controlled system, which mirrors its management style.

Unless an organization wants to overhaul its culture and style completely, the information system must be mapped into the organization to

---

Network topologies can be basic or complex.

---

achieve balance and harmony. The system must *fit* the organization. With this in mind, a diagram that shows how cultural and organizational factors influence the choice of topologies is shown in Figure 3. Because loop and web topologies are special cases, they have been deleted from this analysis.

The top bar represents the topology choices. All the dashed lines running through the vertical arrow represent the organizational factors, and indicate their influence on the topology selected. If a preponderance of the factors in any organization are similar to those pointing to the left, then a star or hierarchical topology is appropriate. If most of the factors point to the right, then the topology chosen should be a bus or ring.

The two strongest influences on topology selection are management style and organizational culture. But if the direction is unclear, or some of the factors vary from one area of the organization to another, the systems analyst may choose a combination of topologies for the design of the total information system, thereby fitting specific topologies to specific situations, and at the same time, achieving total integration.

Advantages/disadvantages

Advantages of star and hierarchical topologies include:

- Controls are easier to implement and monitor.

- In some instances, with the use of large mainframes as the central nodes, economies of scale can be achieved.
- Standards in policies, programming and information system building blocks can be more easily implemented.

Disadvantages of star and hierarchical topologies include:

- The central mainframe is the processor, controller and gateway for all the other nodes in the network. If this central node fails, all the other nodes are effectively out of commission. In the future, to make star and hierarchical topologies meet the widening and varying needs of the organization, meantime between failure (MTBF) must be measured in years, and meantime to repair (MTTR) must be measured in minutes.
- Because of the size of the central node, significant inefficiencies can occur when members of outlying nodes are not using the system.
- In some instances, stringent standards and monolithic design can become a barrier to quick responsiveness to user needs.

Advantages of bus and ring topologies include:

- They are good topologies for supporting integration of all functions.
- They increase direct user access, and greater standalone capabilities are distributed to the point of need.
- Possibility exists for greater user participation in design.
- User expertise and confidence in using the system are increased, presumably resulting in more efficient and effective use of technology.
- The ability to share computing power, data base, input/output operations and models increases, thereby improving productivity and avoiding significant degrada-

tion of the total system because of crashes at one or more nodes of the system.

- Customizing systems nodes to fit user needs precisely are facilitated.

Disadvantages of bus and ring topologies include:

- They tend to allow redundancies to all the building blocks to creep into the system.
- Generally they are more difficult to manage and control

- Because some of the nodes are small, it is difficult to attract technicians to work in a "small shop" environment and, therefore, skills may not be available to remote nodes.
- If the organizational factors and culture were misread, or if they change, a tendency could be set in motion toward fiefdom-building and fragmentation, exactly what was trying to be avoided in the first place. Indeed, the topology begins to break down if coopera-

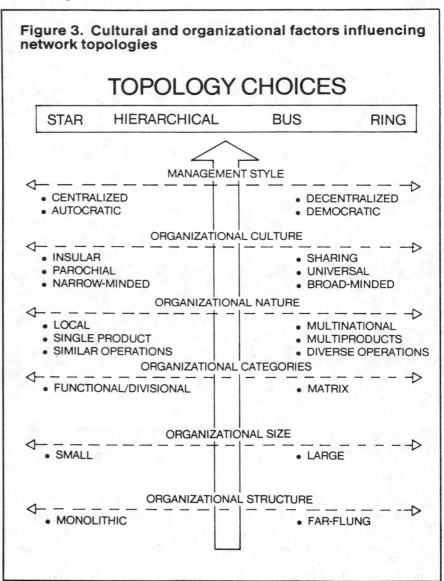

Figure 3. Cultural and organizational factors influencing network topologies

tion and compatibility between nodes begin to diminish.

Summary

Telecommunication networks will significantly change the way information systems are designed and configured in the future. Probably no other technology will have as much impact on information systems as satellites and fiber optics. This technology gives systems analysts the ability to connect a variety of nodes together and quickly transmit high volumes of voice, graphics, images, text and data signals across the hall or around the world. ∎

References

1. *Alexander, Tom, "Computing With Light at Lightning Speeds,"* FORTUNE, *July 23, 1984.*
2. *Bretz, Rudy,* Media for Interactive Communication, *Beverly Hills, CA: Sage Publications, 1983.*
3. *Burch, John G., and Grudnitski, Gary,* Information Systems: Theory and Practice, *Fourth Edition, New York: John Wiley & Sons, 1985.*
4. *Cheong, V.E., and Hirschheim, R.A.,* Local Area Networks, *New York: John Wiley & Sons, 1983.*
5. *Cooper, Michael S., "Micro-Based Business Graphics,"* Datamation, *May 1, 1984.*
6. *Cummings, Thomas G., Editor,* Systems Theory for Organization Development, *New York: John Wiley & Sons, 1980.*
7. *Dix, John, "Sears to Fuse Private Lines Into Unified Net,"* Computerworld, *Nov. 12, 1984.*
8. *Dizard, John W., "Machines that See Look for a Market,"* FORTUNE, *Sept. 17, 1984.*
9. *Ferris, David, and Cunningham, John, "Local Nets for Micros,"* Datamation, *Aug. 1, 1984.*
10. *Frank, Howard, and Frisch, Ivan, "Local-Area Nets: What Matters Most to Users,"* Computerworld, *Nov. 5, 1984.*
11. *Gross, Jerry L., "Components Can be Added Gradually by Logically Mapping Out Present, Future Uses,"* IE, *June 1984.*
12. *Habrecht, Herbert Z., "Is There a Best Way to Deliver Data Services?,"* ABA Banking Journal, *Oct. 1984.*
13. *Hector, Gary, "The Race to Perfect the Flat Screen,"* FORTUNE, *May 28, 1984.*
14. *Hodge, Bartow, Fleck, Jr., Robert A. and Honess, C. Brian,* Management Information Systems, *Reston, VA: Reston Publishing Co., Inc., 1984.*
15. *Kay, Susen S., "How to Choose Electronic Mail,"* Infosystems, *June 1984.*
16. *Krouse, John K.,* Computer-Aided Design and Computer-Aided Manufacturing, *New York: Marcel Dekker, Inc., 1982.*
17. *Lancaster, Kathleen Landis, Editor,* International Telecommunications, *Lexington, MA: Lexington Books D. C. Heath and Co., 1982.*
18. *Landau, Robert M., Blair, James H. and Siegman, Jean H.,* Emerging Office Systems, *Norwood, NJ: Ablex Publishing Corp., 1982.*
19. *Leinster, Colin, "Mobile Phones: Hot New Industry,"* FORTUNE, *Aug. 6, 1984.*
20. *Lipnack, Jessica, and Stamps, Jeffrey,* Networking, *Garden City, NY: Doubleday and Co., Inc., 1982.*
21. *Louis, Arthur M., "The Great Electronic Mail Shootout,"* FORTUNE, *Aug. 20, 1984.*
22. *McManus, Kevin, "Car Phones That Really Work,"* Forbes, *Apr. 23, 1984.*
23. *Micossi, Anita, "The Ten-Second Commute,"* PC World, *Dec. 1984.*
24. *Moss, Mitchell L., Editor,* Telecommunications and Productivity, *Reading, MA: Addison-Wesley Publishing Co., 1981.*
25. *Nilles, Jack M.,* Micros and Modems: Telecommunicating with Personal Computers, *Reston, VA: Reston Publishing Co., Inc., 1983.*
26. *Olson, Margrethe,* Organization of Information Services, *Ann Arbor, MI: UMI Research Press, 1980.*
27. *Otway, Harry J., and Peltu, Malcolm,* New Office Technology: Human and Organizational Aspects, *Norwood, NJ: Ablex Publishing Corp., 1983.*
28. *Peltu, Malcolm,* A Guide to the Electronic Office, *New York: John Wiley & Sons, 1982.*
29. *Sachs, Jonathan, "Local Area Networks,"* PC World, *July 1984.*
30. *Shaw, Donald R.,* Your Small Business Computer, *New York: Van Norstrand Reinhold Co., 1981.*
31. *Singleton, Loy A.,* Telecommunications in the Information Age, *Cambridge, MA: Ballinger Publishing Co., 1983.*
32. *Teicholz, Eric, "Computer Integrated Manufacturing,"* Datamation, *Mar. 1984.*
33. *Uttal, Bro, "The Latest World in Show and Tell,"* FORTUNE, *May 14, 1984.*
34. *Womeldorff, Thomas, "The Pursuit of Data Integration,"* Computerworld, *Nov. 12, 1984.*
35. *Young, Robert E., and Mayer, Richard, "The Information Dilemma: To Conceptualize Manufacturing as Information Process,"* IE, *Sept. 1984.*

Guidelines are suggested to help determine whether DDP is the right solution to a particular firm's computing system problems.

Distributed Processing:
Implications and Applications for Business

BY AVI RUSHINEK AND SARA RUSHINEK

SARA AND AVI RUSHINEK

Sara Rushinek is currently an assistant professor of Management Information Systems in the Department of Management Science and Computer Information Systems at the University of Miami. She received her Ph.D. from the University of Texas at Austin. Her current interests are in the areas of user involvement in computerized management information systems, mini/micro computers, and expert systems. Avi Rushinek is an assistant professor of Accounting and Information Systems at the University of Miami. He holds a Ph.D. from the University of Texas at Austin. His interests include accounting information systems, mini and micro computers, computer-auditing, cost and managerial accounting, financial planning and modeling.

■ All indications point to an enormous growth in distributed data process-systems (DDP) in the years 1982-1983 (Henkel, 1982). No longer is the large generalized central computing facility the only rational choice for providing data processing services. Companies are finding that DDP offers great potential for improving the performance of an organization as a whole. Enthusiasm is strong for decentralization of computing, and the call to acquire more computers is bound to increase (Buchanan and Linowes, 1980).

This article defines DDP as it exists today, and suggests the factors to be considered by management when faced with the possibility of switching to a distributed system. What are the overall implications for the firm's management information system (MIS)? For its data base management system? How will such a system adapt to the future needs of the organization? Examples of successful business applications of DDP as well as user surveys pinpointing some concerns about service and support will be used to illustrate the advantages and drawbacks of these systems.

Analysis, Synthesis and Discussion

The concept of distributed processing as a system was initially implemented in the 1970's. Generally defined, distributed processing is the division of logically related processing functions among geographically dispersed computer systems (Feidelman, 1982). The goals of distributed data processing are to allow an organization to improve responsiveness to users, improve manageability of its data and data flow and optimize the cost-effectiveness of its data processing operations (Whall, 1982). Instead of one computer performing all the jobs, physically separate computers each perform part of the processing function (Feidelman, 1982). Each unit is provided with the capacity and control it needs, thus cutting middleman costs and the compromises represented by the central data processing site (Whall, 1982).

Advantages of Distributed Processing

Distributed processing in lieu of a single centralized computer system provides some significant advantages:

Design modularity. Modularity permits computer power to be added or subtracted according to the user's needs. Furthermore, programs can be easily divided into individual subprograms rather than one large program conglomeration.

System reliability. Through DDP a degradation mode of operation, as opposed to a total system being down in case of componentry failure, is created. The remaining computers can perform individual tasks and may be able to process some additional work.

User interaction. Moving the processing capability to the users is designed for more efficient use of the computer, making information access easier and permitting a more flexible system (Feidelman, 1982).

One of the most common misconceptions of a distributed system is that it and remote job entry are one and the same. The major function of remote job entry is to extend the reaches of a central computer to a remote location. In distributed data processing (DDP), however, the main objective is not so much to extend the reaches of the central computer, but rather to distribute intelligence and computer resources throughout the branch offices and various organizational units. With their own computer resources, each organizational unit can solve their own problems and perform their own processing (Quirk, 1982).

Networks

Distributed processing can take many forms. The actual configuration of a DDP system is known as a network. A network is the interconnection of a number of different locations by communication facilities (Senn, 1982).

When considering a distributed processing configuration, the key factor to examine is how well the network matches the company organization. The type of network selected must blend, not conflict, with the company's structural elements (Feidelman, 1982). Some of the more common configurations are the star network, the ring network, the cartwheel network, the tree network, and the fully connected network.

The star network is the most common configuration. In this form remote minicomputer and microcomputer terminals are connected radially to a central computer (Figure 1). The star network permits independent computer operation at each location with consolidation at the central computer (Feidelman, 1982).

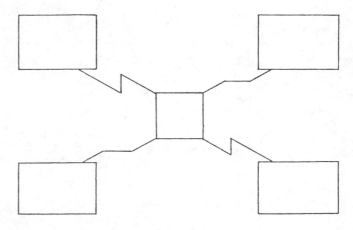

Figure 1
Typical star network
(from Feidelman, *Data Management* June, 1982)

109

The ring network represents an advanced distributed processing system. In this configuration computers are connected via a circular arrangement with data communication between any two computers possible (Figure 2). Each computer node can have its own computer network or be a self-contained unit. The complete modularity of this configuration permits data processing facilities to be apportioned to each user's needs (Feidelman, 1982).

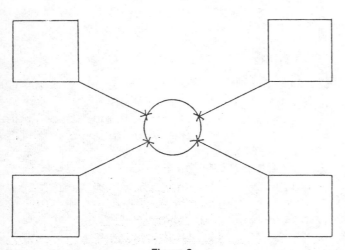

Figure 2
Typical ring network
(from Feidelman, *Data Management* June, 1982)

The cartwheel network is an extension of the star network. Each computer can communicate with the next one in the system (Figure 3). With this configuration the system can operate if an individual computer goes down; however, a certain degree of redundancy exists (Feidelman, 1982).

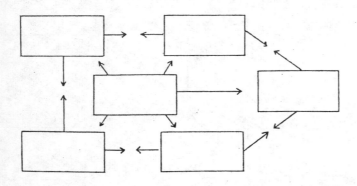

Figure 3
Cartwheel network
(from Feidelman, *Data Management,* June, 1982)

The fully connected network represents an extension of the ring network. There is no central processing unit within the system and all computers are capable of communicating with each other (Figure 4). This configuration provides a high degree of redundancy (Feidelman, 1982).

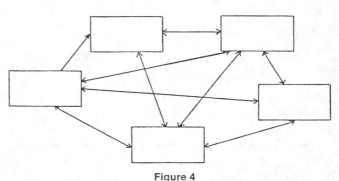

Figure 4
Fully connected network
(from Feidelman, *Data Management,* June, 1982)

The tree network features a central processing unit which communicates with two other processing units, which in turn communicate with satellite microcomputers (Figure 5) (Feidelman, 1982).

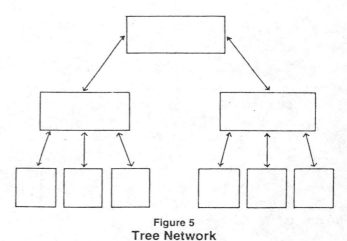

Figure 5
Tree Network
(from Feidelman, *Data Management,* June, 1982)

DDP and Management Information Systems

In many cases, leading-edge distributed processing systems are truly management information systems. Their goal is to place a wide variety of information directly into the hands of the professionals who manage an enterprise. The capabilities of these systems typically include:

On-line availability of traditional programming languages for use by management professionals.

Word processing capabilities that can be used for the creation of large reports, business letters, or interoffice memoranda.

Electronic mail capabilities that allow documents and other material to be distributed locally or throughout the world.

Statistical analysis tools that can be used in conjunction with a high level data base.

The ability to extract data from the operational systems that exist throughout the enterprise plus access to other information sources outside of the organization (Schultz, 1982).

Distributed Data Bases

Distributed processing systems require access to large amounts of on-line storage (Schultz, 1982). As DDP systems evolve, pressure is mounting among users for control of their own data. More data is moving out toward local control every day, thus creating distributed data bases. As this continues, integration among systems and their components must be achieved. Considering the present diversity in hardware, software, and communications methods, integration is only possible using compatibility at the lowest common denominator, that of data itself. This is accomplished through the use of a single distributed data base management system (DDBMS) operating in a loosely coupled network defined by the software operating at each node, where each node can operate independently (Whall, 1982).

The DDBMS at each node has three responsibilities: managing its own local data base, processing requests directed to it, and managing the routing of requests to other nodes. Traffic between nodes is in the DDBMS' own format, suitably sandwiched within whatever protocol requirements a communications link demands. At each node the DDBMS is configured to satisfy its local processing requirements and to operate within the capacity of its host processor (Whall, 1982).

DDP Problems

Distributed data processing is not without its problems and complications. With multiple data bases, interaction between geographically dispersed computers and personnel and multiple points of entry at various locations, security and data integrity can be difficult to maintain. Realizing that data base con-

tamination can be due to hardware, system software, application programs, or the users themselves, it is easy to see why maintaining data base integrity can be a problem with DDP. Likewise, the degree of accessibility and integration required by DDP make unauthorized detection difficult. As a result, the system must include sophisticated security equipment to protect against unauthorized usage (Feidelman, 1982).

Developing a System Structure

When developing a distributed processing plan, the first step is to survey the future needs of the organization. Then the different methods of computing to meet those needs must be examined. The following topics should be addressed:

Corporate direction (long- and short-range objectives and goals, tactical and strategic plans).

User needs (short- and long-term management needs, operational management needs).

Technological directions (mainframes, minicomputers, personal computers, and communications).

The results of such a study should provide enough information for the formation of a plan to establish a distributed processing system for an organization (Woods, 1982).

Grayce Booth, manager of special projects for Honeywell Inc.'s Marketing Support Operations/Large Information Systems Division, proposes a series of ten questions and suggests that the answers to these questions will point the way to the most appropriate choice of system structure. The questions and the directions they suggest are summarized below (*ComputerWorld,* 1982).

1. Are the capacity requirements of the application too great to be implemented in a single computer system? The needed capacity is determined by the total number of users to be served, the number of users who will access the system simultaneously, the volume of transactions to be handled, the response-time requirements, the size and complexity of the data base, and the complexity of the processing functions. It is also prudent to include a cushion of unused capacity to allow for rapid and unpredictable growth.

2. Is a high degree of flexibility for change and/or capacity expansion required? One of the basic rules of information systems is that complexity reduces flexibility. A centralized system with a large number of possibly unrelated applications would be much

less flexible than a distributed system.

3. Are there requirements for a high level of availability and/or a high degree of resilience to failures? Distributed and decentralized systems typically are dispersed over multiple sites and, therefore, are less vulnerable to single point failures than centralized systems.

4. Which mode of processing will predominate: interactive or batch? The more inactive the system, the greater the likelihood that the distribution of at least some functions will be advantageous.

5. Are there clusters of shared functions, each of which serves a separate group of users? The clustering of functions, in effect, defines the distributed systems structure.

6. Are there user groups who need somewhat different functions, methods, interfaces, and/or reports than other similar groups? Customization in a centralized system typically results in increased complexity which limits the flexibility to change. A distributed system can be highly customized without reducing flexibility.

7. Will the system handle data and/or functions that require tight protection for security or privacy reasons? The physical protection provided by a restricted access computer center makes it easier to handle sensitive data or functions. There are ways to partition sensitive data or functions from nonsensitive ones in a distributed system, but it is costly.

8. Are the users widely dispersed geographically? A distributed system will lower cost of communications and may also improve speed of response to terminal users.

9. Does the system consist of a set of loosely related functions or of functions whose requirements are not well-defined? Office systems, in particular, are made up of clusters of related functions. A distributed system provides greater flexibility than a centralized system to change each of the functions as needed.

10. Will a distributed system result in lower total life-cycle costs for the system? If the cost of communication facilities in a centralized system can be reduced by using local satellite processors, total life cycle costs will be lower. However, in general, distributed systems have a somewhat higher expected cost than centralized systems.

There is obviously no one system that would fit the needs of all users of DDP. For example, a bank may have multiple branches all of which provide the same set of services to their customers — or it may have one or several branches that have a much higher than average proportion of savings accounts to checking accounts. Several factories may be building the same product for a company, but local conditions might require different procurement procedures.

Some Successful Applications of DDP

Let us look at some examples of DDP at work in a power plant, a carton maker, and the McDonnel Douglas Corporation, a high technology organization staffed with engineering-oriented employees. Commonwealth Edison Company had three good reasons for switching from a centralized computing system to a distributed processing network, according to Frank Blake, Jr., the company's computer activities director (*ComputerWorld,* 1982): First, the technical directors and management at each of the firm's fifteen power plants wanted to do their own local processing. The second consideration was that with six additional nuclear reactor stations scheduled to come on board in the next five years, the already overworked IBM host computers at the firm's headquarters would be stressed even more. Finally, because of the regulations governing power plant operations, the firm not only wanted a better handle on corporate information, but needed that information in a more timely manner.

Commonwealth Edison recently installed IBM's Systems Network Architecture (SNA) on its two mainframe computers to communicate with Computer Automation Inc. Syfa 1000 minicomputer systems located at each of its remote generating stations. SNA is IBM's plan for DDP that incorporates a hierarchy of hardware and software "layers." Each remote Syfa system has four to six CRT terminals, one or two line printers and one to six character printers at each station. It is one physical unit to the network and locally supports up to fifteen logical units by routing their data to the mainframe. On one Communications line, one sender on a Syfa system can send and receive multiple remote job entry batch transmissions and multiple interactive inquiries under IBM's Time-Sharing Option (TSO). Applications programs are written and maintained by the corporate DP organization. TSO applications involve routine, daily transactions between each station and corporate headquarters. Data entry is performed by a Syfa terminal operator off-line to permit editing and correcting of information prior to transmission. RJE applications occur with a weekly/quarterly frequency and involve reports on station performance and efficiency. Budget programs are the focus of all local applications. When special applications are developed for one station, all stations have the opportunity to use them.

The final and most truly valuable side benefit, according to Blake, is the use of the Syfa systems for budget and work scheduling programs for nuclear stations under construction (*ComputerWorld,* 1982).

Packaging Corporation of America (PCA), a manufacturer of corrugated cartons and supplies, installed a centralized computing system at headquarters and operates a network of fully contained minicomputers at each of its branch offices. At each of its thirty plants located around the country, a Honeywell, Inc. Level 6/43 minicomputer takes care of local business processing and keeps track of the local customer base within a 200-mile radius. When additional information is needed by the regional plants, the computers can communicate with a dual-process Level 66/DPS large-scale computer system located at the firm's headquarters (*ComputerWorld,* 1982).

According to Arnie Rohlwing, director of the firm's systems and computer services operations, "We needed a central computer system that could provide the plants with on-line access to local sales and production information, yet eliminate our need for outside time-sharing and batch processing at our suburban home office."

Gaining a large system capable of supporting on-line data files and a large communications network, as well as versatility for the future, were important requirements for PCA. Their DDP system has enabled them to answer customer queries quickly at remote plants, schedule mill production via daily computer transmission, and learn exactly what roll stock is available and when it will arrive. There is no need to call and check on shipments because of the on-line information they can access through the Evanston Switching Center. The remote computers provide salesmen with cost-estimating information, enabling them to avoid delays in providing customers with price quotes. According to Rohlwing, the combination of a network with the advantages outlined above, and a powerful mainframe that can handle the big jobs generated by their 5,000 customer companies and 8,000 employees, has turned out to be a winner.

Dave Borlin, manager of distributed processing at McAuto, the McDonnell Douglas Automation Cor-

poration (*ComputerWorld,* 1982), reports that the changeover at McDonnell Douglas Corporation came only after long debate and a corporatewide study resulting in the implementation of an information resource management organization (IRM). IRM's officers were appointed at the vice-presidential level within each component of the company and were responsible for reviewing and approving all IRM activities within their respective components, with corporate IRM office acting as chief watchdog.

In order for McAuto to support DDP efforts within the corporation, two DDP-related coordinating functions were implemented: DDP change planning and DDP daily planning. The change planning committee, staffed at the managerial level, with representatives from each of the major areas of McAuto, handles concerns at the mid-management level. Among its goals are coordinating between distributed activities and planning in order to ensure optimum interface, and establishing centralized DDP-related task forces to provide proper DDP planning and installation. The DDP daily planning meetings provide an opportunity for user representatives of DDP systems to sit down on a regular basis with supervisor-level McAuto and vendor personnel to discuss plans for anticipated changes and any problems experienced. The objectives of this cooperative central/distributed approach include:

1. Making maximum use of each DDP site for the benefit of its own users.
2. The availability of 24-hour-a-day support personnel in the central site, thus easing non-prime shift requirements.
3. Consistent documentation and procedures resulting from common expertise and sharing of information between similar sites.

According to Borlin, McAuto's approach to DDP has been to incorporate as many of the centralized techniques as seem applicable, thereby reaping the benefits of distribution while minimizing the impact on the corporation (Borlin, 1982).

These are only three of many successful configurations worked out by DDP users, but it would be erroneous to leave the impression that all attempts at setting up DDP systems succeed to the same degree. What are some of the problems encountered?

User Concerns

Accoridng to a 1982 DDP report published by Management Information Corporation (MIC) in Cherry Hill, New Jersey, "more vendors are getting into DDP, service is getting worse and users are becoming more concerned about interfacing and communications support in distributed application" (*ComputerWorld,* 1982). MIC contacted 210 distributed users with annual sales ranging from less than $10 million to more than $1 billion. The firms were polled on performance, reliability, ease of use, service, and manufacturing support. Users were asked to rate them on a scale of 1 to 4. One was considered poor and four excellent.

Asked how their DDP systems met their needs, 63.2% of 147 respondents said their present system met their needs, and 29.3% said their system did not sufficiently meet their needs. However, 7.5% said their systems had more capabilities than they needed.

When users rated major problem areas in existing DDP systems, the one most often mentioned was interfacing (14% of the respondents), followed by applications software (12.2%), data communications (11.8%), systems software (11.63%), cost (8.4%), support and service (7%), management of facilities (6.8%), compatibility with product line (6.2%), flexibility (6%), and several other problems mentioned by fewer than 4% of the respondents (Henkel, 1982).

Conclusions and Implications

This article reports on developments in the area of distributed data processing and on its impact on the firm's management information system and its data base management system. The focus is on business applications of DDP.

Firms need to approach the DDP concept carefully, keeping in mind the nature of their business, corporate directions, the nature and needs of user groups, requirements for capacity, security, flexibility, and availability, the nature of functions and cost.

Once the decision is reached to go with DDP, the project must be approached with the understanding that distributed processing is not just one way of organizing a company's computing system into a network. Rather, it encompasses a multitude of possibilities. Each firm will have to design the system to suit its own particular requirements. Recent surveys of users indicate that not all systems in use are meeting the needs of their users. Among the most often cited problem areas are interfacing, applications software, data communications, and system software. Successful users report that planning is *the* most important element in creating a viable system that will fulfill the needs and expectations of a firm.

Booth, G.M., "Centralize? Decentralize? Distribute? Where to Put Data Depends on Applications," *ComputerWorld,* special report (February 22, 1982), pp. SR 5-6.

Borlin, D., "Debate over CCP Leads McAuto to IRM," *ComputerWorld,* special report (February 22, 1982), pp. SR 13, 18.

Buchanan, J.R., and Linowes, R.G., "Making Distributed Data Processing Work," *Harvard Business Review* (September/October, 1980), pp. 143-161.

"Carton Maker Packages Data for 30 Different Plants with Mini-Based DDP Net," *ComputerWorld,* special report (February 22, 1982), pp. SR 40-41.

"DDP Gets Glowing Review at Power Plant," *ComputerWorld,* special report, (February 22, 1982), pp. SR 39-40.

Feidelman, Lawrence, "Distributed Data Processing: What It Is Today and What It Will Be Tomorrow," *Data Management* (June, 1982), pp. 38-43.

Henkel, T., "Multifunction Systems Seen Hot Item by Mid Decade," *ComputerWorld,* special report (February 22, 1982), pp. SR 5-6.

Henkel, T., "Survey Pinpoints User's Concerns about DDP," *ComputerWorld,* special report (February 22, 1982), pp. SR 45-46.

Quirk, D.M., "RJE and DDP: What's the Difference?" *ComputerWorld,* special report (February 22, 1982), p. SR 4.

Schultz, J.P., For Top Firms, DDP Means Mix of Capabilities," *ComputerWorld,* special report (February 22, 1982), p. SR 35.

Senn, James A., *Information Systems in Management* (Wadsworth Publishing, 1982), pp. 231-242.

Whall, Curt, "An Attractive Alternative to the DDP Solution: Localizing Control of Data," *ComputerWorld,* special report (February 22, 1982), p. SR 2.

Woods, Larry, "First Step for MIS: Survey Future Needs," *ComputerWorld,* special report (February 22, 1982), p. SR 11.

Distributed data processing 'nightmares' offer valuable lessons

by Jonathan Smith

Smith is senior management consultant, Touche Ross & Co., Chicago, IL.—Ed.

Many lessons learned from minicomputer implementations can be applied to the current issues associated with the widespread use of personal computers.

But, apparently, many people are ignoring or unaware of these lessons and making unnecessary errors in PC implementations.

This article describes some of these lessons and how they can make PC implementation smoother. It also outlines what to do about single-user PCs evolving into the complexity of distributed data processing.

Minicomputers—and distributed data processing (DDP)—were the panacea of the late 1970s. They appealed to many organizations for a variety of reasons, reasons which now make PCs so popular. Like today's PCs, minicomputers were bought because: They promised users independence from centralized DP centers, often perceived as cumbersome and unresponsive; they reflected the business trend of decentralization—a "mini in every division"; they were something the user could get his or her hands around—

the small physical size psychologically appealed to the small user; they promised high technology—nationwide minicomputer networks had pizzazz; they promised easier, user friendly software—no systems software gurus needed (off-the-shelf affordable packages provided the answers); and they were relatively inexpensive and their minimal environmental needs brought them within reach of smaller budgets.

In the 1970s, DP had to use "carrots."

Yet problems abounded with DDP implementations, especially in large, complex organizations. Those problems and the solutions are especially relevant now that multi-user PCs and local area networks are evolving.

DDP-related problems

As minicomputers left the laboratory and entered the workplace, they brought with them a brand new set of problems for corporate DP organizations:

- *Proliferation.* The drastically smaller price of minicomputers when compared to mainframes resulted in their being affordable

for much smaller corporate organizations (e.g., divisons, factories, etc.). Often, corporate entities each bought computers of different models from different vendors, all expecting assistance from corporate DP.

- *Vendor instability.* While some users were faced with vendors who left the minicomputer marketplace outright, many more users were faced with vendors who released unproven products, provided below-standard maintenance or cancelled planned releases of improved systems. Much of this was due to vendors not reaching "critical mass"; thus, they could not provide the support structures (maintenance, testing, etc.) needed. On the other hand, the large vendors grew so fast that their support organizations were outpaced. In either case, vendor support was inadequate.

- *Growth limitations.* The early minicomputers had severe speed, memory, workstation and mass storage constraints that often restricted a user's growth. Aggravating this problem was the constraint of several vendors' product lines requiring software conversions if a larger minicomputer were to be installed.

- *Data control.* Controlling access to and versions of corporate data became far more complex because it no longer physically resided inside the large headquarters mainframe. Multiple versions of data became widespread, and different sets of numbers were being used by varying decision makers.
- *User-instigated changes.* Often, minicomputer networks were originally developed by the centralized DP shop but subsequently modified in different ways by users.
- *Incompatibility.* The minicomputers often could not communicate with each other or the mainframe, sometimes even if they were made by the same vendor. Worse yet, several vendors released—and subsequently pulled back—communications software for computer interconnections.

These issues gave the "unresponsive" centralized DP groups still more headaches—headaches that would not go away. Often, the managers of the DP groups were not at a

---

The central issue is the user's motivation.

---

high enough level to manage by edict, but rather had to persuade users to cooperate.

Solutions

A variety of methods to prevent or resolve these problems were developed by DP managers across the industry. In organizations with strict policy enforcement, strong control mechanisms ("sticks") were used. In the decentralized structures that were common in the 1970s, DP had to resort to inducements and incentives ("carrots"). Figure 1 summarizes several key approaches to each of the problems discussed above. A few of these approaches are worthy of explanation.

Figure 1. The carrot and stick approach

Issue	Carrot	Stick
Proliferation	Establish list of "approved" systems and provide supporting funds for purchase of approved hardware and software only	Prohibit purchase of unapproved systems
	Negotiate bulk discount agreements for approved components, including purchase, lease and maintenance	
	Establish group to test new software packages and coordinate sharing of in-house software	No support for "unapproved" systems
	Establish group of in-house experts and keep them available at bargain rates	
Vendor Instability	Establish performance bonuses for vendors	Restrict purchases to proven vendors with references
	Establish approved vendor list	Establish minimum size and age requirements of vendors
	Participate in vendor's user groups	
Growth Limitations	Identify growth path - and limitations - of approved vendor(s)	Require 3 to 5 year growth analysis prior to approval
Data Control	Provide tools for downloading or sharing data	Use strong data base administration with tight data control
	Provide controls for reconciling or comparing systems data versions	Maintain high system security on obtaining files
User Instigated Changes	Provide internal software support for versions	Remove software tools and source code from user controlled machines
	Keep software up-to-date	
	Maintain expertise in central location	Prohibit changes
Incompatibility	Provide incentives above for staying with recommended vendor(s)	Require approval prior to purchase
	Obtain/develop conversion tools for software and communications methods for sharing data in "approved" systems	Establish communications and software standards

Rules about computer purchases. In order to ensure that the corporation would stay compatible, standards and special approval policies for computer purchases were established. Their effectiveness was proportional to the level of authority that would stand behind the standard. It was also inversely proportional to how wily the user was. For example, a telecommunications company with three mainframe centers found a computer listed under the office furniture budget. A trading company bought new sophisticated minicomputers and developed much software, yet found users unwilling to abandon their old key-to-disk system. Each of these organizations reacted by using "carrot" techniques.

Bulk discount agreements. By negotiating bulk discount agreements with preferred vendors, DP managers did more than save their companies money. Instead of DP managers having to justify why the user should buy the DP manager's preferred system, the user now had to justify to

his own boss why he wasn't taking advantage of the discount agreement.

Vendor qualification requirements. Although using market-tested vendors and vendor products resulted in lagging the leading edge of technology, it certainly reduced the risks of total failure or inadequate vendor support.

Minicomputer-based DDP is no longer in the limelight, partly because these solutions have made the problems manageable. Today, however, the same issues fill pages of journals, but as they relate to PCs. In order to use DDP solutions and tools for PC implementations, one must first examine how applicable the basic DDP issues are for PCs.

DDP problems today

The central issue in comparing minicomputer-based DDP to PC implementations is the user's motivation. Figure 2 compares the way the PC solves some of the user's basic needs even better than DDP

Figure 2.
Comparison of user motivation for DDP and PC use

User Motivation	DDP	PC
Release from unresponsive DP center	Obtaining own minicomputer yielded control but still required system expertise to develop application	Many PC applications, though limited in scope, require no special system expertise at all
		User has complete control of his or her application
Decentralization	System structure should reflect corporate structure	Decentralized to the individual level
Manageable size	User's organization could understand and run system	User himself or herself can understand and run system
High technology	Nationwide minicomputer networks promised far more than technology could deliver	PC's technology has more sophisticated marketing (less puffing) but is also promising great things at user's fingertips
User friendly software without technicians	Reduced need for systems programmers but continued need for applications programmers	User friendly software which can be used without programmer training and often includes tutorials
Low cost and minimal environmental needs	Within department/division factory's budget with simpler environmental needs	Almost an incidental expense with no special space needs

ever hoped to. However, some of DDP's problems are exacerbated by the PC.

Proliferation. Whereas minicomputers appeared by the handful, dozens or, occasionally, hundreds, PCs may be on nearly everyone's desk and obtained by the thousands. This greatly increases the demands on centralized DP for technical support *other than* building, maintaining and operating centralized systems.

Vendor instability. Growth and change on the PC market surpasses that of the minicomputer, to the point where six-month old products are considered established and perhaps even out-of-date. Similarly, products exit the marketplace just as fast. This rapid change increases the need to review the vendor's qualifications as well as the product's.

Growth limitations. The PC's growth capabilities are more severe than those of the minicomputer. Although multi-user PC systems are becoming available, today's personal computer is essentially a single-application, single-user system. Minicomputers ran out of gas when growth required dozens of users and gigabytes of storage; the analogy to the PC is when the application outgrows the eight-hour workday, or two users

want the PC—or just a peripheral on a local area network—simultaneously.

User-instigated changes. In contrast to minicomputers, where most applications were in procedural languages, many PC applications are built with very user friendly packages. This fact, combined with the

---

A "preferred" list of hardware and software is needed.

---

order-of-magnitude increase in the number of direct users, results in a much higher incidence of user modifications to programs.

Incompatibility. Although many corporations have different (and incompatible) types of PCs, the PC market has sorted itself out far more quickly than the minicomputer market did. Although there is a variety of vendors, one microcomputer standard for corporate use dominates the market. This is a contrast to the minicomputer market of DEC, Data General, Wang, Hewlett-Packard, Datapoint, Four-Phase, Texas Instruments, IBM and Honeywell, each with its own substantial market

share. Thus, the compatibility issue for the PC itself is far simpler to establish. (If no standard is established, the current variety of microcomputers is nightmarish.) However, there are two other compatibility issues with PCs that are far more severe than they were with DDP:

✓ *Peripheral standards.* Often the minicomputer peripherals were bought from the vendor who sold the minicomputer. However, PC users may obtain a standard or look-alike PC model, but buy printers, plotters, graphic CRTs, or other devices from a large variety of vendors.

✓ *Software.* Many firms standardized on a single spreadsheet package for the minicomputer only to drop the standard for an improved package six months later. Micro software packages for PCs are more readily available, cheaper and more user friendly than minicomputer software packages. The PC software is, unfortunately, equally incompatible and multiple brands of packages—with similar or different functions—make sharing data and/or applications difficult indeed.

Data control issues were extremely complex due to the use of minicomputer networks for real-time transaction processing of production data. Although PCs are used far less for real-time input, edit or update of production data, they are being used to generate outputs used by management for critical decision making. The accuracy and timeliness of the data used for these outputs is thus critical. Users are currently accessing mainframe data bases via online inquiries and reports for manual or automatic loading into PCs, and subsequently massaging the data. Because this process is extremely difficult to control, PC-produced reports that cover different time periods or different data sources can result in inconsistent or conflicting management information.

Applying DDP methods to PCs

Although there are certainly new issues with PCs that minicomputers never addressed, many of the methods used in DDP management apply to the PC implementation problems. Figure 3 shows which DDP tools are applicable to the PC environment.

The first question is whether a small set of "approved" hardware or software should be established in this rapidly changing environment. Corporations with distributed processing found multiple vendors and different systems extremely prohibitive in the long run; on the other

---

User incentives and controls must be implemented.

Figure 3. DDP tools applicable to PC implementations

Issue	Carrot	Stick
Proliferation	Establish list of "approved" systems and provide supporting funds for purchase of approved hardware and software only	Prohibit purchase of unapproved systems
	Negotiate bulk discount agreements for approved components, including purchase, lease and maintenance	
	Establish group to test new software packages and coordinate sharing of in-house software	No support for "unapproved" systems
	Establish group of in-house experts and keep them available at bargain rates	
Vendor Instability	Establish performance bonuses for vendors	Restrict purchases to proven vendors with references
	Participate in vendor's user groups	Establish minimum size and age requirements of vendors
Growth Limitations	Identify growth path - and limitations - of approved vendor(s)	Require 3 to 5 year growth analysis prior to approval
Data Control	Provide tools for downloading or sharing data	Use strong data base administration with tight data control
	Provide controls for reconciling or comparing systems data versions	Maintain high system security on obtaining files
User Instigated Changes	Provide internal software support for versions	Remove software tools and source code from user controlled machines
	Keep software up-to-date	Prohibit changes to applications
	Maintain expertise in central location	Prohibit changes to package versions
Incompatibility	Provide incentives above for staying with recommended vendor(s)	Require approval prior to purchase
	Obtain/develop conversion tools for software and communications methods for sharing data in "approved" systems	Establish communications and software standards

---

hand, some early PC users mistakenly standardized on seemingly solid products or vendors and found themselves empty-handed or far behind the state of the art. Still, the only way to manage the variety of technology is to set up a "preferred" list of hardware and software packages which is subject to expansion and modification as the technology evolves. Once this step is made, other approaches can be reviewed.

Negotiating vendor discounts. These discounts will save the company money, no doubt. However, the prices of personal computers are so low that the discounts alone may not influence a user if he or she prefers the features of another system. Price discounts however, put the "burden of proof" on the user to explain why he or she did *not* take advantage of the corporate-level negotiated prices. Similarly, the PCs are so reliable—again on an individual basis—that negotiating any type of special maintenance agreement will have little impact on the user's choice. Volume discounts will help centralized DP management save money and influence user decisions, but they are not enough.

Prohibiting purchases of unapproved equipment. If the company structure permits such dictates, it certainly enables standardization. Enforced standardization, however, may result in missed opportunities. Letting the user balance his specific needs against the carrots dangled by the DP manager (for going the "standard" way) often results in optimal decisions.

Establishing an expert group. The user is always interested in his contingencies if the technology fails him. A good incentive is an internal group which is up-to-date on the best package for the approved systems, and has in-house experts to diagnose and perhaps fix problems. On the other hand, a centralized group that is interested *only* in tracking users' hardware configuration, software packages, number of applications, hours in use, etc., may prove to be inefficient and annoying. These groups must be structured to be supporting, not controlling. Similarly, *voluntary* user groups for sharing of software and techniques also help. The PC users set quicker implementations and advice. And centralized DP also benefits because there will be less custom software as users borrow programs and techniques from each other. For instance, one large oil company has an information center that supports PC users as well as users of fourth-generation languages, and constantly tests new technology as it appears on the market.

Data control tools. If established standards exist, then it is possible to set up data base extracts for personal computers that can be commonly used. Information from systems such as the general ledger, inventory and sales is widely used. Establishing a simple method to access it for further manipulation will help ensure that users are using the same versions of data. Summarization and downloading techniques used in the multiple-location DDP world should also be used for PCs.

Internal software maintenance. Many users are now being confronted with personnel changes that result in *all* knowledge of the PC applications leaving their department. User-generated documentation helps, but the user has even less incentive than DP to keep it up-to-date. In contrast to DDP, modifications by users to user-developed programs on PCs should be tolerated and not discouraged; most DP center managers would probably do best to let the user handle his own applications (*not* package) software maintenance.

Communications standards. The latest fad—local area networks—brings a whole new set of communication problems to the data center manager, not to mention to the end user. This is the one area similar to DDP where the technology has not kept pace with the marketing. Corporations would do well to establish easy methods to communicate from PC to mini or mainframe. But it is probably too early to establish strict standards on local area networks. The lesson learned from DDP is that intercomputer communications among "peer" systems (e.g., mini-to-mini, PC-to-PC) has a host of technological and procedural issues, and many vendors in the DDP world failed with their first public attempts to deal with these. The history of DDP would indicate a "wait and see" attitude at this point, until user-tested technology is available.

Future directions

The trend toward PCs becoming multi-user, both by themselves and as part of local area networks, results in a new style of DDP. Former-

ly, applications on large multi-user mainframes migrated "down" to minicomputers; now, applications will migrate up to PCs. All the problems confronted in peer system relationships in DDP will soon be confronted in PCs:

- *Inadequate communications technology.* In spite of all the press on local area networks, the technology is still too complex for user friendly systems. A "wait and see" attitude is most appropriate here.

- *Data synchronization issues.* Controlling data contention, multiple update, data versions and user access will be more complex with

---

Stay closely involved in all in-house implementations.

PC networks due to the limited tools available. This technology will also evolve soon.

- *More components that can fail.* Just as in DDP networks, component failure in PC networks will affect far more users than just the system owner.

More of the DDP techniques used for PCs will be required. Management will have to:

- *Get involved.* In contrast to stand-alone applications, where the user often needs no DP support, the complexity of DDP and PC networks require technical expertise in design, testing and implementation.

- *Use only proven products.* Many vendor-supplied DDP communications products flat out did not work. The potential number of system paths and conditions resulted in high failure rates and bug incidences. Wherever implementation of the communications is critical, use only proven products. Reference checks and even field inspections are critical here.

At the current time, there are very few acceptable products available.

- *Anticipate human resource needs.* DP will eventually assign far more staff to networks than originally anticipated. Monitoring, operating and expanding networks—even minicomputer or PC networks often keeps several people fully occupied.

The anticipated growth of PCs into multi-user environments highlights the criticality of establishing corporate standards and of DP becoming involved. As the systems grow in size, number of users and general visibility, corporate DP will again be called in for technical expertise.

Summary

DDP implementations taught us several key things that are applicable to PC implementations:

✓ Establish a small list of standard PC hardware and software as a framework; obtain bulk discounts to save money and further encourage standardization.

✓ Use centralized support (in-house experts, technology reviews, user groups) as the "carrot" to induce users to choose the standard.

✓ Sponsor software clearing houses and user groups for sharing of programs, techniques and experiences, and for quicker and better implementations.

✓ Develop a standard method, standard tools and a basic set of files for users to obtain corporate data.

✓ Do not commit too early to a single PC-to-PC network strategy, but stay closely involved in all in-house implementations.

✓ Use only proven communications products.

In light of the trend toward multi-user PCs, it is becoming more critical that the user incentives and controls for PCs be implemented. ∎

Planning, user needs determine final shape of local area networks

by Yvonne Lederer

Lederer is a member of the Penn-Del Chapter. She is a Media, PA-based independent computer consultant specializing in systems analysis and systems design programming. Lederer also teaches MIS courses in the School of Management at Widener University, Chester, PA.—Ed.

Most organizations realize the need for a local area network (LAN). Yet there continues to be a reluctance to meet that need because of a lack of technical understanding.

Let's take a "simple and sane" look at LANs. And let's answer some of the most-asked questions on the topic. These questions include:

- Which network topology is most suited to our needs? (Network topology is how the network is configured.)
- What are the differences between baseband and broadband and which should be used?
- What equipment can or should be included in a LAN?

Market segments

Presently, there are three major segments of the LAN market. These are:

High-speed data links between mixed mainframe and minicomputer networks. This enables the connection between various types of computers.

The integration of office equipment such as print servers, printers, hard disks, etc.

LAN features

There are three basic features of LANs.

The first feature is bandwidth, which is the range of frequencies a circuit will pass. The greater the bandwidth of a particular communi-

---

There are three types of LAN protocols.

---

cation channel, the greater the capacity and speed of the information.

There are two types of bandwidth—baseband and broadband. Each has advantages and disadvantages over the other. Baseband sends signals without modulation (the translation of digital signals to analog signals), which means only digital signals are used. As seen in Figure 1, this type of bandwidth has an overall lower cost. There are limitations in capacity and distance. Broadband, on the other hand, can

also carry analog signals and has a higher capacity and distance. Broadband, though more complex and costly, is the preferred technology—when it can be cost justified.

The end choice between broadband and baseband should meet the specific requirements of the user.

The second feature involves the type of rules and regulations of how each node (workstation) talks and order of use on the line. This is known as protocol.

There are many protocols available from various vendors, usually offered with the use of the vendor's LAN. Remember—not all organizations are able to use a LAN pre-established by the vendor.

Protocols

There are three major types of protocols used in conjunction with a LAN:

✓ **Polling**—This is usually used when a central computer or intelligent workstation exists in a LAN. This central computer controls which node uses the line as well as time limitations of line use.

✓ **Token Pass**—This protocol includes destination and source addresses which accompany the message. This "token" is passed along the network until it reaches the destination address. After the message has been received correctly, an acknowledgement message is returned to the source address.

✓ **CSMA (carrier sense multiple access)**—This protocol has the ability to "sense" or monitor the line. A message is only sent when the destination node is idle.

One should select a protocol based on the topology of the network being used. Figure 1 summarizes each protocol's strong points.

The network topology or physical design of the system is a key factor of a LAN.

The organization should consider the user when planning the location of the nodes and how they're connected. Equipment, location and connection can be very important to future expansion. The three common LAN topologies are Star, Ring and Bus or Tree.

The *Star* topology, as shown in Figure 2, makes use of a central computer or intelligent workstation. Each additional node has a direct point-to-point connection to this central node. In a LAN, the central node performs a type of circuit switching. Star topology is commonly used with polling to control the resources. Because there is only one main computer, there is tighter network control. However, failure of the central node will cause a disruption in the network. For this reason, the central node of a Star topology network is called the critical node. An appropriate use of a Star topology would be the sharing of data base, or other valuable software.

A *Ring* topology, as shown in Figure 3, consists of a closed loop. Data is circulated around the ring in the form of a packet. A node wishing to transmit waits for its turn (when the packet passes by). It then sends data onto the ring by adding to the packet.

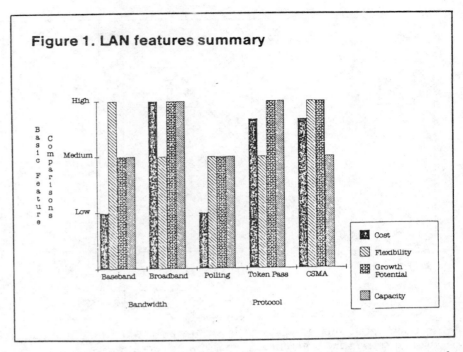

Figure 1. LAN features summary

Source and destination addresses must accompany the data to ensure destination and acknowledgement. The Token Pass protocol is commonly used with this topology. If the ring is large, the message (Packet) can lose its signal. In this case, each node can be attached to a repeating element which renews the signal power.

The major advantage to Ring topology is the relative low cost per node. Also, there is no need for a central controlling computer. However, there are a number of disadvantages.

These include: Security of a Ring network depends on the nodes themselves. Expansion can be difficult; distance and repeaters must be considered. Longer response time may result. There is greater dependency upon the equipment; if one node point fails, the message is lost. Because of those disadvantages, the Ring network has not been widely accepted in the United States.

The most common topology is the *Bus* or *Tree*. As shown in Figure 4, nodes are attached to a single (or dual) coaxial or fiber optic cable. This is commonly used with CSMA

to ensure a node is idle before sending a message.

The message also is formed into a packet which contains source and destination addresses. This network topology does not require a centralized controller and is able to operate effectively if one or more nodes malfunctions. It also allows easy expandability and modification along with the combination of voice, data and video signals. With Bus topology, only one pair of nodes can communicate at a time. This factor enables Bus topology to be used effectively with CSMA protocol.

Figure 5 summarizes the performance of each topology relative to certain characteristics.

Network considerations

A problem may arise when an organization combines one or more network topologies.

This cannot be done without an intermediate device—a Gateway.

Gateways are used to attach dissimilar LANs, as shown in Figure 6. The configuration of each LAN is such that data cannot be understood in an unfamiliar line design. There-

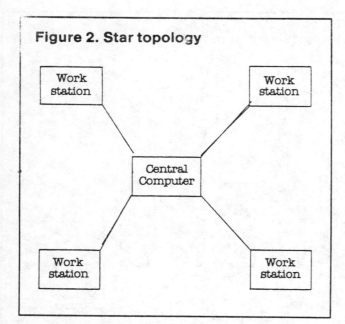

Figure 2. Star topology

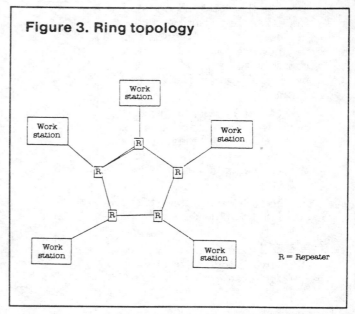

Figure 3. Ring topology

R = Repeater

fore, a program such as a gateway is used to correct the differences.

An additional problem occurs with line distance. A LAN has a limited distance. Once exceeded, the signal begins to distort. A repeater can be used as shown in Figure 7 to boost the signal, renewing the signal strength to continue its destination path. Each repeater may add static

to the line which may limit the number of repeaters used on one line of transmission.

A local area network is better than other networks for several reasons. The relative cost is low compared to alternative networks. LANs are accessible and available from many vendors. And once installed, LANs are easy to use.

On the downside, among the problems which may occur with LANs are:

- Distance limitations. A LAN may have node distances from 500 feet to 5,000 feet depending on the type of LAN. The option of a repeater is available to extend this limitation.

- Data can be lost or distorted over

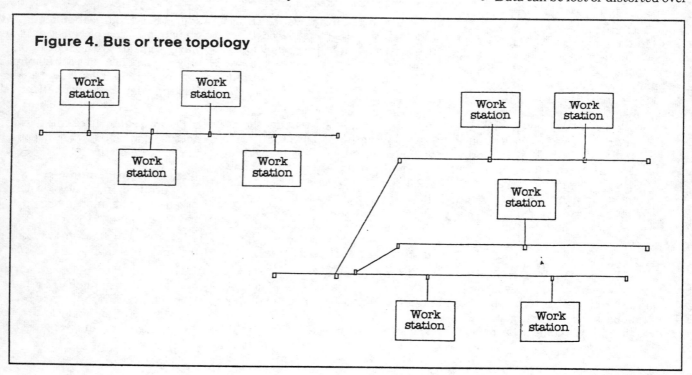

Figure 4. Bus or tree topology

distance. This is the risk taken when node distance is extended.

- An additional device known as a gateway is needed to connect dissimilar LANs.

- Once a LAN is installed, it may be limited and difficult to change. Careful planning must be done prior to installation. Where to install the communications line, what type of line is required for each piece of equipment, and the best location for each piece of equipment are factors to be considered. These are important considerations for future expandability and use. If the building is not wired for desired use, a large expense could be incurred for remodeling.

- User acceptance has been a past problem because of unresolved network standards, which are still existing today. With careful planning and knowledge of the technology, Local Area Network acceptance and success should follow.

Vendor LANs

LANs can be purchased from a variety of vendors.

An important innovation in the LAN market was the late 1985 release of the IBM Token Ring LAN. IBM has tried to overcome the disadvantages presently facing the ring

Optimized information flow should not be the only goal.

topology with this network. The network uses conventional telephone wiring, which eases expansion and has a capacity of 260 PC connections (which is much larger than PCnet, which IBM now offers). The network incorporates a simple scheme using three pieces of hardware, designed to link personal computers in a LAN environment to share peripherals and servers. The approximate cost

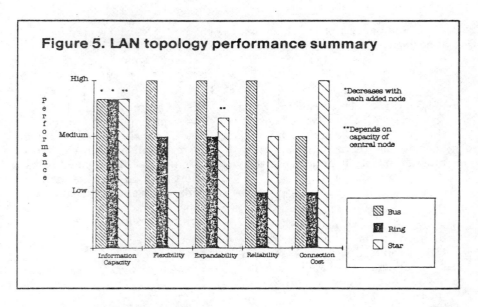

Figure 5. LAN topology performance summary

*Decreases with each added node

**Depends on capacity of central node

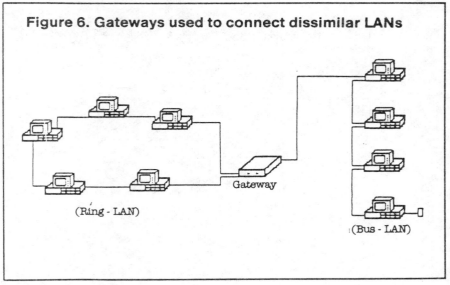

Figure 6. Gateways used to connect dissimilar LANs

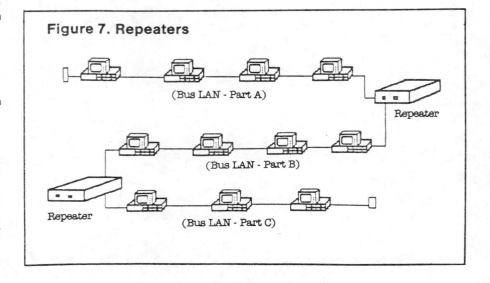

Figure 7. Repeaters

runs $828 per station (not including the cable). This is only a small step toward IBM's goal of creating a layered system of networks.

There are mixed opinions of the new IBM LAN. One benchmark test showed very little network degradation during 90 to 95 percent network capacity, as compared to large degradation at 30 to 40 percent of Ethernet's network capacity.

However, there are some limits of this first release. This release has a 4-MBPS capacity, not the 16-MBPS to which IBM is building. The release was introduced without immediate host connection capabilities. Without additional gateways and servers, the LAN only exists for the PC market.

IBM introduced this network to get an "edge" on the market, and has started a cluster of third-party vendor LANs who waited for IBM to set a standard. The result has encouraged vendor competition to increase network functions for less money.

The key to a successful LAN is proper planning. Optimized information flow should not be the only goal in establishing a LAN. Information customer involvement is just as important. Consider the customer's needs as well as organizational needs. LAN acceptance and success are sure to follow. ∎

References

1. BIS Applied Systems with Mackintosh International, The Local Area Network Reference Guide, Prentice-Hall, Inc., Englewood Cliffs, NJ, 1985.
2. Churchill, Bruce, Jordan, Larry E., Communications and Networking for the IBM PC, Robert Brady Co., 1983.
3. Cooper, E., "Broadband Network Designs Issues and Answers," Computer Design, March 1983.
4. Derfler, Frank Jr., Stallings, William, A Manager's Guide to Local Networks, Prentice-Hall Ind., Englewood Cliffs, NJ, 1983.
5. Greene, William H., Moss, Gary G., Pooch, Udo W., Telecommunications and Networking, Little, Brown and Co., Boston, MA, 1983.
6. Haugdahl, Scott, "Local Area Networks for the IBM PC," Byte, Dec. 1984.
8. Sherman, Kenneth, Data Communications A User's Guide, Reston Publishing Co., Reston, VA, 1981.
9. Webster, Roger, "Building a Microcomputer Local Network," Data Communications, Feb. 1985.
10. News Scan, "IBM Announces Token-Ring Network for Micros," Computer Decisions, Nov. 5, 1985.
11. Feldman, Robert, "Host to Token Ring Links Not Expected," MIS Week, Nov. 13, 1985.
12. Feldman, Robert, "TOKEN GESTURE: Ring Rossed," MIS Week, Oct. 23, 1985.
13. Greenstein, Irwin, "TI Dumping Ethernet for Token Ring," MIS Week, Nov. 20, 1985.

Telecommunications: Trouble in Paradise

By Gail Thackeray

There's always trouble in paradise. When FCC Chairman Mark S. Fowler in 1983 called the marriage of computer and telephone the most beneficial union since Adam and Eve, he didn't have fraud in mind. But the growing army of communication-services thieves would agree with him. Events of the last few years have provided an ideal environment for the explosive growth of telecommunications crimes.

During the boom years of the microcomputer revolution, direct access to computer and communications facilities have moved from the controlled setting of the computer room to the comparatively unsupervised individual work station and home. At the same time, the proliferation of communications carriers and breakup of the Bell System have decentralized security and investigation functions. This has given more people the opportunity to steal, with few of them punished.

Communications fraud has been around longer than the computer, of course, and can be accomplished simply by putting a slug in a pay telephone or falsely denying responsibility for a toll call. There is also the familiar corporate headache of employees using company facilities for personal calls. This is a problem which has given way to a whole range of frauds, many perpetrated by outsiders taking advantage of the new technology.

In the early 1960s, "phone freaks" combined technology and fraud to produce a variety of devices to circumvent billing systems. Among these were the "black box," which allowed incoming calls to be received without a toll charge to the caller. Another was the "blue box," a multifrequency tone-generator which enabled the caller to gain access to a long-distance circuit by dialing a toll-free number and then using the "box" to imitate AT&T audio-switching signals. These disconnected the original call, but left the circuit open. The thief then could use his box to produce the tones necessary to "dial" his fraudulent call, while the telephone billing equipment failed to record it. Only after the telephone company's security efforts were intensified and dozens of successful prosecutions handled were dishonest callers dissuaded.

Today, calling-card or code fraud is the technique of choice. While MCI Communications Corp. claims to hold fraud losses between $400,000 and $500,000 a year, AT&T, with the largest subscriber base, suffered a 36% increase in calling-card fraud between 1982 and

> *"Proliferation of common carriers and the breakup of Bell have decentralized security and investigation functions. This has given more people an opportunity to steal . . ."*

1983. According to Neal Norman, a corporate security district manager for AT&T, the company's losses reached nearly $150 million in 1983, with calling-card fraud accounting for $108 million of the total.

Losses of this magnitude have pushed all long-distance carriers to beef up efforts in fraud control and investigation, with some unexpected consequences. According to Mr. Norman, until early 1983, AT&T's method for assigning account numbers and authorization codes was relatively uncomplicated. Consequently, thieves could create calling-card numbers which, though never legitimately issued to anyone, would be accepted by the system. In response to mounting losses, the company made modifications. Now the system requires a valid calling-card number and code.

Diabolically adaptable, however, the criminals stopped inventing fraudulent numbers and began stealing real ones. Hence, the recent rash of news stories about people, like one New York State woman whose $109,000 home phone bill ran over 2500 pages, and had to be delivered by UPS.

The crooks obtain valid codes by various means. They overhear executives in hotel or airport telephone booths reading their company card number to an operator, or they may steal a wallet containing a card or authorization code. Thousands of people belong to computer bulletin boards, where "good codes" are listed and constantly updated. There can be lots of trouble should a code fall into the hands of a thief. Testimony to this was a recent case in which 12,000 attempts were made to fraudulently use a number within a 24-hour period, said Mr. Norman, noting that codes can be transferred with incredible speed.

Sometimes the crook's job is made even easier when the victim innocently parts with a code. Such was the case of one female victim who was using her son's calling card while visiting Florida. She asked the hotel operator for assistance in placing a call. She got help and he got the code, which he gave to his girl and a few friends. Together, the pals ran up $1 million in fraudulent calls.

Private corporate networks, whether designed for voice or data transmission, offer a whole universe of free rides. While investigating a group of computer "hackers," Philadelphia detectives discovered that they were accessing a large corporate telephone network designed for communication with branch offices and travelling executives. The hackers had valid authorization codes belonging to various employees, but were blocked from stealing services when the codes were changed. Another major corporation got out of the private telephone system business when outside abuse of its 800-number network soared. That company now obtains a telephone billing card for each authorized employee and makes the individual responsible for protecting and monitoring its use.

Finally, in a telephone version of the double-whammy, computer hobbyists who spend their energies invading other people's systems, often employ public networks like GTE Telenet or Compuserve, which bill the "host" organization for calls received. A Canadian corporation suffered a system crash last winter when an American teenager tried to explore its operating system. The youth dialed his local Telenet access number, which connected through the Canadian Datapac network to the com-

> *"Computer hobbyists who spend their energies invading other people's systems often employ public networks which bill 'host' companies for calls received . . ."*

pany. He succeeded in logging on to the system. After the crash, the company changed the passwords to prevent further entry, but as a network "host," it was charged for the original call and each subsequent unsuccessful attempt.

The first problem when a serious communications fraud is uncovered is catching the criminal. Sophisticated thieves are hard to trace, because they don't dial direct. Computer hackers are fond of "looping" a call around the country, or combining several carriers to link them to their victim. Tracing back the call, investigators come up against one local access number after another. This makes it hard to trace incoming calls to identify the origin of a fraudulent one. It can be done, however, as increasing numbers of "hackers" and "phone freaks" know to their regret.

The second problem can be even worse: finding an agency able or willing to prosecute. Larry Newman, senior director of corporate security for Western Union's Metrophone service, complains that he has found several prosecutors un-

willing to handle even a well-documented case with substantial losses. They are also reluctant to prosecute locally a crime which they believe is federal in nature, or difficult to prove because it is "technological."

The statutory framework necessary for successful prosecution of these crimes is already in place in most jurisdictions. About half the states now have computer-abuse statutes on the books or awaiting passage. In addition, most states have a fraud or theft of services statute which covers communications theft. At the same time, jurisdictional problems plague the local prosecutor trying to prove a complex scheme which extends across county or state borders.

If he can persuade federal authorities to investigate, the victim will benefit from a statute specifically designed for such problems: the wire-fraud statute. Federal courts have more experience with these cases, the prosecutor has no jurisdictional problems, and the resources of federal agencies concerning technological expertise are far greater than those of local agencies. However, the FBI and U.S. Attorneys' offices have declination policies which permit them to reject even substantial felony cases. This leaves the victim a choice of either a civil suit for damages, local criminal prosecution, or both.

Clearly, even successful prosecution is less important than a good security system for the corporate communications network. Organizations should guard their communications assets as carefully as their financial ones. But too

> *"The statutory framework necessary for successful prosecution is in place in most jurisdictions. About half the states now have computer-abuse statutes on the books."*

often, security is not considered when deciding on the purchase of equipment and services. When planning a corporate communications network, it is wise to consult the security officer and the data-processing and procurement professionals.

Henry Kluepfel, an AT&T district manager, and an expert on computer fraud, recommends consideration of the access requirements and sensitivity of the information of each user when determining the level of security appropriate to each work station or individual employee. Where outside access to or from the internal network is required, he says, detailed message-billing, broken down by work station, should be considered. This will enable monitoring of the system and facilitate early discovery of fraudulent use of company resources, along with providing documentation needed to prove a crime. Since each vendor's products have different levels of controls available, managers should compare security elements when adding new equipment. Mr. Kluepfel also recommends isolating the internal network from outside access.

> *"Even successful prosecution [of crimes] is less important than a good security system for the protection of the corporate communications network . . ."*

Individuals and organizations with sloppy control over their calling cards and codes also face a hazard seldom recognized until too late. As the losses from fraud mount, carriers are more willing to let those whose carelessness made the thefts possible share the financial damage. The consumer credit-card statutes which protect retail cardholders from bills run up by a thief do not currently apply to telephone authorization codes and cards.

Therefore, parents who allow the family electronics genius to use their codes, or companies which fail to adequately protect themselves against employee abuse, risk more than the annoyance of a fraud investigation. They may foot the bill, along with the rest of the honest subscribers who have suffered through higher phone bills over the years. **TO**

GAIL THACKERAY is an assistant district attorney with the Philadelphia (Pa.) Economic Crime Unit. Her responsibilities include investigation and prosecution of computer and other white-collar crimes.

PART VI

APPLICATIONS OF MIS AND DSS

LEARNING OBJECTIVES:

. Differentiate between information needs for small and large businesses.

. Appreciate the use of Decision Support Systems in marketing and manufacturing management.

. Recognize the effect of MIS technology on choices now available to the personnel manager.

INTRODUCTION

In Part I the definitions of EDP, MIS, and DSS were discussed in terms of the major changes in computer technology during the past forty years. In this part the selected articles provide the reader with an opportunity to experience the application of EDP, MIS, and DSS in a variety of settings as they relate to the functional areas of the firm and decision making within the firm.

The structure of the firm will determine the relationship between managerial decision-making and the functional subsystems within the organization. Information systems, in turn, are the glue that ties the organization together and make it function as an organized whole. Within the managerial decision-making hierarchical structure, there is a bi-directional flow of data and information up and down the structure. At the top level, the strategic level, there is responsiblity for decisions relating to directing the firm's resources in terms of overall goals and objectives. At other levels, namely, middle or tactical and lower or operational, the responsibility changes from more planning activity to controlling. However, within each managment level there are basic functions to be performed. These functions relate to planning, organizing, staffing, directing, and controlling. For example, in terms of planning, strategic level management is responsible for developing long range plans relating to the products or services to be produced. At the operational level, planning would include detailed forecasting of demand for the product or service to be produced and the translation of this forecast into a production schedule. At the operational level, responsiblity is assigned for tracking the daily output of goods or services and planning the schedule of operational activity for the following day. Hence, each level effects other levels and in turn is effected by activity at another level relative to the data or informa- tion generated and how this information is presented. At the top level of the firm, information relating to the external environment is more important to making policy decisions which set the direction of the firm in terms of overall goals and objectives. At lower levels, the internal information becomes the most important in performing the functions at that level. One other factor, which may have an important bearing on how information generated within the firm affects managerial decision-making, is related to the size of the firm. Although all firms have basically the same set of functions to be performed, in smaller firms many of the functions are aggregated and decision-making may, in some instances, be based more on soft information. That is, intuition, as opposed to hard information based upon a quality data processing and information system.

Each of the functional areas has well defined responsibilities in meeting the overall goals and objectives of the firm. For example, in the functional subsystem relating to the financial function, the information needs of the managers must be identified and an information system created to meet these needs. The financial subsystem, which generally includes the accounting function, is basically responsible for money flows. Data are gathered on the internal operations of the firm and along with external data relating to money market conditions, are input into a database. From this database, data and information relating to the flow of funds in and out of the system, budgeting and control of expenditures within the firm, and future market conditions which affect the firm are provided. In essence, managerial efforts are directed toward financial analysis and control.

Areas of responsiblity within the marketing function include planning, promoting and sale of existing products, and the development of new products. That is, they are the revenue generating function of the firm. The marketing information system involves the assimilation of data and information on internal conditions relating to such factors as distribution center, inventory status, transportation, shipping plans, production schedules, capacity availability, production alternatives, financial capital availability, etc., and this, coupled with external data generated through marketing research on products and customers, is input into a database. The output from this system provides data and information for planning and control with regard to market planning, managing the sales resources, sales forecasting, product development and brand management, advertising and promotion, and marketing intelligence.

The personnel function is somewhat different from the other functional areas discussed in this section in that it is generally considered a line function and serves all functional areas of the organization. The responsibility of the personnel function is the development of human resources. The information system related to this function includes data and information on recruitment, education, training, payroll, and employee benefits. Outputs from this system include reports on the budget and financial status of the personnel function, and reports relating to hiring, separating, promoting, transfering, and training which are the major areas of responsibility for the manager within this function. However, with computerized information systems, the personnel manager must also be cognizant of other conditions imposed on the firm in the form of affirmative action legislation, privacy of records, and security of information in the personnel database.

In terms of MIS design and implementation, there is a significant difference between the information provided by each system. Therefore, the types of data gathered by each system, types of analysis, and types of information provided is significantly different. Also the users of these systems may occupy different roles and responsibilties within the organization.

The major questions(s) encountered by the user(s) and the designer(s) of these systems are directed at the type of information which should be provided by each system. In order to provide an answer, one should first identify the types of data gathered and analyzed by these systems. From this process, an answer to the question can be formulated.

In terms of policy related to information systems design, there are two alternatives. The first alternative suggests one information system for the whole organization. This policy would require a corporate database which could be accessed by all functional managers. The second alternative favors a separate information system for each functional area of the business orgnization. We believe the second alternative is more evolutionary and responsive to the specific needs of different functional managers.

Functional information systems in a business organization are generally associated with the financial, production, marketing, personnel, and manufacturing functions. Let us briefly describe the basic input/output operations of each system.

Financial information systems provide information regarding funds management and financial control. The information regarding funds management assists decision makers in maintaining a balance between the cash inflow and the cash outflow. In order to achieve this goal, sources and uses of funds should be identified and carefully monitored.

Information related to financial data serve as a control mechanism. By generating a series of financial ratios, the business organization may assess its financial situation by comparing its ratios with industry ratios or with a series of predefined standards. Also a sophisticated financial information system should provide projected information about future activity of the organization. Probably the most important projected information would be the sales projection.

Most of the input data to a financial information system comes from the accounting information system. However, other data regarding the environment of the business organization must be collected externally. These data may be derived from a variety of sources such as labor, customer, financial community, and government.

Marketing information system has received a lot of attention during recent years. This system provides valuable information regarding the marketing mix, e.g., product, place, price and promotion. The product component of this sytem provides important information about the product life cycle. Knowing the current stage in the life cycle dictates an appropriate decision which should be made by the marketing manager. The price component provides information related to the effects of different pricing policies on sales, profit, and competition. To provide information regarding the price component, marketing information system collects and analyses variety of data on such factors as the national economy, competitors' pricing strategy, etc. The promotion component is responsible for providing information regarding the most effective ways to promote the firm's goods or services. This may include types of advertising, budget, theme, and media selection. The place component of this system traces the link between the manufacturer and the customer which may also include a wholesaler and retailer. This subsystem seeks to identify the most efficient and effective communication channels between these parties.

To provide all this information, the marketing information system gathers data both from inside and outside of the organization. The internal data are mostly collected from the accounting information system. The external data may be collected from variety of sources by using variety of means. Industrial espionage may be one of these means. Also marketing research may provide valuable data to marketing information system regarding current and future product needs and trends.

During recent years, decision support systems have been playing an important role in marketing information system. A variety of end user mathematical models related to pricing strategy, media selection, and distribution centers have been employed in marketing's DSS to generate valuable information for determining the firm's marketing strategy.

Another important functional information system within an organization is the personnel information system. An effective personnel information system can provide the personnel professionals with valuable information related to basic employee tracking, equal employment opportunity reporting, affirmative action reporting, skills inventory, benefit and salary administration, analysis of training and turnover, job requisition, selection list, etc. Most of the input data to this system are collected internally. However, some external data related to the labor force and the governmental regulations are also collected.

The production or manufacturing information system provides information regarding the status of the transformation from raw material to finished product. Information provided by this system focuses on the most efficient and effective utilization of raw materials, labor and existing machineries. A sophisticated manufacturing information system provides valuable information regarding cost and the quality of the products manufactured. To provide this information, the manufacturing information system utilizes accounting data and external information related to labor force conditions and availability of material inputs from current or potential vendors.

DISCUSSION QUESTIONS

1. What is the main impact of CBMIS on small business operations?

2. In dealing with a CBMIS, what is the difference between efficiency and effectiveness?

3. How will future changes in CBMIS affect the personnel manager?

4. In the personnel area, is data security a major problem?

5. To date, where has the major emphasis been placed in developing a CBMIS for the marketing area?

6. What are the major differences between a traditional and DSS approach in defining managerial information needs?

7. How is the term "what if" related to DSS?

8. What primary conditions must be addressed in order for DSS to have a positive impact?

Decision Support Systems Are for Small Businesses

DSS helped reduce the actual weekly variance for direct labor from 20-25% to 6% of the budgeted amount, which could mean savings of $15,000 on sales of $500,000.

John S. Chandler is assistant professor of accountancy at the University of Illinois at Urbana-Champaign. He received a doctorate degree in computer and information science at the Ohio State University. He is a member of Sangamon Valley Chapter, through which this article was submitted.

By John S. Chandler, Thomas Trone, and Michael Weiland

Small businesses need Decision Support Systems (DSS) just as much as larger firms, and they can be built cost effectively for the small business. In support of that statement, we offer as evidence the system set up in a food service operation.

The goals of a DSS are threefold: to facilitate decision making (as opposed to merely aiding a clerical function); to support, but not automate, decision making; and to be able to adapt to the changing needs of decision making. A DSS, then, is in stark contrast to the structured, repetitive environment of transaction processing systems.

Figure 1 shows the commonly accepted components of a DSS. There are several aspects to note. First, the decision maker/manager/user does not directly interface the computer-based systems but goes through an intermediary. Second, there may be more than one intermediary if more technical expertise is required. And, third, the computer support may take the form of some very sophisticated hardware and software. A key role in the DSS is the intermediary, translating in both directions: from management's decision-making needs to computer support and then back from the computing environment to the user's decision-making environment.

The typical decision-making environment supported by a DSS can be determined by looking at some of the reported decision support systems now in operation.[1] The organizations are very large, both commercial and governmental, and have very complex problems to be solved. They have large budgets to support extensive and expensive computer development and testing. The decisions directly supported have a significant financial impact: for example, banking institutions have developed portfolio analysis DSSs that aid in multimillion dollar investment decisions; a U.S. government agency uses a DSS constructed to investigate the impact of government regulations on the country as a whole; and large corporations have developed DSSs to aid them in financial planning. All of these organizations have ample technical staff and resources from transaction-based computer operations, so that the development of a DSS is not a significant burden.

Why Does a Small Business Need a DSS?

There are several aspects of the small business environment that makes a DSS appropriate, or at least, potentially helpful. The management of a small business is of a different character than a large business. In general, small business operators are of two types: craftsmen and opportunists. Craftsmen enter the business environment because they feel they have a comparative expertise; they can prepare food better, make furniture different or rewire houses better. Their main objective is to be able to continue to perform their craft. Profitability of the business is only a means to that end, not as a factor in growth. Although they do not have, in general, the management background necessary for growth management, they also have little desire to acquire such a background, and thus, are not likely to benefit from a DSS.

The opportunist is a different case, however. He, too, has typically found a comparative niche in the current business environment, but sees it as a beginning, not as an end. He is growth oriented, interested in running a productive and efficient operation. Unfortunately, like the craftsman, the opportunist is also naive at management; but, unlike the craftsman, the opportunist wants to learn how to make the critical management decisions. Because of his lack of management background, the opportunist sometimes is forced to make these decisions in an unorganized, unsupported manner. He needs aid in learning not only what decisions need to be made, but also what data is needed to make them. As will be shown, a DSS can be an effective mechanism for these purposes.

The operational constraints on the small business manager, craftsman or opportunist, are also different than a manager in a large business. The small businessman spends more time in the operation of the business than in any other aspect, resulting in a minimum amount of time for management decision making. The overall time horizon for small business decisions is much shorter than for larger businesses. A major portion of small business failures occur in the first year of operation, and, therefore, management information is needed on a quicker basis than for a large business. The time horizon is also much shorter for reacting to changes in the environment. Because small businesses do not have the large capital base and credit level of the large business, small variations in demand can cause catastrophic consequences. A small business needs to be able to adapt quickly to changes. Viewed on absolute scale, the financial impact of a small business decision may be much less than that of a larger business, but in the context of the continued existence of the firm, the small business decision may be even more critical.

Thus, the small business manager, in particular the opportunist, needs a mechanism to direct him toward the appropriate decision-making functions (i.e., facilitate decision making). He also needs a mechanism to provide him with the relevant data and tools to make those decisions (i.e., support decision making). And, finally, this mechanism must be able to react quickly to the ever changing, decision-making environment of the small business manager (i.e., ability to adapt). Can a DSS be developed that provides the nontechnical small business manager with these capabilities?

Implementation: Two Key Considerations

There are two key considerations that affect the small business person's decision to implement a

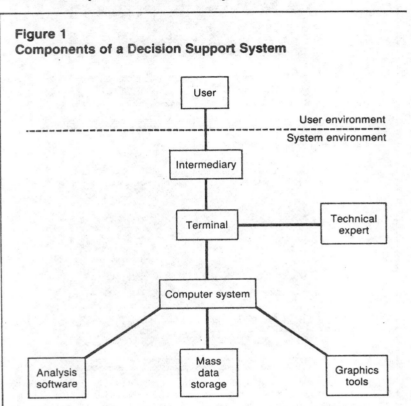

Figure 1
Components of a Decision Support System

DSS. The first is the cost of development and operation of the decision support system. The second is the capability of the DSS to interface with a nontechnical user and operate without a technical intermediary on site.

Any decision aid must be cost effective; this constraint is an acute concern for the small business because funds are of such a critical nature. The computer industry has continued its phenomenal reduction in unit costs while still increasing performance. The current explosion in the personal computer market has opened the door for many small businesses to enter the computer-based processing arena. Computer systems can be purchased for as little as $500, but the more common range for small business systems is $2,000-$5,000. Thus, it is now technically and financially feasible for a small business to obtain computer-based support systems.

The bottom line for successful DSS implemen-

Figure 2
Conversational Mode for Input/Update Sales Data in a Decision Support System

Displayed initially to refresh user of current data.

First question asked by the DSS. The system waits at the position of the cursor for user response. If NO is the response, the DSS skips all further change questions and asks for the daily sales percentage only. Note that both lines of the question are displayed and the cursor returns to position so that the user can see the full consequences of his response.

If YES is the response, each attribute of the sales item is reviewed. Again both the question and its consequences are displayed. The cursor first stops at A and if YES is input it then moves to B, awaiting the new value. This is crucial in the DELETE question.

After all (or no) changes have been made to the current attributes of the sales item, the actual days sales percentage is requested. This same process is repeated for all items. Note if there are no changes, the only input by the user is an initial NO to the first change question and then the daily sales percentage.

tation then lies in the user-machine interface. The small business has neither the time nor the money to support an intermediary; therefore, the small business manager, in most cases, will end up being not only the user of the DSS, but also the intermediary. The large-scale DSS assumes a technically proficient intermediary so the challenge for the small business is to modify the design of a DSS to accommodate limited resources and make it cost effective.

One of the most important design considerations is the language of the user-machine interaction and operation. The system should be able to operate so that the user does not need to program. The commands to run the systems should be as nontechnical as possible. For example, a menu approach to data entry or report generation can provide a mechanism for the user with little knowledge of programming to operate the system.

The absence of the intermediary expert affects the translation process in both directions. To overcome this problem, the DSS must have design features that can provide the small business user with similar "expertise." The steps that must be performed in either translation, that were known by the intermediary but may not be known by the user, must now be carried out by the system, or at least controlled by the system. The DSS design essentially must "lead" the user through the necessary steps in operation. One appropriate approach is a conversational/explanatory interactive mode, in which the system requests information from or action by the user in English, based on an *a priori* set of alternatives.

For example, to enter sales data for a sales analysis report under this approach, the DSS would request data items from the user, one-by-one, prompting the user with the correct order and format (Figure 2). The production of the resulting report could then be automatic or by single command. This feature may limit the flexibility of a DSS to generate ad hoc reports, but the small business manager first needs assistance in making the fundamental business decisions.

A second important function performed by the intermediary is in error detection and correction. In the typical DSS, if data is entered incorrectly or a command is misspecified, the intermediary can remedy the problem. In a DSS for a small business manager, however, any errors, data, or command, would be the immediate problem of the user. The solution to handling errors is much the same as above; the DSS has to lead the user through the detection and correction process.

For detection, the DSS can have built-in limits and tests on the reasonableness and accuracy of data being entered. It can also have predefined conditions under which certain commands are or are not allowed. The DSS can test these conditions on each communication with the user and alert the user of any problems. The correction mode may be even more difficult for the user than the initial input of data and commands, but, again, the system should know what form the data or command should be in so it can direct the user through the correction process. Explanatory material also can be provided at user demand to increase familiarity with the system.

Finally, the retranslation process from computer processing to the user, sans intermediary, must be addressed. The user must not be overwhelmed by an impressive battery of output possibilities. Having to choose between statistical analyses, graphs, and charts may only confuse the user. The trade offs among the possibilities could be evaluated by the intermediary but probably not by the user. Accordingly, the output first should be similar to the reports that are now produced without the DSS, so that the user's familiarity with the DSS can be increased. Second, the output should be as concise and direct as possible because the user may be learning the decision process from the DSS.

DSS at Lox, Stock and Bagel

We developed a DSS for an independent food service operation in Champaign, Ill., named Lox, Stock and Bagel (LS&B). In addition to the restaurant, a bakery on the premises provides all of the bread products used in the business. The computer system used was a Digital Equipment Corp. VT78 (containing a PDP-8), running with the operating system COS 310. The language used in the programs is DIBOL, a business-oriented language similar to COBOL. The system was developed by a computer specialist but daily operation and use are the responsibility of LS&B staff, all nontechnically oriented. The owner, and main user, is a growth-oriented opportunist. Although this DSS was developed for a small food operator and several of the examples are food service oriented, the underlying structure of the DSS can be generalized to any small business environment.

How the DSS is integrated into the normal flow of operations is a key implementation issue for small business. The small business manager does not have much time to spend on management decision making and even less time to operate and maintain a DSS. The duties of data entry and report generation, therefore, should integrate with functions that the manager already has to perform, instead of imposing an additional task on him.

Although there are many decisions that the small business manager needs support in making, one of the most important is the planning and control of daily operations. Because the small business typically is resource poor (i.e., inade-

quate capital, credit, cash flow and personnel), small miscalculations in either planning or control over a very short time period can be disastrous. Figure 3 presents a model of the necessary functions that must be performed by the manager on a periodic basis. In Step 1, the manager plans for the coming period by scheduling (or budgeting) his resources of direct labor and direct materials, resulting in the work schedule for the period or purchase orders. In Step 2, the actual daily operations of the business occur and, from a control point of view, the key function for the manager is to measure (record) these events. The plan and reality come together in Step 3 when an analysis of variance report is generated. In Step 4, the manager then analyzes this report to determine the causes of any variances so that corrective action (Step 5) can be taken for the next period.

The DSS developed at LS&B fits well into this flow. The system is actually an integrated set of individual computer programs. The program NPARAM handles the initialization of key parameters (e.g., hourly wage) and constructs the framework for the budgeting process. Facilitating

Thomas Trone is president and chief executive officer of Lox, Stock & Bagel, Champaign, Ill. He has an advanced degree in finance from the University of Illinois.

Michael Weiland is a systems programmer at UOP Processing Co., Des Plains, Ill. He has a master's degree in computer science from the University of Illinois.

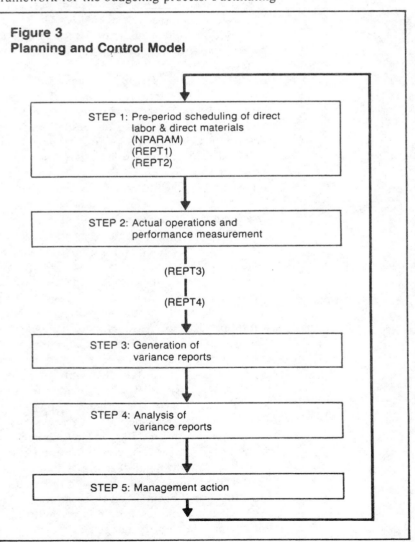

Figure 3
Planning and Control Model

STEP 1: Pre-period scheduling of direct labor & direct materials
(NPARAM)
(REPT1)
(REPT2)

STEP 2: Actual operations and performance measurement

(REPT3)

(REPT4)

STEP 3: Generation of variance reports

STEP 4: Analysis of variance reports

STEP 5: Management action

the allocation of resources to this budget are the programs REPT1 for direct labor and REPT2 for direct materials. These programs not only produce a printed schedule, but they also establish the basis for subsequent control. Entry of daily operational data is the function of program REPT3 for direct labor and of program REPT4 for direct materials. They also automatically produce the required variance reports. These reports are structured to allow the small business manager to identify areas of concern quickly.

A Walk Through the System

The first step in the operation of the DSS is initialization. A number of parameters must be input: the prevailing wage rate, projected weekly gross sales, the daily sales breakdown, and the budgeted percentages of gross sales for each type of expense. The program NPARAM (for New PARAMeters) maintains this list of parameters.

The actual input of the data is controlled by programs REPT1 for direct labor and REPT2 for direct materials. (Note: for clarity, we will only discuss the direct labor sequence of decisions.) From the values stored via NPARAM, REPT1 determines the labor-hour available for a given day as [(daily sales × percent sales for direct labor)/wage rate]. The DSS then asks the manager for the allocations of that labor hour pool to the specific service periods or categories. As in NPARAM, the conversational mode is employed, asking the manager a series of questions and verifying the response.

This schedule may be relatively constant over the short run, and, therefore, only modifications to the existing schedule are of concern to the user. The DSS only requests new data when necessary. This request may occur as a result of a change in NPARAM; for example, changing the wage rate but not the budgeted amount will cause the amount of labor hours to decrease. In this case, REPT1 automatically positions the user to that part of the schedule that must be amended. If the old schedule is still correct, however, the schedule will simply be displayed for verification and information purposes. Even at this point, the user can change a particular portion of the schedule as the DSS steps through the schedule. Only after an affirmative response will REPT1 update the stored schedule and make it the permanent copy.

As a precautionary measure, any new schedule is compared against the allowed labor hours determined in NPARAM. For convenience, the screen displays a running total of hours as they are entered. If the sum does not agree with the budgeted total, the user is again asked to assign hours. The DSS will not allow a schedule to be built that is not compatible with the budget.

To simplify the user's session at schedule mak-

ing, only one system command need be given to run the entire schedule-making portion of the DSS. A control file takes care of initializing the logical devices for the disk data files and of running NPARAM, REPT1, and REPT2. From the user's perspective, all three programs meld into one.

The analysis of the variance between the actual operations and the budgeted operations level is greatly simplified by the DSS. As the policies of the manager are carried out during the week in the small business, activity takes place and that activity must be measured and captured. The programs REPT3 and REPT4 aid in this endeavor. For each day in the period, these programs query the user for the actual sales and direct labor (or direct materials) costs. These figures are readily available on existing media, time cards, and register tapes.

The budgeted amounts of each of these items also are already stored in the DSS as a result of REPT1 and REPT2. Thus, programs REPT3 and REPT4 can easily finish the comparison automatically by retrieving the stored budget data. The programs calculate the actual and the unexpected variance for each day, broken down into periods or food types. The expected variance is based on the actual day's sales level versus the budgeted sales level. In each day's summary, the day's total variances are summarized (Table 1). Furthermore, a weekly summary is prepared, showing the variances for each period or food type for the entire week.

Because the variances are summarized both on a daily and weekly basis, the causes of the variances can be more readily identified. If a variance is prominent throughout the week for a given time period, this fact may indicate either that an inappropriate method has been used to estimate this time or that an actual shift in demand may have occurred. In either case, it gives the small business manager at least some initial leads on solving the problem. On the other hand, if a variance is prominent for all periods, but only on a given day, the performance for that particular day is suspect, either from a management or sales demand perspective. These programs can be used to generate a five-page output showing the individual variance analyses for each day, plus the weekly summary, the weekly summary only or nothing at all. In parallel, sales data is analyzed via program SAL-MIX. Input is again conversational (Figure 2) and the output allows for analysis of daily trends.

What this DSS Has Accomplished

The impact of this DSS on the daily operations of the business has been gratifying. Prior to the implementation of the DSS, the actual weekly variance for direct labor was 20-25% of the bud-

The small business needs a mechanism to enable it to react to changes quickly.

geted amount of 15% of sales. By the end of only the first month of use, the actual variance had been reduced to less than 6% of the budgeted amount. Assuming an annual sales level of $500,000, the savings in this area alone could amount to an increase in profit of $10,000-$15,000 in this current year. This savings easily recoups the initial investment the company made in the DSS.

Besides being a cost-saving process, the system also satisfies all the design requirements for a small business DSS. No programming is required of the user. To operate the system, the user enters only a couple of simple system commands and then merely responds to requests for data. The system continuously requests the user for the most up-to-date data and parameter values to keep the user cognizant of the crucial parameters of the business. In each iteration of the system (i.e., each week), the system forces the user to go through each step in the budgeting and control process, re-inforcing ("teaching") this management function to the user. The system employs an English conversational mode, designed to be as "personal" as possible (Figure 2). By continuously comparing check figures (e.g., total allocated hours vs. budgeted hours), the system prevents the user from entering erroneous data. And, finally, the output of the system—the printed schedules and variance reports—is integrated, as is, into the normal flow of operations.

Although a typical large-scale DSS design has to be modified to fit the small business environment, there are general design guidelines for such modification. These guidelines were followed in the design and implementation of an operational DSS for a small food service operator. The benefits in control and profits were evident in only the

first months of operation. Other small businesses should investigate the possibilities that a DSS can offer them.   □

Table 1
Direct Labor Variance Analysis
(sample daily results page)

	Prod 1	Prod 2	Serv 1	Serv 2	Serv 3	Serv 4	Serv 5
Friday							
Budgeted hours	18.0	10.0	8.0	55.0	14.0	54.0	14.0
Actual hours	18.0	10.0	10.0	58.0	20.0	57.0	16.0
Labor-hour variance	.0	.0	2.0	3.0	6.0	3.0	2.0
Expected variance	1.1	.6	.5	3.5	.9	3.4	.9

	Budgeted	Variance	Actual	Expected variance
Man-hours	173.0	16.0	189.0	11.0
Dollar pool	656.25	62.95	718.20	41.62
Sales	4,375.00	277.50	4,652.50	

	Prod 1	Prod 2	Serv 1	Serv 2	Serv 3	Serv 4	Serv 5
Saturday							
Budgeted hours	22.0	10.0	8.0	68.0	20.0	46.0	20.0
Actual hours	22.0	10.0	8.0	68.0	22.0	46.0	20.0
Labor-hour variance	.0	.0	.0	.0	2.0	.0	.0
Expected variance	.0	.0	.0	.0	.0	.0	.0

	Budgeted	Variance	Actual	Expected variance
Man-hours	194.0	2.0	196.0	.0
Dollar pool	738.75	6.06	744.80	.00
Sales	4,925.00	.00	4,925.00	

[1] P.G. Keen and M.S. Scott Morton. *Decision Support Systems*, Addison-Wesley, 1978.

CREATIVE NUMBER CRUNCHING
Why Marketing Managers Love DSS

by Michael Dressler, Ronald Beall and Joquin Ives Brant

In last month's BUSINESS MARKETING (INDUSTRIAL MARKETING), newly promoted marketing VP Dave Shaker told his assistant marketing manager, Bill Mover, all about marketing decision support systems (DSS) and their three essential characteristics: databases, a user interface and a library of analytical and modeling tools.

In this month's episode, we get to look over Dave's shoulder, so to speak, and share his thoughts as he manipulates marketing data with his DSS. He'll be working through three typical marketing problems:

- *Examining sales data for product line analysis;*
- *Forecasting;*
- *Modeling price and profit expectations.*

Each of Dave's inquiries will illustrate one or more of the common DSS capabilities: "what if" analysis, statistical analysis and quantitative modeling.

Each example will show how DSS is prescriptive; it suggests what data and analytical approaches are needed for problem solving and decision making. Importantly, the DSS follows the decision-maker's thought process step-by-step as he selects data, chooses techniques, and refines and interprets his findings.

With pencil and pad in hand, marketing VP Dave Shaker sits at the keyboard of the microcomputer in his office. He turns to the decision support system programmed on it to learn if he's allocating his ad budget and his marketing effort correctly among his company's different products.

Continued on page 78

Michael Dressler is managing partner at Dressler/Davison & Associates, San Francisco. Ronald Beall, a partner, is also an assistant professor of marketing at San Francisco State University. Joquin Ives Brant, until recently, was staff consultant at the firm.

SALES AND PRODUCT ANALYSIS

In a previous DSS session, Dave reviewed how his advertising expenditures are divided among his product lines. "Let's see, I need to see what each of my product lines has sold, in dollars, each month, for the year to date," he says to himself, setting the criteria for his information. "The decision I'm making is rather general; so product line data should be the right level of detail to look at.

"Because I want to sort out the winners and losers here, I could do some kind of ranking. Should I rank the product lines by dollar sales this year?"

But Dave also knows that he wants to compare product line actuals to forecasts, to see where performance is seriously off-target. He concludes: "I'll compare year-to-date sales against the forecast targets, with variances expressed as a percentage. And I'll rank the product lines, starting with the most positive variance above forecast, going down to the most below-target product line."

Exercising his judgment about the best way to massage a large quantity of data, he decides to go a bit further. "Let's see, I could also use a comparison of sales with last year's sales to date. If there are any strange changes, I'll see if my resource allocations have changed, or figure out what else is the cause." Dave's next step is to select the report format, and to tell the computer to execute the report. The computer assembles the report from two sources; the sales history database and the forecast database.

Dave studies the report on the screen, and runs off a copy on his printer for later use. He notices almost immediately that all lines are on target except product line A, on which he has been spending almost 15% of his advertising budget. It has fallen to 8% of his dollar volume and sales are growing at a rate of 5%.

"Last year this product line increased to 10% of sales volume and grew at a rate of 13%. That made our forecast for this year very optimistic, and of course we missed it by a mile," Dave acknowledges.

Sales analysis is a core feature of a marketing DSS; it's the application managers tend to think of first because of its critical role in decisions. Microcomputer-based DSS is now powerful enough to allow executives to create their own analyses with a choice of criteria—such as dollar or unit sales, by product and by sales representative and customer segment, by time period, geographical location, etc.—as long as a company's database captures sufficient sales detail.

Strategic product line analysis is Dave's next step. He'll alter information in specific ways—asking "what if" questions—to see how sensitive the overall picture is to changing assumptions.

He'll use an 'electronic spreadsheet,' a software program that displays numbers in rows and columns. He can change some of the numbers to test his assumptions, in the same way that an accountant—or an overworked marketing executive—totals up columns and grinds out percentages and variances by hand. The

> 'Sales analysis is a core feature of a marketing DSS; it's the application managers tend to think of first . . . Micro-based DSS is powerful enough to allow executives to create their own analyses . . .'

computer does all the work, almost instantaneously, however.

The electronic spreadsheet remembers the calculations needed; change one number, and it will automatically recalculate all the others as required. Because spreadsheets save time and improve accuracy, DSS software often allows reports to be displayed and changed directly on the CRT (cathode ray tube) screen. It's one of the most important features of a DSS. (But it is not the only feature, which is one reason why "true" DSS is a more powerful tool than spreadsheet software such as the popular Visicalc package. See last month's issue, p. 62.).

Facing his CRT, Dave examines different scenarios. He asks, for example, "Suppose product line A had kept its 13% share of total volume, and its price had stayed at $5,900."

He calls up a "template" for price/profit analysis that he had already designed for himself and his staff. It's an overlay for the electronic spreadsheet, with row and column designations and calculations predetermined by Dave to standardize everyone's calculations in a consistent format. Using it, and trying different assumptions of his own, Dave watches the rows and columns change as the spreadsheet incorporates his new assumptions to recalculate the product line's profit level. He tries a new scenario: "Suppose I had budgeted media for $900,000, volume increased to 15% of company sales as I had forecast, and we hiked the price to $6,500. What would have been the profit impact?"

Dave is fortunate. His DSS spreadsheets offer an enhanced "what if" analysis which shows not only the new calculation result, but also a comparison between the new and the previous result. It makes evaluation much easier.

Dave also has "goal seeking" capability in his DSS. He can designate a target profit level, set some of the conditions such as price and a first month sales volume, and then ask the computer to suggest what rate of sales growth is needed to reach the profit target. The spreadsheet works backwards from the outcome, filling in the sales growth for each month, for example.

FORECASTING

Managers forecast constantly. Sometimes they use large computers, large committees and large memos in their forecasting process. Other times, they forecast implicitly without even realizing they're doing so, as when deciding during a meeting to make a statement about next quarter's sales and profits. In either case, making forecasts is intrinsic to the management function. Good forecasting is one very important aspect of a DSS.

Dave Shaker needs to forecast product line A sales for the rest of the year. "I'd better update this forecast, not just for my own use, but also for the production and finance departments that need to know how the picture has changed since we made our last prediction." He realizes that the results will depend largely on factors within the company, such as managerial effort and ability, sales force effectiveness, and the promotion budget. External factors will also matter a great deal, such as the health of his customers' industries.

He also knows that in picking vari-

consider the time horizon for his forecast. He decides that it's short term, only five months.

"My other big consideration is that demand fluctuates seasonally," he reasons. "It wasn't really obvious just by looking at the sales figures, but we analyzed the data using a technique called auto-correlation. At any rate, I'll need a forecast technique which accounts for seasonality."

After some reflection, Dave chooses a technique called 'classical decomposition,' chuckling over the name. In MBA school, they joked that it was a Greek mummification ritual. Yet among available forecasting methods, it's readily understood, and it's effective.

Dave instructs his computer to base the forecast on data starting five years back, up through the most recent month. In so doing, he assumes that that five-year period is relevant to current and expected future business conditions.

"Well, the last five years should be relevant, shouldn't it?" he asks himself. "Maybe I'd better check." He turns to the DSS's graphics feature, and he displays the last five years of monthly sales for product line A in a bar graph on the CRT screen.

"Sales have increased steadily during the last five years, as my customer industries have grown. I think we are on an upward trend, basically, and demand stumbled this year only because my customers were hurt by the soft economy. But that should turn around, according to all the economic predictions I've been hearing."

Studying the graph, he spots a marked plunge in sales during the last quarter of year four. "How could I forget that? That was when we lost our production machinery in a fire at the Wichita Plant." Exercising his management judgment, which is essential to successful DSS use, Dave adjusts the misleading data. "As I recall, we were shipping out of stock from earlier overproduction, and we could fill only a third of our orders during that quarter. So I'll triple those figures, and assume that is close to what we would have sold had the fire not occurred."

When Dave next runs the classical decomposition technique, the following things happen:
• The data is deseasonalized, adjusted for the ups and downs of winter and summer. When the seasonal fluctuations are removed, the data looks like a wobbly, but generally upward-inclined line.
• The microcomputer runs a linear regression analysis on that wobbly line, to isolate the underlying trend. Creating the regression 'curve' removes the occasional 'spikes' in the sales line and eliminates the wobbles, or 'errors.'

"The world out there doesn't know it is supposed to be right on my trend line," Dave reflects. "Some months, the marketplace gets a bit ahead of itself and buys in January when it really could have waited until February. At least the randomness isn't too severe; the errors are pretty small."

Having decomposed the data into seasonality, trend, and random error components (with enough data, classical decomposition can also account for multi-year economic cycles), Dave is ready to extend the historical trend line into the future. He'll add back seasonality, but he cannot put random error back into the estimate. (If he could, he might have perfect forecasts and he'd get rich playing the stock market!)

Of course, Dave is sensitive to the 'confidence interval' around the forecast (a statistical estimate telling Dave how certain he can be that his prediction, based on historical data, will fall within the interval). But does Dave blithely accept the forecast? No, because he again exercises that DSS essential—management judgment—and decides that even though the numbers look very good, "I just don't think we can get back on the track so fast." So he reduces each month's estimate by 5%. "Now these are numbers I can believe, and they are numbers that I can get the sales force to believe in. I should save this forecast."

Dave knows that it's a good idea to forecast often and to keep the fore-

casts around. One reason is that previous forecasts are useful for learning how to forecast more accurately, as long as one keeps a record of the assumptions and thinking behind a particular forecast.

Otherwise one has dozens of forecasts in the files, with no idea on what they were based.

Note that Dave's thinking followed patterns that are familiar to most marketing managers. Faced with a decision which led to specific questions, he gathered data and organized it into information which was relevant to his decision. He analyzed it, drew inferences from it, and changed parts of it to test his inferences.

Rather than do the work arduously by hand, his computerized DSS provided all the number crunching, including generating statistics such as a regression curve which are a practical impossibility by hand.

Importantly, he was able to use a computer dedicated to the DSS; he didn't have to wait hours or days for computer runs to be completed by other departments. The computer was able to provide answers to questions while they were fresh in his mind, and he could interact with it creatively, following the information wherever his intuition led him.

But while the computer flows with a manager's thoughts, it influences those thoughts as well. It helps bring discipline to the manager's thinking.

Of course, the software must be powerful enough to give the manager enough room for thinking. For example, had Dave not had a classical decomposition package in his DSS, he could not have used it on his microcomputer. So choosing a DSS requires that managers' likely needs be known in advance. Missing pieces in a DSS package could leave dangerous blind spots in a manager's strategic planning.

MODELING

Just as managers forecast constantly, they also use models constantly.

Models are descriptions of the real world and relationships in it, boiled down to something orderly and understandable. As descriptions, they can either be verbal or numerical. And they can be as simple as "I sell two widgets every week, so I will sell 104 widgets this year."

Models can be made complex enough to suit every taste, or to intimidate those who aren't cognoscenti. But from the simplest to the most complex, models share the common characteristic of abstracting real events and causes. That virtue helps the model user clarify his thoughts on the important relationships between critical factors. They can turn an undisciplined ocean of information into an understandable description.

Models are integral to the DSS because they help support decisions. But they do not provide conclusions. For example, Dave Shaker reviewed the results of his classical decomposition forecast and concluded that they needed adjustment.

Furthermore, blind reliance on the effectiveness of any one model is like always using your favorite socket wrench when working on your automobile, regardless of whether the wrench fits the bolts. Even the best of analytical tools are not universally appropriate, except for old-fashioned common sense. And sheer volume of analysis never substitutes for understanding the situation or problems at hand.

Dave Shaker, schooled in the promise and pitfalls of using analytic models, has found the price modeling capability of his DSS particularly useful. He knows that although pricing is an obviously important marketing decision, relatively few companies take the time to carefully develop pricing strategy.

One problem is that of setting pricing objectives. The traditional fixed markup approach, simple assuming that true costs of goods are known, is only one way to approach the pricing problem. There are others such as:
- Maximizing short term profit;
- Maximizing long term profit;
- Achieving a specified sales level;
- Maximizing return on investment, in either the long or short term;
- Achieving a specified market share;
- Achieving breakeven in a specified time.

The DSS presents a model to match each objective the manager chooses, then generates the optimum price. Usually a manager will test several objectives, running different models to see how much their recommendations vary.

As Dave Shaker reviews the price of one of his products, he selects the pricing subsystem from the different subsystems on the DSS menu. (See last month's story, p. 50.)

He can choose from a number of objectives listed within the pricing subsystem.

Because he has an established prod-

uct, his main objective is profit maximization.

He needs two pieces of information, product costs and the product demand curve.

Dave already has cost information in his company's database, so he doesn't have to enter additional data unless he wants to override what's already there. Demand information is not likely to be in a database, however; Dave finds that that's the case with his.

So he'll enter demand information in one of two forms: a demand curve equation, or historical data. If Dave provides a demand curve equation, the computer can use that information directly. If he provides historical data, the computer will have to generate its own demand curve equation, generally by computing a linear regression curve (unless some non-linear curve seems to be more appropriate).

If Dave wants to continue the analysis, he can ask the computer about pricing to meet different objectives or he could provide different data and hence a different demand curve. He could see quickly how modeled optimum prices vary by objective, or by changed demand conditions. That allows him to refine his judgments and pick what he considers the best price.

The DSS not only shortens the time required for price analysis, it probably improves the quality of decisions compared to the way prices are established at most business/industrial product and service companies. Having the manager focus on objectives is almost certainly going to improve the quality of the final price even if he doesn't use computer modeling. Without a DSS, however, most managers do not have the time, the energy, or the technical background required to calculate optimum prices under even one set of assumptions, much less under several.

Dave Shaker's experiences discussed in this article hardly describe all that marketing managers can accomplish with marketing DSS. How much more they can aid their decisions and cut uncertainty depends, of course, on the extent of the data and the power of the DSS software they employ.

The keys are flexibility in the software, and creative intuition in the manager for DSS to achieve its potential as a marketing management tool. ∎

141

Decision Support System for Human Resource Management

BY DR. K. H. CHAN

■ Increased computerization in business data processing is one of the most notable trends of the past two decades. With the speed and capabilities of the computer, much more data and information can now be maintained and many sophisticated analyses, previously limited by mechanical considerations, have become practical applications. These developments have led to greater reliance on computers and growing data processing budgets. Even with the price reduction of some EDP equipment and the expanded use of mini and microcomputers, total EDP costs in many organizations are rising significantly. It has not been unusual for data processing budgets to grow at a steady twenty five percent a year; measured in absolute terms, the annual expenditures for EDP related activities in many organizations have now exceeded the total cost budgets of some major operating divisions.[1] Many companies are increasingly concerned about this phenomenon.

Manpower cost for systems development is one of the largest components of a typical EDP budget.[2] This has risen rapidly due to the short supply of skilled people in the field. Moreover, system development projects have all too often degenerated into costly overruns and incomplete technical performance. These facts indicate that efficiency in EDP centers warrants special management concern. To improve efficiency requires better planning, control, and scheduling of costly manpower resources. Many companies are now seeking for advice on how to do so. This article will show how a network technique, namely the minimum slack time heuristic (MINSLK), can be used for this purpose.

Efficient Management Helps Control Costs

Project management for EDP centers has been discussed by a number of authors.[3] The management planning and control techniques proposed include conventional budgets, transfer pricing, organizational control such as user interface and internal communication, detailed flowcharts, detailed file design layouts, program evaluation and review technique (PERT),

DR. K. HUNG CHAN

Mr. Chan, Ph. D., CPA is an Associate Professor of Accounting with the Faculty of Management Studies at the University of Toronto, Canada. He was previously associated with a major public utility in Canada. Professor Chan's research interests include computerized planning and control systems and energy accounting issue.

FIGURE 1   COMBINED NETWORK

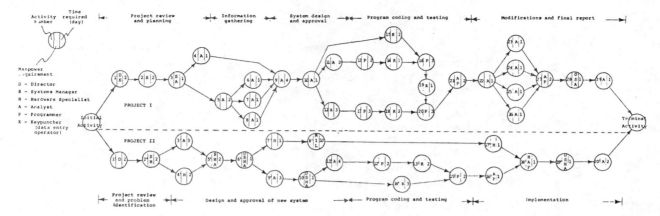

Gantt charts, and progress reports. This article presents a different technique called MINSLK, which extends the usefulness of PERT for planning and controlling EDP projects. MINSLK shows the way to the optimal or near-optimal allocation of manpower resources in EDP centers by bringing complex projects to completion at the earliest possible time for the given level of resources. The technique is particularly helpful when the project is complex but structured, when the resources are expensive, and when heavy work pressure is expected. These factors are normally present in today's high cost EDP projects.

A recently developed concept intended to reduce the workload of the main data center and thus reduce the possible delays of system development projects is that of information centers providing information to allow user departments to develop their own applications. These applications tend to be small in scale and specialized in their applicability. Large and corporate-wise projects normally remain the responsibility of the data center. Thus, there remains the need for operational efficiency in the data center.

Data Processing Activities

Activities in a data processing center can be segregated into two distinct categories: systems development and systems operations. Development includes system upgrading as well as the analysis and design of new information systems or system components. Two factors contribute to the need for frequent changes and new developments in the information systems of business organizations. The first is the growth of business organizations themselves in a dynamic society, which creates new demands for information for more timely and better decision making. The second is the rapid improvement of information technology, offering a competitive advantage to those firms which are among the first to innovate. Operations activities include the running of application programs and the preparation and maintenance of files. These latter activities are normally carried out by lower salaried personnel in the center, such as operators and keypunchers (or equivalently data entry operators). Usually a development project is a one-time task, but requests for different projects may arrive at the center at irregular times. Operations activities, on the other hand, are routine and must be performed regularly. In this article, the main concern is with the scheduling of development activities even though the techniques discussed may also be applicable to operations activities.[4] Systems development costs are the largest but also the most controllable elements in a typical EDP budget.[5] Manpower costs for development activities normally outweigh those for operations activities as the former usually involves high salaried personnel such as systems managers, systems analysts, and programmers. Proper scheduling of development activities would lead to a more efficient utilization of these high salaried personnel and could contribute substantially to cost savings.

Scheduling of Systems Development Activities

I. Defining Systems Development Activities

Typically, a data processing center will be faced with several system development projects simultaneously. These projects may include, for example, a request for the development of a system for capital budgeting analysis from the production planning department, a system for cash flow analysis from the accounting department, a corporate strategy simulation program from the president's office, a sales analysis program from the marketing department, and a system upgrading project initiated by the EDP center itself. After receiving a request for a system development project, an EDP center will generally proceed through the following five phases:[6]

1. Review the request, investigate manpower and machine availabilities, outline project plan, and estimate costs.

2. Gather the information necessary for a comparison of the requirements of the present system and the new system.

143

TABLE 1   ACTIVITY LIST - PROJECT 1

CAPITAL BUDGETING ANALYSIS FOR THE PRODUCTION PLANNING DEPARTMENT

Activity Number	Activity	Preceding Activities	Manpower Requirements*	Time required (day)
	(A) Project review and planning			
1	Review proposed project from the production planning department	Nil	D,S	2
2	Analyse information required, work involved, estimate cost	1	S	2
3	Discuss project with analyst	2	S,A	1
4	Discuss cost of the analysis with the production planning department	3	A	1
	(B) Information gathering			
5	Meet with accounting department and internal auditor to discuss information required and the analysis	3	A	2
6	Obtain information on alternative equipments	5	A	1
7	Obtain marketing information needed in analysis	5	A	1
8	Obtain financing information needed for analysis	5	A	1
	(C) System design and approval			
9	Summarize requirements, design system structure and prepare written specifications	4,6,7,8	A	4
10	Report design and specifications to systems manager and production planning department for approval	9	A	1
11	Design detail of Part 1 of program (cash flow analysis)	10	A	2
12	Design detail of Part 2 of program (other aspects)	10	A	3
	(D) Program coding and testing			
13	Program Part 1	11	P	2
14	Keypunch Part 1 of program	13	K	1
15	Prepare input data for Part 1	10	K	2
16	Test Part 1	14,15	P	3
17	Program Part 2	12	P	3
18	Keypunch Part 2 of program	17	K	2
19	Prepare input data for Part 2	16	K	1
20	Test Part 2	18,19	P	3
21	Integrate & test all parts of program	20	A,P	2
	(E) Modifications & final report			
22	Send preliminary report to production planning, marketing, finance, and accounting departments on test results, solicitate suggestions	21	A	1
23	Obtain and analyse response from production planning department	22	A	1
24	Obtain and analyse response from marketing	22	A	1
25	Obtain and analyse response from finance	22	A	1
26	Obtain and analyse response from accounting	22	A	1
27	Modify program according to suggestions received	23,24,25,26	A,P	2
28	Report to systems manager and director for approval	27	D,S,A	1
29	Report to all departments concerned	28	A	1

* D - Director   S - Systems Manager   H - Hardware Specialist
A - Analyst   P - Programmer   K - Keypuncher (data entry operator)

3. Design the new system based on user specifications. Include one or more proposals with a cost/benefit summary for each design proposed. The design will have to be reviewed and approved by user departments.

4. Code and test the programs for the new system. Printed outputs would be compared with the written specifications.

5. Prepare a final report and implement the new system.

To analyze each request, the project manager will first break down each phase into clearly defined activities according to specific requirements of the project. He will then have to define each activity by describing the work content, the expected time and the resources required to complete it. These activities are interrelated and can be graphically represented by a network. Some activities precede others and an activity may not be started until all of its preceding activities have been completed.

A clear and precise definition of each activity and an accurate estimate of its time (duration) and resource requirements will contribute to the successful completion of the project. Normally, a combination of management and software engineering techniques is needed to improve the accuracy of the time and resource estimates.[7]

TABLE 2   ACTIVITY LIST – PROJECT II

SYSTEM UPGRADING

Activity Number	Activity	Preceding Activities	Manpower Requirements*	Time required (day)
	(A) Project review & problem identification			
1'	Review management recommendations	Nil	D	2
2'	Analyse system performance & identify problems	1'	S,H	2
	(B) Design & approval of new system			
3'	Analyse possible solutions (software aspect)	2'	A	3
4'	Analyse possible solutions (hardware aspect)	2'	H	2
5'	Select an alternative	3',4'	S,H,A	2
6'	Acquire director's approval	5'	D,S,H,A	1
7'	Order hardware	6'	H	1
8'	Wait for hardware to arrive	7'	Nil	10
9'	Analyse & design structure of software	6'	A	3
10'	Present specifications to manager and director for approval	9'	D,S,H,A	1
11'	Design detail of software	10'	A	4
	(C) Program coding and testing			
12'	Program	11'	P	2
13'	Keypunch program	12'	K	2
14'	Prepare input data for testing	10'	K	3
15'	Test program	13',14'	P	2
	(D) Implementation			
16'	Demonstrate test result	15'	A,P	1
17'	Inspect hardware on arrival	8'	H	1
18'	Test software on new hardware	16',17'	H,A,P	1
19'	Demonstrate final result	18'	D,S,H,A	1
20'	Document improved system operation	19'	A	2

* D – Director   S – Systems Manager   H – Hardware Specialist
   A – Analyst   P – Programmer   K – Keypuncher (data entry operator)

Contingencies to be expected, such as attrition, absence, temporary duties, computer turnaround time, computer system failure and late delivery from user departments must be built into the estimates. Familiarity with the problem, knowledge of the working environment, and experience on similar projects should help improve the accuracy of the estimates and the representativeness of the network in portraying the project. Network methods such as PERT can be useful tools for project definition. PERT provides a systematic and logical way to describe the activities and the interrelationships among them. Figure 1 shows a PERT network, representing a capital budgeting and a system upgrading project. (It should be noted that each firm is different. Therefore, Figure 1 may not be representative of all capital budgeting or system upgrading projects. Furthermore, these two examples were chosen to demonstrate that the network techniques described in this article are applicable to the planning and control of quite different development projects. When budget allows, it would be more efficient to have one group of EDP personnel to handle similar projects.) A circle in the network represents an activity; an arrow indicates the flow of work through the network. Description of the activities for the two projects can be found in Tables 1 and 2.

II. Scheduling Personnel

After defining all the activities involved in a project, the project manager would have to schedule the personnel to carry out each activity. This scheduling process can be very complicated, especially when there are several projects competing for the same resources and each project consists of a large number of interrelated activities. The complexity of this process multiplies when only limited manpower resources are available.

Manpower utilization can usually be improved if the resources are pooled together instead of assigning each person exclusively to one project. This is feasible for most types of manpower resources in EDP centers. Director and systems managers are usually involved in most or all projects. Programmers, keypunchers and operators can easily be assigned to handle activities of different projects and still maintain roughly the same level of efficiency. Only systems analysts would perform significantly better if he or she can concentrate on one project at a time. Consequently, the project manager can treat all the projects he has on hand as one big project. Using PERT, he will construct a network for each project and combine the networks to form an overall network for all projects to be completed within a given time period.

III. PERT Analysis

Once the combined network is constructed and the time estimates are obtained, the project manager can determine the critical path. (Methods for determining critical path and other PERT statistics can be found in any standard quantitative text.[3]) The critical path is the longest (in time) path through the combined network. The length of the critical path represents the length of time required to complete all the projects included in the network. Any delay in completing activities on the critical path will lengthen the critical path and thus delay the project completion date. The staff must therefore devote special attention to these activities. They should remember, however, that the critical path is not fixed. It may shift to another sequence of activities due to a significant delay in any noncritical activity or because the time estimates have been revised. Should either of these occur, the critical path may have to be recalculated.

In addition to determining the critical path, one may also compute the "earliest start time", the "latest start time", and the "slack time" for each activity. The earliest start time is the time before which an activity cannot start due to its relationship to preceding activities. The latest start time is the latest time that an activity must begin to ensure that the combined project will be completed on time. The slack time indicates the amount of time an activity may be delayed without delaying the final completion date of the combined project. It is seen that, by definition, all critical activities have zero slack. With the earliest and the latest start times, the project manager will know when to start an activity. The slack time reflects the criticality of an activity and signals the manager which activities deserve more attention. However, while PERT provides useful information for project management, its validity lies in the assumption that the resources needed for each activity are always available when needed. When manpower resources are expensive and limited (which is often the case in practice for EDP centers) so that the demands of concurrent activities cannot be met, some activities will have to be delayed and the project completion time may also be delayed. Under this circumstance, additional techniques must be employed in order to obtain a feasible schedule with minimum delay. This will be a schedule which satisfies all manpower constraints and completes the project at the earliest possible date. As will be seen later, the results produced by PERT analysis are required to implement some of these techniques.

Scheduling Approaches

When resource constraints exist, there are two basic approaches for finding a feasible schedule with minimum delay: (1) the judgemental approach and (2) the scientific approach.

The judgemental approach is often used in practice and is essentially a manual process. By using a manpower loading chart to graph the amount of every type of manpower needed over the project duration, the project manager can reschedule some activities to achieve a smoothing effect, i.e., to bring demand closer to the availability of manpower at any one time.[9] The manager, using his professional judgement, subjectively decides which activities are to be deferred so that manpower constraints can be satisfied.

The judgemental approach requires a considerable amount of managerial time, effort, and thus, cost, to set up, monitor and revise schedules. This is especially true when the number of activities is large and the inter-relationships are complicated. Thus, judgemental procedures often result in poor resource utilization.

With the scientific approach, some systematic methods would be used to analyse the projects and to obtain a schedule that meets the manpower constraints with minimum delay. The existing procedures in this approach can be grouped into two categories: (1) optimal procedures that aim at producing the best or optimal schedule, i.e., the shortest schedule that satisfies all the constraints; and (2) heuristic procedures which aim at producing good schedules, i.e., schedules that do not deviate much from the optimal ones.

All the optimal procedures involve a systematic search for the optimal solution considering all the constraints. Different procedures represent different strategies for performing the search. Integer programming, dynamic programming and branch and bound are some typical techniques used in the search.[10] These procedures guarantee an optimal schedule and can be computerized. However, they are only useful in solving projects of limited size. The computation time or storage required increases exponentially with an increase in the number of activities.[11] Thus, when the number of activities is large and the interrelationships are complicated, even today's fastest computer may not be able to complete the search for the optimal schedule.

Heuristic procedures on the other hand provide a practical alternative. They are good rules of thumb, simple to apply, intuitive, but nonetheless quite reliable in producing good schedules. Furthermore, they can easily be computerized and require little computation time or storage. It is even feasible to run these procedures in microcomputers such as APPLE, HP and TRS-80. Many scheduling heuristics have been developed. However, for reasons stated later, we will only present the MINSLK procedure.

The Minimum Slack Time Heuristic (MINSLK)

There are several reasons why data processing managers will find MINSLK of particular interest:

1. It applies to the scheduling of manpower, which is the greatest concern in the planning and control of development activities. Improved manpower utilization in systems development can lead to substantial cost reduction both in the center and in the departments that it services.

2. Research shows that MINSLK is the best among leading heuristics commonly used. For example, Davis

and Patterson showed that MINSLK performs better than seven other leading heuristics.[12] On average, MINSLK establishes activity schedules that are only 5.6% longer than the optimal schedules. Adam, et al. found that MINSLK outperformed competing alternatives and it gave solutions within 5% of the optimal solution for 90% of the cases tested.[13] Kohler also compared the performance of MINSLK with the optimal branch and bound procedures.[14] He concluded that the difference in performance was so small that the additional cost of implementing optimal procedures is not justified even for a small network of 30 activities.

3. Compared with other approaches, MINSLK is a least-cost method. In virtually all cases, it takes less than 2 seconds of CPU time to determine the schedule of a 100-activity network on an IBM/3081 computer. Due to the simplified implementation procedure discussed later, computer programs can easily be developed to implement MINSLK. These costs are nominal when compared to the time and cost the project manager may expend in scheduling the activities manually.

4. Alternative schedules for different time and manpower requirements can readily be prepared because of MINSLK's least-cost feature. The cost associated with the implementation of alternative schedules can be estimated and the most cost-effective schedule can be selected. Furthermore, when significant delays or unexpected events occur during the project, revised schedules can be prepared with minimal cost. This capability facilitates the planning and control of manpower resources.

Procedure for Implementation

The basic idea of MINSLK is that the most critical activities should be performed first because their delay will most likely delay the projects' completion. How critical an activity is — the "criticality" — is measured in terms of slack time. The smaller the slack, the more critical the activity. Any activities that have been completed will no longer be relevant to the scheduling of future activities and should therefore be eliminated from the network. Once a network has been reduced, the criticality of the remaining activities may also have changed from their initial criticality and thus have to be re-calculated. This process continues until all activities are scheduled.

Although re-evaluating criticality is cumbersome, it can be achieved by the following simplified procedure:[15]

1. List the activities in the multi-project network in ascending order of their latest start times obtained from PERT analysis. In case of a tie, the tied activities can be listed in arbitrary order. (The possibility of a tie in real projects is minimal.)

2. Available personnel should be assigned to the first unexecuted and ready activity on the list where the man-

147

power requirements can be met. An activity is ready for execution only when all of its preceding activities have been completed. The personnel will once again become available when this activity is completed. If no activity is ready or if available personnel cannot meet the manpower requirements of the activities that are ready, the personnel will be "idle" until an activity where the manpower requirements can be met becomes ready.

3. Repeat the second step until all activities are scheduled.

An Illustration

Assume an EDP center is assigned two systems development projects: the production planning department has requested a system for capital budgeting analysis to be developed, and the EDP center, after receiving management review concerning the response time of a data base system, has decided to upgrade the system to provide better response times. The activities required and the time and manpower estimates for the two projects are listed in Tables 1 and 2, and the combined network is shown in Figure 1. For easy identification we have labeled the activities of Project II with primed numbers.

It should be noted that computer time is required for the program testing activities in these projects. The time estimates for the completion of these activities should take into consideration the computer time available for systems development activities. That is, when the computer is heavily used for operations, the turn-around time would be slow and thus the program testing activities would require more time to complete.

Assume that the center has assigned two system analysts, two programmers, and two keypunchers to these projects. The director, the systems manager and the hardware specialist are also involved. Due to the nature of the work, each analyst is best assigned to a project exclusively while the programmers and keypunchers can form a pool of manpower resources and handle both projects simultaneously. We assign analyst 1 to Project I and analyst 2 to Project II.

In applying MINSLK, the project manager will first list all forty-nine activities in ascending order to their latest start times (as shown in Table 3). In case of a tie, the tied activities are listed in arbitrary order.

Following the MINSLK procedure, the director and the systems manager will review the proposed project from the production planning department (Activity 1) on the first two days. During these two days, Activity 1' is ready but cannot be started since it requires the director who is currently tied up with a higher priority activity, Activity 1, according to the priority list. The analysts, programmers and keypunchers as well as the hardware specialist will be idle on these two days since there is no activity ready for them (Activities 2 and 3 are not ready). Since the time that they will be idle is known in advance, they can be given other assignments during the idle periods.

TABLE 3
PRIORITY LIST

Activity Number*	Latest Start Time	Activity Number*	Latest Start Time
1	0	16	18
2	2	8'	18
3	4	11'	18
1'	4	18	20
5	5	19	21
2'	6	20	22
4	7	12'	22
6	7	14'	23
7	7	13'	24
8	7	21	25
9	8	15'	26
3'	8	22	27
4'	9	23	28
5'	11	24	28
10	12	25	28
11	13	26	28
6'	13	16'	28
12	14	17'	28
9'	14	27	29
13	15	18'	29
15	16	19'	30
14	17	28	31
17	17	20'	31
7'	17	29	32
10'	17		

*A description of these activities is given in Tables 1 and 2.

After reviewing Project I, the systems manager should analyse information required, work involved and estimate the cost of implementing Project I (Activity 2). The director can turn to Project II to review management recommendations for system upgrading. Activities 1' and 2 will be finished after day 4 at which time Activities 2' and 3 will become ready. Activity 3 will be done first because it is higher on the priority list. Activity 2' will be delayed as its manpower requirement cannot be met when Activity 3 is being worked on. At the completion of Activity 3, in addition to Activity 2', two more activities (4 and 5) will become ready. Since both Activities 4 and 5 require analyst 1, Activity 5 is higher on the list, it will be scheduled while Activity 4 has to be delayed. Activity 2' gest scheduled at this time since its manpower requirement has no conflict with that of Activity 5. This scheduling process continues until all activities are scheduled. The entire schedule is shown in Gantt Chart 1 of Figure 2. Such a Gantt Chart can be useful for keeping track of the staff assignments each day. The shaded areas represent idle staff time and the activities assigned each day to each of the staff are indicated by the activity numbers within the appropriate spaces.

FIGURE 2 GANTT CHARTS

Gantt Chart 1: Assign Analyst 1 to Project I, Analyst 2 to Project II.

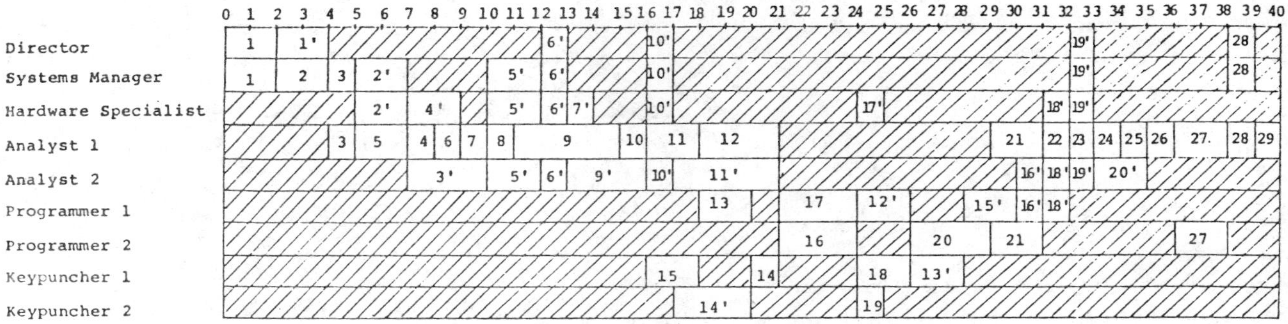

Gantt Chart 2: Assign Analysts 1 and 2 to Project I, Analyst 3 to Project II.

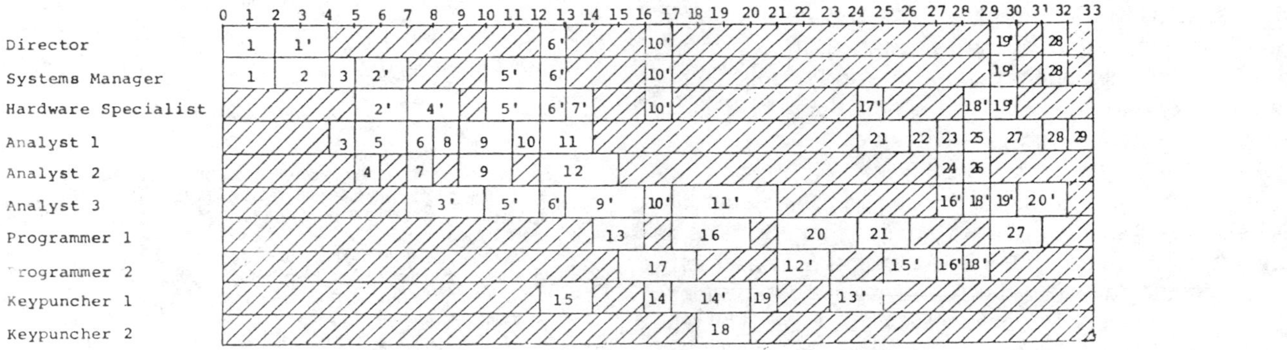

Project Acceleration and Other Considerations

Gantt Chart 1 shows that Project II is expected to be completed in 35 days whereas Project I will need 40 days. If these completion dates are found to be unacceptable, the project manager can accelerate the projects by adding additional manpower. What kind of manpower and how many should be added could be a difficult decision. Fortunately, due to the least-cost nature of the MINSLK procedure, the project manager can perform a sensitivity analysis by trying out a number of alternatives to find out the most cost-effective assignment. For example, adding one analyst for Project I will lead to an overall schedule of 33 days (a saving of 7 days), as shown in Gantt Chart 2 of Figure 2. However, having two analysts for Project I and three programmers in the programming team will again yield a schedule of 33 days; that is, an additional programmer will have no effect on the completion date of the projects. These alternative schedules will help the project manager decide on the size and the mix of manpower resources that should be employed. Because the Gantt Chart shows in advance who and when will be idle during the project duration, idle staff can be assigned temporarily to other assignments. Sometimes they can be assigned to help out busy members and thus speed up the completion of other activities. Such a sharing of work will normally require additional time for co-ordination, however. When additional manpower required to accelerate the projects' completion is not available, it may be acquired on a part-time basis, or overtime may be required. The Gantt Chart shows when this additional help will be needed.

Time and resource requirements may change after the projects have been started and significant delays may occur for one reason or another. Under these circumstances, the project manager should review the situation carefully, obtain new estimates of time and resource requirements, and prepare a new schedule for the remainder of the network. Because MINSLK is inexpensive to implement, revised schedules can be readily prepared without any undue additional effort.

It often happens in EDP centers that projects arrive continuously and may have to be fitted into the schedule for previously received projects. Again because of the least-cost nature of MINSLK, a MINSLK schedule can be generated periodically (say once a week) for the set of jobs currently available, i.e., old projects not yet completed plus newly arrived projects. Some projects may be more urgent than others. Priorities can be imposed by means of a pseudo activity appended to each urgent project with length sufficiently enough to reduce the slack time of the activities in the urgent projects to some appropriate level of criticality.[16]

Finally, it should be noted that although this article addresses the manpower management problem for EDP projects to control and reduce costs, the MINSLK procedure applies equally well to other types of professional organizations such as law firms, accounting firms and engineering consulting firms. MINSLK can also be used when different times are required for different categories of manpower to complete the activities, and when there are changes in manpower availabilities during the project duration. This makes MINSLK very flexible in the scope of its application.

Promoting Efficiency and Controlling Costs

Increased computerization in the business world has resulted in heavy investment in data processing equipment and great demand for skilled manpower. Thus, efficiency in operating a data processing center becomes a major concern in most organizations that computerize. As equipment costs begin to drop due to advance in computer technology and as manpower costs keep on rising due to the short supply of skilled people in the field, manpower utilization becomes essential in controlling the costs for operating a data processing center. Therefore, those who want to control or reduce EDP costs should consider the network techniques described in this article.

The major responsibility of most high salaried personnel such as systems and operations managers, systems analysts and programmers is to develop or revise computerized information systems and system components. A data processing center typically will be faced with several systems development projects simultaneously. Efficient management of the center's manpower resources in carrying out these projects will reduce project delays, improve manpower utilization and often result in substantial cost savings. This article has demonstrated how a network technique, namely MINSLK, when applied in conjunction with PERT, can be used for optimal manpower scheduling. In particular, MINSLK offers several features that are important to efficient project management:

1. It is easy to apply because it is tied to the conventional PERT concept and because the scheduling process can be readily computerized, thus saving the managerial effort required to schedule manpower resources manually.

2. The cost involved in preparing and revising and schedule is minimal when compared with other approaches or with the time and cost the center may save by properly scheduling the development activities. This least-cost feature facilitates project planning and control because the project manager can now try out alternative manpower assignments to find the most cost-effective alternative. Revised schedules can readily be prepared should time and resource estimates change or unexpected events occur.

3. It is very flexible in the scope of its applications.

4. It gives optimal or near optimal schedules in terms of minimizing project completion time and maximizing manpower utilization.

5. The resulting Gantt Charts show in advance (a) the expected project completion times, assuming alternative manpower availability, (b) the overall use of manpower resources, and (c) the timing of the idle resources. Needless to say, this information is useful for manpower planning and control.

Finally, it is important to realize that whereas PERT and MINSLK are useful tools for EDP project management, other tools such as budgets, transfer prices, organizational control, documentation, and progress reports are necessary components of a project control system. They should all be used together for effective project control. Scientific Techniques such as MINSLK and PERT are not meant to be rigid mechanistic "numbers game" seeking to supplant professional judgement. They are used to complement professional judgement and insight and to improve planning and control in complex environments. ●jsm

References

1. D. H. Drury and J. E. Bates, Data Processing Chargeback Systems: Theory and Practice, a research monograph prepared for the Society of Management Accountants of Canada (April 1979), p. 1.
2. See Drury and Bates (1979), p. 28.
3. See for examples:
   H. Kerzner, "Tradeoff Analysis in a Project Environment — Part 1," *Journal of Systems Management* (October 1982), pp. 6-13. Also Part 2 of the series in the November issue of the same journal. J. Finney, "Controlling EDP Costs," *Journal of Accountancy* (April 1981), pp. 63-67. J. Cooke and D. Drury, *Management Planning and Control of Information Systems,* a research monograph prepared for the Society of Management Accountants of Canada (April 1980). R. C. Rettus and R. A. Smith, "Accounting Control of Data Processing," *IBM Systems Journal,* No. 1 (1972), pp. 74-92. T. R. Gildersleeve, *Data Processing Project Management* (Van Nostrand Reinhold Company, 1974). D. Norton and F. W. McFarlan, "Project Management," in F. W. McFarlan and R. Nolan, eds., *The Information Systems Handbook* (Dow-Jones and Irwin, Inc. 1975), pp. 517-28. R. Nolan, *Management Accounting and Control of Data Processing* (National Association of Accountants, New York, 1977).
4. E. J. Niemoth, "Scheduling of EDP Operations," *Data Management* (September 1971), pp. 43-46.
5. Drury and Bates (1979), p. 28.
6. P. Anthony, "Functional Cost Accounting for D. P. Centers," *Management Accounting* (October 1976), pp. 33-41.
7. See W. J. Pierce, "Improving Project Estimates," *Journal of Systems Management* (December 1978), pp. 12-15. E. Chrysler, "Improved Management of Information Systems Development," *Journal of Systems Management* (March 1980), pp. 6-13. A. Ferrentino, "Making Software Development Estimates Good," *Datamation* (September 1981), pp. 179-182.
8. See, for example, H. Bierman, C. Bonini and W. Hausman, *Quantitative Analysis for Business Decisions,* 5th edition (Irwin, 1977).
9. See P. H. Burgher, "PERT and the Auditor," *The Accounting Review* (January 1964), pp. 103-120, esp. p. 117.
10. F. B. Talbot and J. Patterson, "An Efficient Integer Programming Algorithm with Network Cuts for Solving Resource-Constrained Scheduling Problems," *Management Science* (July 1978), pp. 1163-74. C. V. Ramamoorthy, K. M. Chandy and M. J. Gonzalez, Jr., "Optimal Scheduling Strategies in a Multi-processor System," *IEEE Transactions on Computers* (February 1972), pp. 137-46. W. H. Kohler, "A preliminary Evaluation of the Critical Path Method for Scheduling Tasks on Multi-processor Systems," *IEEE Transactions on Computers* (December 1975), pp. 1235-38.
11. T. L. Adam, K. M. Chandy and J. R. Dickson, "A Comparison of List Schedules for Parallel Processing Ssyterns," *Communications of the ACM* (December 1974), pp. 685-90.
12. E. W. Davis and J. Patterson, "A Comparison of Heurisric and Optimum Solutions in Resource-Contrained Project Scheduling," *Management Science* (April 1975), pp. 944-55.
13. T. L. Adam, K. M. Chandy and J. R. Dickson (1974).
14. W. H. Kohler (1975).
15. E. W. Davis and J. Patterson (1975).
16. J. D. Wiest, "A Heuristic Model for Scheduling Large Projects with Limited Resources," *Management Science,* 13 (1967), pp. 359-77.

Developing an Effective Manufacturing Decision Support System

MOHSEN ATTARAN and HOSSEIN BIDGOLI

The variety and complexity of decision making in manufacturing has increased the need for timely and accurate information, thus opening the door to comprehensive, integrated decision support systems.

As today's technologies integrate the work of production from design to implementation, manufacturing inevitably must rely more and more on sophisticated information systems, such as decision support systems (DSS). While there is no common and acceptable definition for DSS, most authors define them as a series of integrated computer software for computer-based information systems that help decision makers with semistructured and unstructured tasks.[1]

Decision support systems have been applied to many different disciplines, including manufacturing, marketing, human resource management, accounting, small business, purchasing, sales, banking, office automation, life insurance, and facility planning.

The effectiveness of these systems has been demonstrated in the business world; however, few (if any) guidelines have been provided for establishing these

Dr. Attaran *is Associate Professor of Management Science at California State College, Bakersfield.* **Dr. Bidgoli** *is Professor and Director of the MIS program at California State College.*

systems specifically in the manufacturing area. Therefore, this article presents an integrated approach for the establishment of a decision support system for manufacturing. This presentation will include a general model with a detailed explanation of its different components.

What Is a DSS?

For the past 40 years, electronic data processing (EDP) has been applied primarily to structured tasks. The tasks suitable for EDP application are programmable and need little human intervention, such as recordkeeping, simple clerical operations, and inventory control. These systems emphasize data collection and data processing. The collected data are generally regrouped, reorganized, and mathematically processed to provide the final result.

Since the mid-1960s, management information systems (MIS) have been used for information processing. These systems produce timely, accurate, integrated, and useful information, including scheduled

Reprinted by permission from BUSINESS Magazine. "Developing An Effective Manufactuing Decision Support System," by Mohsen Attaran and Hossein Bidgoli, October-December 1986.

for different decision-making purposes. They have, however, experienced many failures. The major shortcomings of MIS are lack of flexibility, and lack of user involvement in all phases of analysis, design, and implementation.

DSS differ from traditional EDP and MIS in many ways. DSS provide a means to assess complex, ill-defined problems through systematic methods. The most impressive characteristics of these systems are their flexibility, interactiveness, discovery orientation, and ease of use for noncomputer decision makers. DSS actually use a wide variety of technologies such as EDP and MIS. A comparison of EDP, MIS, and DSS, and descriptions of unique DSS characteristics can be found in Exhibit 1.

What DSS Can Do

The following are some of the operations performed by a typical sophisticated DSS:

● *What-if analysis:* Illustrates the effect of a change in one variable over the entire system. For example, what would be the impact on profit if sales grew at a rate of 10% to 12% instead of 5%? Or, if the cost of labor increased by 4%, what is going to happen to the final cost of a unit?

● *Goal-seeking:* This capability is the reverse of what-if analysis. It provides answers to such questions as, how much should a particular unit sell for in order to generate $200,000 profit? Or, what level of growth must be generated in sales to double the profit every five years?

● *Sensitivity analysis:* Management operates in a dynamic environment. This means that costs and prices change, resources diminish or become more rapidly available, and technological changes affecting production occur. A company using any model must be able to explore the sensitivity of the best (optimal) solution to changes in the data and parameters used to build the model. This capability enables decision makers to see how sensitive the optimal solution is to model assumptions and data. For example, what is the maximum price that can be paid for a particular raw material and still make a profit? If additional resources such as ten hours of machine time should become available, would this change the solution mix or total profit?

● *Exception reporting analysis:* This capability monitors the performance of the variables that are

Exhibit 1: **Unique characteristics of DSS**

Key factor	DSS
Central focus	To aid decision making and decision implementation
Mode of usage	Active use—each instance of system use is initiated by user(s) and designer(s)
Types of activities	Line, staff, and management
Orientation	Overall effectiveness of the system and organization
Time horizon	Focus on present and (mostly) future
Design emphasis	On flexibility and ad hoc utilization
Key words	Interaction and support for decision maker
System evaluation	Mostly based on behavioristic criteria, for example, user satisfaction and decision-making improvement
Computational focus	Basic and complex
Output orientation	Mostly for planning and forecasting
Problems addressed	Qualitative, quantitative, unstructured, and semistructured
Output format options	Numerous (for example, hard, soft, graphic, exceptional reporting, tabular)
Design principles	User initiates, designs, and controls the implementation of the system
Design tools	Prototyping, iterative, and adoptive design
Flexibility of the operation	Quite flexible—responds quickly to the changing environment
Organizational target group	All levels—proportional, tactical, and strategic

out of the range. An example would be the production line that generates the highest profit or the production center that spends more than the predefined budget.

Some other capabilities of a typical DSS include graphic analyses, forecasting, and different modeling analyses.

DSS in the Manufacturing Environment

Rapid changes in manufacturing technology, business, and the work environment have brought attention to the need for timely decisions on the part of manufacturing management. Conventional management science tools, such as linear programming, queuing, and network analysis, are no longer adequate for planning and controlling all aspects of manufacturing operations. The need for better flexibility, shorter production runs, more customized products, faster responses to changes in market demand, and greater control and accuracy of processes will inevitably force managers to attempt to increase the effectiveness of manufacturing decisions. More important, because manufacturing decisions will increasingly affect and be affected by a wider range of strategic operations implicit in manufacturing technology, managers

must be able to coordinate various departments in making operational decisions. This requires more effective teamwork to ensure prompt responses to unexpected situations. These, in turn, could be improved by the speed and effectiveness of a computerized support system.

By using data, quantitative and statistical models, and "what if" analyses, a DSS can provide valuable information for decision making in all of these areas.

MDSS Framework

A manufacturing decision support system (MDSS), like any other DSS, should include the following three important components: a data base, a model base, and dialog management. Exhibit 2 illustrates the relationships of these components. In the following paragraphs each component will be discussed in detail.

Data Base: A data base is the upgraded version of a file cabinet that stores data for decision-making purposes. This data may be from internal sources, external sources, or syndicated services and should include data regarding the economy, the legal environment, technology, consumers, competition,

Exhibit 2: **Components of MDSS**

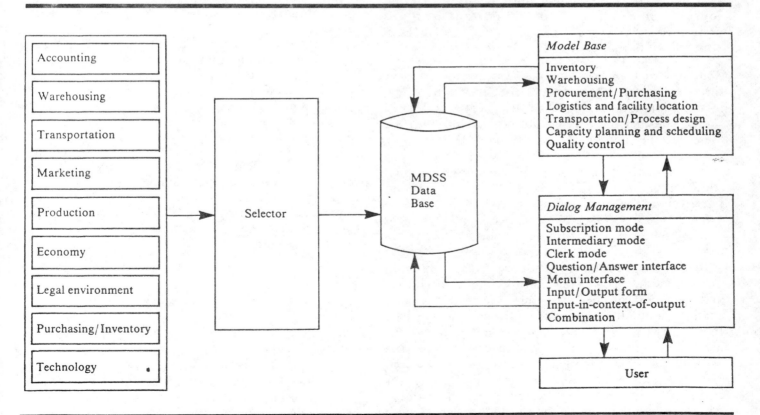

sales, markets, and costs. Exhibit 3 illustrates the types and sources of data that should be stored in the data base.

For effective decision making, the collected data in the data base must be accurate, recent, and preferably disaggregated (itemized). The data base must also include past, present, and projected data concerning the operations of a particular organization.

The data base of a MDSS can be organized in several different ways, such as relational, network, hierarchical, record types, and so forth.

However, any type of data base and data base management system must provide basic data base operations such as data insertion, data retention, data extraction, and data recovery. These capabilities are available for the majority of data base packages, both for mainframes and microcomputers.

Model Base: The MDSS provides the user with a range of models that will support all levels of decision making. The MDSS not only includes the ability to do inquiry and report generation but also the ability to interface with a large number of subroutines that can be linked into a selection of models. Integration and linking should allow the user to continue to adapt and become more familiar with the system. In order to grow with the system, the user must be able to redefine, generate, restructure, and incorporate new information into the modeling analysis. Hence, the system must be from external sources. Some of the most important analyses performed by the model base component of MDSS are outlined in Exhibit 4.

Dialog Management: Dialog management involves the user/system interface and the format in which information is provided. The designer of a MDSS should consider these important factors and integrate them into the conceptual model of the MDSS.

Different users of the MDSS may have different information needs, as their personal and organizational status differs. A sophisticated MDSS should respond selectively to these differences.

There are four types of system/user interaction or "usage" patterns: subscription, terminal, clerk, or intermediary.[2]

In a *subscription* mode, the user receives information on a regular basis. This method lacks flexibility and does not consider changing user needs. A good example is monthly reports from the computer center. In contrast, the *terminal* or *direct* mode allows the user to use the MDSS as it is needed. Thus, the user will not be bombarded by masses of information. However, the user still needs minimal computer training in order to use the system. An example of the terminal mode is the 24-hour teller used in

the banking industry. The teller is available when the user needs it. It reduces interruptions of daily routines considerably because of its after-hour access feature.

Terminal or direct mode could include several types of interfaces such as question-answer, command language, menu interface, input form/output form, input-in-context-of-output, and combination.[3]

In the question-answer interface, probably the easiest to use, the system asks the user a question and the user responds. Although this may be a slow process, the user does not need any special training to use the system.

In command language, the user employs a series of short commands to interface with the system. This may be more challenging for experienced users, but requires some basic training.

Menu interface is probably the most versatile. The user is given a series of options. He or she chooses one option and the conversation continues.

In input form/output form interface, the user enters commands and data and the system provides an output. After viewing the output, the user may respond to another input form. If there is a correspondence between the input and the output, this type of interface could be very successful. Input/output may be used for situations that have many predefined items.

Input-in-context-of-output interface is an extension of the input/output interface. The system provides an output and, based on that output, the user answers some questions in order to modify the existing output or generate a different type of output.

In *clerk*, or off-line mode, the user does not need special training, but this type of interaction is slower. All batch processing applications—such as payroll, inventory control, or any types of billing—can be classified within this group.

Finally, in the *intermediary* mode, the user receives special advice from another individual about the provided information. An example of the intermediary mode is the statistician within the organization who interprets the correlation analysis computer output for the vice president of personnel.

A MDSS with all these options should be extremely effective.

Integration of the Components

The model of the MDSS presented in Exhibit 2 collects the most relevant data using a selector, which can be either a series of predefined forms or the person inputting the data at the computer. The *data base* generally contains two types of data: external and internal. Exhibit 3 presents the types and

Exhibit 3: **Types of data needed by MDSS in its data base**

Area	Type of data needed	Source of data
Accounting	Invoicing Order scheduling Credit control and collection	Accounting information systems
Warehousing	Receipt data Shipping Storage Replenishment Packing	Accounting information systems
Transportation	Loading Trip log Overall costs/units/miles Commodity movement information Carrier movement patterns	Accounting information systems Trade publications
Marketing	Current and potential customers Customer service demands Current and potential competitors Competitors' strategies Market potential Market share Demographic profiles Geographic changes and shifts	Marketing research Sales force reports Trade publications Syndicated services Census guide data Survey of buying power Marketing information guide
Purchasing/Inventory	Vendor file (lead time, price, financial strength, etc.) Procurement Bidding Overall purchasing Inventory records Lot sizing Overall inventory management	Accounting information systems Trade publications Securities and Exchange Commission reports
Production	Aggregate scheduling Priority planning Capacity planning Facility planning Production control Material planning Work force planning Shop floor data collection R & D planning Output design Layout of facilities Overall production management	Industrial engineering information systems Personnel information systems
Economy	General level of economic activity Economic activity within industry	Economic indicator *Survey of Current Business* *U.S. Industrial Outlook* *Standard & Poor's Industry Survey* *Across the Board* Trade publications
Legal environment	Changes impacting all businesses Changes impacting industry	General business publications such as *Business Week* and *Wall Street Journal*
Technology	Available technology and expected trends	Trade publications Trade shows

sources of data needed by the MDSS. These data should be indexed and stored, preferably in their original form (disaggregated versus aggregated).

The *model base* of the MDSS provides the tools and techniques to analyze and solve problems and support the user for a range of decision situations. The model base of the MDSS should include two types of models and/or routines. The first group

Exhibit 4: Examples of types of analyses and models needed for MDSS

Types of analysis	Description	Examples of models
Inventory	When to order and how much Cost calculation Safety stock Priorities for inventory management	EOQ (Economic order quantity) ELS (Economic lot size) MRP (Material requirement planning) TPOP (Time-phased order point)
Warehousing	Storage structures Space utilization analysis Control of equipment	AS/RS (Automatic storage and retrieval systems) Simulation modeling
Procurement/Purchasing	The supplier rating/selection decision Vendor rating/selection decision Price change/discount analysis Bid evaluation	Vendor rating/selection models
Logistics and facility location	Distribution improvements Routing/scheduling Selection of modes of transportation Transportation budgeting Shipment planning Regional/international selection Community selection Site selection	Transportation method Center of gravity/incremental analysis Weighted score model Breakeven model
Transformation/Process design	Selection of the process Design of the transformation process Layout design Balancing a line Tools/equipment/facilities selection	Computerized line balancing CPM/PERT CRAFT (Computerized relative allocation of facilities) ALDEP (Automated layout design program) CORELAP (Computerized relationship program)
Capacity planning and scheduling	Short-term capacity planning Long-term capacity planning Capacity versus investment Aggregate scheduling Priority planning Sequencing Detailed scheduling "What if" production/inventory trade-offs	CPM/PERT GERT (Graphical evaluation review technique) Learning curve Linear programming Decision tree Linear decision rule MRP II (Manufacturing resource planning)
Quality control	Design quality Quality/cost analysis Where to inspect/how to inspect Handling of defects Setting optimal control limits Process control Acceptance sampling	Fraction production charts (P charts) Number of defects (C charts)

is process independent routines that perform basic data manipulation operations. In other words, they are not involved in modeling analysis. Some of these operations are available in most data base management systems. The second group consists mostly of mathematical models outlined in Exhibit 4.

The user can query or access the system by one of the interface modes detailed in Exhibit 5. If the request is only for data manipulation, procedure independent routines—such as regression analysis, graphic routines, and any types of data analysis routines—will process the data in the data base and provide the user with an appropriate response. If these operations fall within the standard capabilities of data base management, the user can directly query the data base. The data base management system (DBMS) is capable of handling standard data base operations such as extraction, insertion, search, and sort. Otherwise, the model base of the MDSS will query the data base and provide suitable analysis. In other words, the available data will be manipulated by one of these models and the necessary response will be provided.

The *dialog management* component provides the interaction between the system and the user. Recent developments in "user-friendly" software have provided excellent conversational power that leads the manager through sets of input/output decisions.

As an example of how the MDSS supports the day-to-day activities of manufacturing operations, the remaining discussion will deal with the application of the MDSS model to inventory management.

MDSS and Inventory Control

Manufacturing management has always been responsible for inventory control. The objective is to reduce the total inventory costs to the lowest possible level consistent with desired service. The total inventory costs consist of carrying or holding costs, which vary directly by inventory level, and purchasing or ordering costs, which vary inversely with the number of units ordered. The two key decisions in inventory management are when to order and how much to order.

If the demand for finished goods inventory is constant and known in advance, the Economic Order Quantity (EOQ) model balances these two inventory costs and identifies the optimum order quantity.

These two decisions can be made with little management intervention using the MDSS. Management uses the accounting and purchasing/inventory files in the data base to determine the total holding and ordering costs. The EOQ model will determine the optimum quantity to order. The specific vendor is then selected from information provided by the procurement/purchasing file.

Another area where MDSS can be helpful in inventory control decisions is with material requirement planning (MRP). MRP schedules "what we want"

Exhibit 5: Important user/systems interfaces and organizational decision making

Types of interface	Characteristics of the users	Types of decisions	Organizational focus
Subscription mode	Inexperienced	Routine and recurring detailed response needed	Operational management
Intermediary mode	Both (mostly inexperienced)	Ad hoc decisions Analysis of the response needed	Middle and mostly strategic level
Clerk mode	Inexperienced	Ad hoc and one-shot decisions Summary response needed	Middle and strategic levels
Question/Answer interface	Inexperienced	Infrequent use Summary response needed	All levels (mostly middle and operational)
Menu interface	Both (mostly inexperienced)	All decisions with several options Summary or detail response needed	Mostly middle and strategic level
Command language interface	Experienced	All decisions Summary response needed	All levels (mostly middle and operational)

For Further Reading

Alter, Steven L. *Decision Support Systems: Current Practice and Continuing Challenges.* Reading, Massachusetts: Addison-Wesley, 1980.

Bennett, John L. *Building Decision Support Systems.* Reading, Massachusetts: Addison-Wesley, 1983.

Chan, K. H. "Decision Support Systems for Human Resource Management." *Journal of Systems Management* (April 1984): 17-25.

Chandler, John S., Thomas Trone, and Michael Weiland. "Decision Support Systems Are for Small Businesses." *Management Accounting* (April 1983): 34-39, "Decision Support Helps Dominion Choose Store Sites." *Canadian Data Systems* (October 1983): 85.

Dressler, Michael, Ronald Beall, and Joquin Ives Brant. "Why Marketing Managers Love DSS." *Business Marketing* (April 1983): 77-81.

Goldberg, Joan B. "RB 3 Boosts Personal Selling, Enhances Bank's 'Pro' Image." *Bank Systems & Equipment* (April 1984): 72-73.

Jaffe, Merle. "Decision Support Systems for Manufacturing," Infosystems (July 1983): 112-114.

Johnson, Bart. "Why Your Company Needs Three Accounting Systems." *Management Accounting* (September 1984): 39-46.

Keen, Peter G., and Michael S. Scott-Morton. *Decision Support Systems: An Organizational Perspective.* Massachusetts: Addison-Wesley, 1978.

Krajewski, Rich. "Database Types." *Byte* (October 1984): 137-142.

Sprague, Ralph Jr., and Eric D. Carlson. *Building Effective Decision Support Systems.* Englewood Cliffs, New Jersey: Prentice-Hall, 1982.

Taylor, Thayer C. "Honeywell's Computer Makes Managers Out of Sales People." *Sales & Marketing Management* (May 1984): 59-61.

"User Friendly Software Now Available for Purchasing." *Purchasing World* (October 1984): 70-71.

Viste, Gerald D. "Making Decisions Are a Snap Because of DSS at Insurance." *Data Management* (June 1984): 22-24.

Walkinshaw, Ian. "Development and Users of a Flexible DSS." *Data Processing* (United Kingdom) (October 1984): 37-40.

in each time period and plans the acquisition of the items. To derive maximum benefit from a MRP system, a large integrated data base is needed.

The input requirements of the MRP model are information regarding what should be produced, when it is needed, and a record of the actual inventory level and lead times, product structure, raw materials, and components and subassemblies. These data can be obtained from various files in the MDSS data base. For example, data regarding lead times and on-hand balance will be obtained from inventory files. The number of finished goods needed during each time period, and component part numbers required to make each individual part, will be gained from production files, and so forth.

Management will then use the MRP model (computer software) to determine the quantity to order and to generate some optional management reports. The output usually includes (1) what should be ordered, (2) what order should be canceled, (3) exception reports (items that need management attention), and (4) how well the system is operating. Properly designed and integrated, the MDSS is a powerful support tool that enhances the effectiveness and capabilities of today's decision makers in a manufacturing environment. By using a MDSS, it becomes easier to collect more data, make forecasts, schedule operations, remove bottlenecks, perform sensitivity and "what-if" analysis, and optimize, monitor, and control the system. These features offer today's production manager—pressed more than ever to maximize efficiency, quality, and flexibility—unprecedented benefits in the management of resources. ∎

1. Rector L. Robert, "Decision Support Systems—Strategic Planning Tool," *Managerial Planning* (May/June 1983), 36-40.

2. Steven L. Alter, *Decision Support Systems: Current Practice and Continuing Challenges* (Reading, Massachusetts: Addison-Wesley, 1980), 111-116.

3. John L. Bennett, *Building Decision Support Systems* (Reading, Massachusetts: Addison-Wesley, 1980), 65-88.

PART VII

FUTURE: THE CHANGING ENVIRONMENT

LEARNING OBJECTIVES:

- Be able to understand several scenarios about the future of CBMIS.

- Recognize the important present and future roles of technology in CBMIS design and utilization.

- Be able to appreciate some of the organizational problems associated with information management.

- Get some idea about articifical intelligence and expert systems.

- Be able to see the trend and direction of the future technology.

INTRODUCTION

For the past forty years the world of CBMIS has witness significant changes in both the computer and information systems. The next thirty years appear to promise a continuation of this dynamic change. In terms of the computer, the computer of the future will be smaller, faster, more powerful, able to store large quantities of data and make it available to users via distributed systems within the firm, and in terms of cost/performance, be less expensive. In terms of users, the users will be more knowledgeable about the computers. Along with user knowledge and the development of sophisiticated management information systems, organizational issues relating to such issues as, changing areas of responsibility, changes in functional line and staff reporting, and the integration of information technology within the organization. The human element will remain a critical factor as these issues become more pressing in the immediate future.

Microprocessors are changing from 8 bit to 32 and eventually a 64 bit machine which will significantly increase the speed of the computer and when coupled with the futuristic 256k RAM chip, the microcomputer will truly resemble the capability of some current mainframes. These changes will be significant in many areas where microprocessors can be employed because they will provide relatively cheap processing power.

The microprocessor is presently being integrated into most facets of both business and personal environments. Within the firm, microprocessors are being employed to control the air temperature, lighting, security, production tools, etc., in productive facilities. They are also affecting both the firm and personal environments through providing a means for paying bills, transferring funds, scheduling emergency responses in time of need, etc. However, problems and costs relating to changes in the organization in terms of distributed data processing, end user modeling, communications, along with the current and growing backlog of requests for applications programs, will remain a significant challenge for the information system professionals. The computer of the future will be accompanied by significant changes in the organizaton. That is, there will be changes in the workplace, market place, relations with customers, and management, especially top management.

The future will see a change in the way work is performed as it is manifest in the work station. The work station will not only give support and technical personel the ability to access and interpret large databases but will also provide top management with immediate access to data and information for decision making.

Concurrent with the development of the concept of work stations, information technology will also significantly be affecting the area of office automation. To date, the office has been a labor intensive operation mainly devoted to the use of typewriters to generate documents based on correspondence. As the demand for all kinds of information grows, the computer has provided an opportunity to convert to an electronic office and give the worker greater control over the functions and responsiblity of the office. In part this was stimulated by the increasing cost of office workers and a recognition of the need to improve productivity in this sector. As technology advances become available, the office of the future will be mainly an electronic office and an integral part of a CBMIS. In particular, one area that will continue to advance is word processing. Microcromputers will increasingly be used to store and edit texts, check for spelling errors, and print documents. The storage feature is very important because many business documents contain common information and the word processing system allows for text modification and adaption to new requirements as well as dealing with repetitive requirements.

Another electronic information feature of the automated office is electronic mail. Electronic mail allows messages to be electronically endcode, stored, distributed, or held in an archive. The mail messages can be retrieved on a screen and thus, the necessity of printing and storing the printed message is deleted. However, with electronic mail the recipient has the option of reading the message from a screen or having a printed copy made of the text. Other electronic information techniques which will be employed in office automation in the future include audio processing of voice messages and image processing of pictoral or graphical material.

The concept of networking is a major key factor in expanding the capabilities of office automation. The processes of electronic mail, audio processing, image processing all depend upon the ability of the information system to communicate with or link users in the system and this ability is directly linked to the concept of networking. The development of a network may involve multiple physical facilities which may be located at great distances from the main office or it may involve linking departments within a building which is defined as establishing a local area network (LAN).

In the area of systems development "prototyping" will continue to be examined and evaluated as an alternative to the serial approach prescribed by the traditional system design methods. Prototyping is a methodology which emphasizes fast initial development of an information system coupled with on-going monitoring of the system in terms of use, feedback, and modification. Prototyping philosophy is based on the idea of end-user involvement in the quick design of a system and alteration and enhancement of the system on a continuous basis. Since the end-user is heavily involved in the process, turn around time is minimized and a final product, which meets the user's specifications, can be developed very quickly. This, in turn, provides for greater utilization of information systems in support of managerial decision making.

A logical question one may ask is, where do we go from here in the dynamic and changing environment of CBMIS? Some experts predict that the next generation of computer systems will involve not only end-user modeling languages, the so called fourth generation programming languages, but the concept of artificial intelligence. Artificial intelligence involves the study of how humans think and how these processes can be transferred to a computer. That is, the concept involves research in processes which will give machines the capability to reason, make judgements, and learn, or in other words, mimic human thought processes. To date, this research is still in the embryonic development stage and there is wide disagreement among experts as to when such a system will in fact be developed. Most of the success in this area has been in developing the so called "expert systems" which are currently used in areas of medical diagnosis, business consulting, and industrial applications on a limited basis. Research in both artificial intelligence and expert systems will continue to grow.

DISCUSSION QUESTIONS

1. What types of changes we may be witnessing in work stations of the future?

2. What types of organizational changes we may be witnessing in the future?

3. From users' perspectives, what types of changes we may observe in the near future?

4. What is the direction for computer hardware?

5. What is the direction for computer software?

6. Many people believe the direction for computer software would be "integrated software". What is this and why?

161

7. What is the direction for CBMIS cost? Which component of CBMIS will be more costly? Why?

8. What is office automation?

9. What are some of the differences between today and future offices?

10. What are some of the components of an automated office?

11. What are the technologies involved in automated office?

12. What is the role of telecommunications and local area network in the automated office?

13. What is artificial intelligence?

14. What are expert systems?

15. Do you think the future computers will really think? Why and why not?

Six issues that will affect the future of information management

by John Diebold

The organizational questions that most of us face with regard to information management are becoming very important.

Following is a look toward the future at some of the issues that will be important questions, or are already questions, that will have to be addressed in the years ahead.

Organizational issues

The first question relates to the organizational issues associated with computers and communications.

There are six pieces of this organizational puzzle, all of which are starting to come to a head.

✓ The first element in this is your own normal area of responsibility— MIS. Generally, it is highly organized, well developed and generally reporting at an officer level in large companies.

✓ Second is the office automation function. Typically it has reported at a lower level of responsibility, but reports at a very wide range of different ways—you can find any model you want. All too often the motivation behind automating the office today has been clerical savings. The real focus ought to be in terms of the improvement of productivity of professionals, whether the profession-

als be managers or engineers or scientists, or you name it, in an organization.

✓ A third element in this picture is the communications function, again reporting in all manner of ways, although more and more reporting to the MIS director. Mostly it has been organized in a helter-skelter way, and mostly it has been fairly low

level in organizations. It has also tended to focus on one source of supply: AT&T. Suddenly we have what my colleagues have been describing as "option shock," a vast number of alternatives available in terms of the combination of voice and data communications. The problems in network analysis, for any large company, generally far exceed

the capability at the command of the individuals responsible for handling this fuction.

✓ A fourth element in the organizational picture for those engaged in manufacturing is the problem of the impact of manufacturing systems, including CAD-CAM, but also increasingly complex factory systems integrated with corporate informa-

The CEO is saying, "Who's going to tell me how we should be doing business tomorrow?"

tion systems. As soon as the investment level picks up, which is about to happen, in terms of the US economy, the developments in the manufacturing area will be a very intense and very interesting part of this total picture.

✓ The fifth element of these half dozen elements in organization is the end user. In many organizations, computing is beginning to become a user-driven activity and a user-driven development, with all kinds of implications for MIS managers. It means that you go from being a wholesaler to a retailer, something that has not likely been done in most industries without the most fundamental soul searching. It means all sorts of questions in terms of what policy you really want to emphasize for the organization. I'm not going to spend a lot of time on this, as you're all very familiar with the problems posed by the users suddenly emerging as a very important driving force in computing through the expanding use of microcomputers.

✓ The sixth element is one that I believe very strongly will become increasingly important, and that is the role of information technology as a determinant of competitiveness within more and more industries. This poses a whole series of very

interesting questions for the MIS manager. If you look across the gamut of different forms that this can take, you have incorporation of the computer into the product, whether that be a credit card which has a chip in it, or an automobile with microcomputer-based controls, or a dishwasher that depends for its sales appeal by having a processor built into it. I'm not talking only about products, but the impact of micro chips on the distribution system: How an insurance company equips its agents, how you begin in a manufactured product to change the distribution channels, what levels you jump over, how you handle the information system as a competitive weapon and how it becomes a determinant of change in the parameters of the whole business system. You begin to have a very new element here. You've seen the financial services industry change, you're beginning to see the publishing industry change.

You have these six elements, all relating to the organizational issue, and all of this relates to your own job: What do you want your own job to be? What ought it to be for the best interest of your own enterprise? And from your own personal standpoint, you have more options than you had a couple of years ago, because you have a very interesting array of possibilities coming out of this.

Human development

Let me move into my second point, on the problem of staffing and human development in your own field.

If you understand that information technology comes increasingly to be looked on as a determinant of competitive effectiveness in businesses, it means quite a different kind of profile for the people you're developing to succeed you and the people you're developing in your organizations. It also poses a question for the organization as a whole: You want entrepreneurial-type peo-

ple to be concerned with this, you want people who are interested in the question of what the product is, whether it's an insurance company or a manufacturing company or you name it. You have a different set of individual human requirements in this picture.

Clearly it's a big problem, and we know it because increasingly CEOs are raising with us the question of what to do about this. They say, "We have a super MIS activity, but basically, what kind of policies do we offer and how is our distribution system going to be changed?" or "How do we compete?" Whether it be the automobile business or the appliance business or the publishing field, the pattern of competition is changing. The CEO is saying,

Very few corporate decisions are made on the basis of the time value of information.

"Where do I get this talent from? Who is it who's going to have the imagination not to do a first-class job on yesterday's method of doing business, but who's going to tell me how we should be doing business tomorrow? What kind of businesses do we need to acquire? What kind of distribution channels should we have? How will the payment system be altered?"

You have a whole set of entrepreneurial issues being raised. Those of you who are interested in that area have an absolutely open sesame in that field. Those of you who are not have still the question that you are logically the individuals to be looked to by your own senior management to help in this area. The question is, what kind of people do you develop? What kind of people do you bring along? And what should your own interface be, if indeed the choice is to try to look to other elements in the business for providing, from a human standpoint, this kind of development? Very key questions on both my first and second points.

Accounting

My third point, very briefly, in the kinds of questions to look for in the future are the accounting conventions that are used with respect to information systems.

These have an awful lot to do with the way our economy moves, and the way individual companies move and, in the MIS area, with the question of what it is you really accomplish and what you do. The way you play chargeback systems, the terms of reference that are used, determine an internal market, determine a whole lot as to what kind of software products and systems will be developed.

For example, what do you capitalize, what don't you capitalize? This question gets very important when you're talking a couple of hundred million dollars a shot on some of the systems requirements that are coming out. How do you treat it? The conventional thing is to say we ex-

---

Most businesses try to go on just as they were before, and they fail.

---

pense everything, but you're beginning to get into areas where the scale is so great very few businesses can talk about expensing some of those. It's a question of what is indeed in the best interest of the business.

We don't even have yet one of the first items that we raised 20 years ago, an area in which we've made very little progress any place, and that is the time value of information. Most of our decisions are made on displaced costs of equipment, of people; very few of the decisions are made on the basis of the time value of the information; that is, the value

of more effectiveness and better decision making and more time freed up for management, as opposed to the cost displacement value. Instead, we cross our fingers and say, "Well, we think we need this and therefore we're going to do it." But if we could make a few serious moves in better understanding time value of information, it would be helpful in determining where we go. It's a big issue; we all run away from it, but it's a big issue.

It relates to this analytical void that we have in the field of methodology. You see it most pronounced in office automation where there really are very few solid analyses of the role of information in an organization; the interfaces, how the internal interventions are made in this, the very delicate and constantly changing balance between machine and people. You have a whole set of big problems with regard to methodology which we're not putting the resources into.

Human change

Fourth of my half dozen elements immediately follows from this and it relates to information technology as an agent of human change.

The first thing that happens with computers is that you change the way a job is done. The second thing that happens is that you change the job. And the third thing that happens is that the technology changes the society, and that opens the real issues as to what the enterprise's opportunities are.

We're now getting to the point where you can start to see examples of the third thing happening. At one extreme, you have the hackers—"the 414s"—and all of their pranks and serious crimes by using computers to break into various networks. While the 414s may have done damage and may indeed have committed crimes, I think basically that the kids doing that did a great deal of good for all of us, because it shook everyone up and brought to the

forefront the fact that this is very serious.

Well, you have indeed this extraordinary phenomenon beginning to occur in which society's patterns are changing as a result of the technology. That opens all the opportunities for business as well as all the problems, because if you read business history at all thoroughly, the great opportunities occur when you get changes in the society.

Most businesses try to go on just as they were before, and they fail. As it gets more expensive and more difficult to do things the old way, a small number decide the rules of the

---

Human factors determine whether or not you get productivity.

---

game have been changed and they see great opportunities in this change—and *they* become the great growth businesses.

You have the human factors related to this kind of change which are becoming absolutely crucial; the human factors become the key factors as to whether you get the productivity or don't get the productivity. And there's surprisingly little original work on this.

Future technology

The fifth point relates to technology and to the question of looking ahead at the technology.

The ability to look ahead has always been the driving force of this field. The techno-economic changes, the technological changes with the cost changes that follow them, will continue to be the major driving force in terms of the motive power under the field.

Some of the aspects that are coming up have considerable significance. The problem is, I think, one hears about them too early, when they seem to take a long time to develop. You tend to discount them, and then suddenly they're on top of you and making a big impact.

The voice response systems are a good example of this, I think. There are always new acronyms, and I'm always appalled by them—bips for billions of instructions per second, for example. Suddenly I found that I was starting to have notes about inverse transformational structures, semantic interpretation rules, string transformations and all sorts of other things. A whole string of PhDs were linguists, and what they were concerned with was trying to solve the language problems.

The cost of processing will no longer be a problem by the time they get the language problem solved, and this is very serious stuff. The role of spoken language and man-machine dialog is something we've all discounted because we all know the problems in it. You all know that when the machine tries to translate "out of sight, out of mind," it comes across "blind and crazy." There are a whole series of very funny problems in translation. We all know all the difficulties, but the realities are that this is the way the systems are going to be, really before not many years go by, and that becomes a tremendously important factor.

I've often cited something which after all these years I think still stands up very well, and that is a Charles Addams cartoon now standing behind my desk, which I got 30 years ago by writing to him. It was a cartoon that ran in *The New Yorker*, and it shows two caterpillars talking to one another. Above the caterpillars a moth emerges from a cocoon, and for the first time unfurls these lovely wings. One caterpillar says to the other caterpillar, "You'll never get me up in one of those things."

Well, that's been consistently good for the last 30 years, and as far as I can see that is consistently good today. All the areas that are really

going to affect all of us in this next period of time are viewed by everybody the same way: "You'll never get me up in those things." And the day afterward, you sort of shrug and say, "Yeah, that's what happens."

Competitive weaponry

My last point of the six key questions is information technology as a determinant of international competitiveness. Not only is it a determinant increasingly of individual firm competitiveness, but it clearly is a determinant of international competitiveness.

Japan's MITI puts it in a class by itself. MITI does not assign a yearly quota to it because, according to their printed statement, information technology is so fundamental to Japanese competitiveness in any other industry category that it simply is a category by itself. It's not a question of how many computers are sold, or word processors, or terminals or anything else; it's a question of how the economy internationally depends on, and will be determined by, this field.

French President Francois Mitterand has made exactly the same kind of statements. I find it fascinating that this issue is a big issue. You always have the question, what can I do about it? You can always run

---

The cost of processing will no longer be a problem by the time we solve the language problem.

---

away from it, but you can also think about the extent to which each of us can try individually to help in some collective realization of the importance of this field.

The United States is the area that is ahead in this field. We're ahead for a variety of reasons: We have a highly mobile population; we have an ability to fail without stigma—

you can leave a large company and fail and go back to work for a large company, or start again, and that is not true in Japan and it's not true in Germany. We have a whole lot of characteristics which help innovation. The question is, how do we maintain some of those characteristics? There are a whole series of issues developing that are important internationally. I think that this is an increasingly important factor. We tend to shrug it off. Most other countries are focusing very hard on it.

Those are the six issues I would choose as being ones that ought to be looked at hard in terms of the period just ahead of us. As I say, some of these are more pressing than others, but some of the ones that aren't so pressing may be more important.

I'd like to end with a comment of a favorite author of mine, Alfred North Whitehead, the British philosopher: "It is the business of the future to be dangerous, and it is among the merits of science that it equips the future for its duties. . . .In the immediate future there will be less security than in the immediate past, less stability. It must be admitted that there is a degree of instability which is inconsistent with civilization, but on the whole, the great ages have been the unstable ages." ∎

About the author

Diebold—a past recipient of the DPMA Distinguished Information Sciences Award—is chairman, The Diebold Group, Inc., New York, NY, an international management consulting firm. This article is based on a recent speech presented by Diebold at the 61st Plenary Meeting of the Diebold Multisponsor Continuing Programs in Grenelefe, FL.—Ed.

Artificial Intelligence: An Overview of Research and Applications

by Alec Chang
Michael Leonard
and Jay Goldman

Over the last decade, a significant body of information concerning artificial intelligence (AI) has been produced. Technical books and research papers on AI are published every year, and now and then introductory books for the general public appear on bookstore shelves. In addition, numerous brochures describing upcoming technical conferences devoted to AI and its applications appear in the mail every month.

But what is AI really all about? Unless industrial managers keep up with technical journals or work closely with university faculty or research engineers in the AI field, it is unlikely that the concepts of AI are clearly understood. However, it may soon be critical for industrial managers to understand basic AI concepts. New computers, the so-called fifth-generation computer system which employ AI concepts in their basic operating systems, are currently being devel-

Dr. Alec Chang is an assistant professor and director of graduate studies in the Department of Industrial Engineering at the University of Missouri-Columbia. He is currently responsible for teaching and research in the areas of automated inspection for computer integrated manufacturing systems, MRP modeling analysis, and robotics.

Dr. Michael Leonard is professor and chairman of Industrial Engineering at the University of Missouri-Columbia. He is currently serving as a project co-director for the Team Effort Advances Missouri Productivity and Quality Enhancement program for Missouri industry. He is a past division director for IIE Health Services division and past Chairman of the ORSA Health Applications Section. His list of publications includes over twenty articles in the area of health care delivery and information systems design.

Dr. Jay Goldman is dean of the School of Engineering at the University of Alabama at Birmingham. He was previously chairman of the department of industrial engineering at the University of Missouri-Columbia. He has made numerous presentations before business and professional organizations and has published widely in technical literature. He has been an active member of the Institute of Industrial Engineers and was vice president for education and professional development and executive vice president of the Institute. He is also a Fellow of the Institute.

oped. Japanese computer firms are deeply involved in this development effort and many experts believe that Japan will overshadow the world's marketplaces unless competitive computer systems are developed and used by U.S. companies.

AI is not an easy topic to discuss. The technologies that make up AI are constantly evolving, and some AI terms are not well-defined. This article will provide managers with an insight into the basic technical aspects of AI as well as some of the current applications of AI concepts. Within the next few years it will be particularly important to understand the concepts of AI, since its use is likely to cause essential changes in the operating practices and managerial functions of almost all industries.

An Introduction to AI

Although there is no uniform definition of the term "artificial intelligence," it is generally considered to be a subject concerned with applying computers to tasks that require knowledge, perception, reasoning, understanding, and cognitive abilities. An AI system should have the ability to accept data and analyze it in order to understand what the data represents. The system must be able to find a relationship between different sets of data, if one exists. The system should be able to effect the proper action based upon the understanding it has achieved. An AI system, therefore, should be able to exhibit true learning so as to improve its level of performance based on past experiences. Most importantly, an AI system must be able to deal with new situations based on previous learning.

Two major objectives of current AI research are 1) the understanding of the fundamental nature of "intelligence" and 2) the applications of computers to problems which lack organized computational methodologies. In order to achieve these research objectives, both the engineering approach and the modeling approach have been used. Researchers using the engineering approach attempt to create a computer system that is able to deal with interesting and difficult intellectual tasks. It does not matter to these researchers whether the methods and techniques used are similar to those used by humans. Patrick Winston suggests that the engineering approach to AI is characterized by its focus on objectives rather than on the use of specific tools. Examples of research using the engineering approach are studies of pattern recognition, language translation, music composition, and facility location.

Researchers using the modeling approach to AI attempt to imitate the actual process of a real-life system. The initial efforts of the modeling approach are directed toward gaining an understanding of the human thought process. This understanding would then be used to develop computer programs that think in much the same way as people do. This approach requires an AI system to be able to think and to learn. Examples of research using the modeling approach are studies of simulated human problem solving, human decision making, learning, natural language understanding, and neural network analysis.

Each of the approaches has its limitations. The engineering approach tends to develop analogy programs based on the paradigm of describe-and-match, and to develop integration programs based on the paradigm of if-then rules. Many experts question the level of intelligence that can be achieved by these two paradigms. On the other hand, there are also limitations in the modeling approach. Little is known about how the human mind works. As a result of the individual limitations, AI researchers may use both approaches. The differences of these two approaches typically exist only in the system architecture rather than in system performance. In general, current AI research is focused on two major areas: problem solving and comprehension.

Problem Solving

If there is a gap between the perceived and the desired state of the world, one might conclude that problems exist. These problems are solved by either filling the gap or by altering the world so that the gap disappears. Problem-solving systems attempt to find and select processes by which appropriate actions can be taken to close the gap. The missionaries and cannibals problem, the tower of Hanoi problem, and chess problems are well-known problem illustrations. A problem-solving system which specializes in a specific problem domain has been called an expert problem solving system, or in short, an "expert system."

In problem solving, researchers deal with symbolic representations of problems rather than the problems directly, primarily because computers operate best with symbols. The translation of states and actions in the real world into symbolic representations becomes the first and most important step of the problem-solving process. Currently, list representation, graph representation, or matrix representation are used to accomplish this translation. However, one must be satisfied that a representation is a sufficiently accurate model of reality. Other concerns about symbolic representations are whether a representation is easy to use by a human being or a machine or both, and how the representation can be modified to make it suitable for use by both human beings and machines.

Knowledge representation—Problem-solving systems rely on a collection of facts and rules of information processing, called a knowledge base, which supplies knowledge of problem areas. These systems use search schemes on the knowledge base in order to find a sequence of moves, a proof, or a solution for a problem. The understanding of so-called "knowledge" is still incomplete, since the nature of knowledge and intelligence has been pondered since the age of Aristotle. But it is generally agreed that the components of human knowledge are facts and rules necessary to perform specific tasks productively. Methods used to represent facts and rules in a domain of knowledge are the most active areas of AI research at the present time. Knowledge representation schemes enable computers to manipulate data and make inferences through the combination of data structures and integrating procedures.

Typical strategies for representing knowledge include semantic networks, object-attribute-value triplets, production rules, descriptional frames, and logical expressions. The most important factors in the selection of strategies for knowledge representation are: 1) the flexibility of the selected strategy to add new knowledge and code different types of knowledge, and 2) the robustness and clarity of the selected strategy in semantic interpretation.

Search and inferences—The use of the knowledge in AI systems includes knowledge acquisition, a learning stage, a retrieving process, and a reasoning procedure. Search schemes are used to gain access to relevant information for a given task. The search tasks are defined by "initial state" and "goal-state" descriptions. An effective search scheme must perform better than a random search, and must operate within whatever time limits and resource constraints apply. Blind search methods treat a search syntactically, while heuristic search methods utilize information about the nature and structure of the problem domain to reduce the effort required in finding acceptable answers.

Search tasks that are difficult for AI systems include those with an infinite search space, as in theorem-proving, or those with a very large search space, as in selecting moves for a game of chess. Therefore, a new problem is created—how to reduce the search space by using knowledge about the problems under study, by using experience gained with similar search tasks performed previously, and by choosing acceptable criteria for search-stopping rules.

Inferences are often required in the reasoning procedure in order to generate implicit answers from explicit information already in the knowledge base. The selection of inference schemes often comes very early in the development of AI systems, since this choice influences the selection of strategies of knowledge representation and search schemes. Many AI system designers utilize off-the-shelf inference models to reduce the system design effort. Most of the existing inference models use logical inference or plausible reasoning. The logical inference successively applies relevant axiomatic knowledge by following strict logic inference rules in order to reach a conclusion. The plausible reasoning approach attempts to draw a tentative conclusion from incomplete or uncertain data, and then checks to see if the tentative conclusion conflicts with stored knowledge. If there is a conflict, the tentative conclusion is modified. This cycle is repeated until the conflict is resolved.

Comprehension

Humans learn about the physical world through five major senses: vision, hearing, touch, smell, and taste. AI research is moving toward an understanding of the physical world using these sensory channels. In human learning, vision and hearing are by far the most important channels, but initial human perceptions about image and acoustic signals provide ambiguous representations of the physical world. It requires a tremendous amount of previous knowledge of the physical world for a human to construct a reasonable interpretation of these sensory inputs. Unfortunately, it is very difficult to present such a tremendous amount of knowledge of the world to a computer.

Two major problems must be overcome in the development of vision and hearing for AI systems. The first is a machine perception problem. For optimum machine use, the sensations of the physical world have to be organized into discrete entities. Then an internal representation of the external world has to be established so that the discrete entities can be linked with this representation. The second problem is a machine comprehension problem. To achieve comprehension, the system's internal representation must be manipulated in some manner to reach a conclusion about the entities.

Vision can be made available for an AI system by using a set of points pictured by a video camera in order to represent objects in a scene. The problem is how to reconstruct the scene from the set of points. In typical scenes, there will be more than one object. Any given object can be recognized as an isolated component or can be recognized through an analysis of the scene given its relationship with other objects. The scene analysis procedure is very complex, and the amount of data to be handled is extremely large. More than a million bits of data are required for just one binary image of a picture with a resolution of 1024 x 1024. The number of data bits required will increase exponentially if gray level is used instead of a binary image. A real-time processing environment may need to process 30 to 100 of such images in one second, and the processing time must include the data input and operation of the analysis algorithm, and color constancy remains a major problem. Therefore, computer vision systems have not yet been used extensively on production lines.

Auditory perception requires the translation of acoustic signals into a digital code. Currently, speech perception is the most studied domain of auditory perception. In speech perception the voice recognition problem is reduced to a conceptually simple pattern recognition problem so that the spoken word can be identified. Normally, the cipher method is used. This method is based on a direct mapping of acoustic features, first into phonemes and then into words.

One significant problem in speech perception is syntactic recognition, which operates at the phrase level. A syntactic analyzer is used to propose syntactic hypotheses about each word grouping. An even more difficult problem is the semantic recognition which must operate at the level of a complete sentence or sentences to express a complete thought. Currently, systems exist that can deal with a predetermined subset of words and phrases. A tremendous amount of research is still required on the problem of comprehension of natural language.

Pattern recognition—To facilitate many comprehension tasks, it is convenient to classify objects into typical or representative categories or sets, so that information concerning all of the members of a set can more easily be added to the database or retrieved at some later date when it is needed. The characteristics of the objects in typical categories determine their classification. A pattern recognition procedure is an algorithm that formulates a pattern classification rule for organizing the categories or sets. The ability to perform such a classification is basic to intelligent behavior. On many occasions people do not realize the broad background of knowledge required to make routine classifications in many daily tasks. The difference between a trivial change in characteristics and a change sufficient to require a new category is not always obvious and is a difficult decision to make.

Sometimes, objects can be reduced to a set of measurable characteristics. In many of the current pattern-recognition studies, these measurements are defined by a Euclidean space, and each object is treated as a point in the space. At other times, objects are characterized by attributes with nominal values, such as sex, place of birth, and race. In the attribute characterization process, the description of an object usually results in a list of features and an indication of the importance of each feature by assigning relative weights to each. A structural feature description stresses the relationship among the features such as linguistic objects rather than the values of a series of measurements. The identification of features and the assignment of weights for different features is generally a very difficult task in the development of a pattern recognition system.

Several important aspects of pattern recognition are closely related to classical statistical techniques used in multivariate analysis, sampling, and decision making. Sequential sampling is often used in AI for classification purposes and in changing and/or generating new classification rules. The procedure of creating new classification rules is often called machine learning.

Most current work in pattern recognition is in the area of comprehension. Other AI problem-solving tasks do not yet use pattern recognition methods. However, the use of pattern-recognition algorithms will be increasingly recognized as an important factor in the design of new AI systems. Some experts in the problem-solving area have already observed that master chess and checker players do not try to remember every step in previous games played by themselves or by other masters. Rather, these masters have their own specific ways to classify game patterns. The masters then use these patterns as a reference for their game playing strategies.

The three basic methods generally used for classifying objects in pattern recognition systems are:

1) Member Roster Method—Characterizes a pattern class by a roster of its members. Objects are classified by template matching.

2) Common-Property Method—Characterizes a pattern class by common properties shared by all of its members. Objects are classified by the identification of similar features.

3) Clustering Method—Characterizes a pattern class by its clustering properties in a pattern space. Objects are classified by measuring distances among pattern members.

Current AI Applications

The general goals of AI researchers specializing in business and industrial applications are to develop applications which share precious expertise, relieve humans from hazardous or boring jobs, substitute for intensive and costly manpower, and maintain competitive industrial strength through increased operating efficiency. To date, the areas in which AI systems have been most successful in terms of producing industrial application results are expert systems, natural language understanding, speech understanding, computer vision, robotics, and game-playing systems.

Expert systems—Most industrial managers had anticipated that it would be many years before AI research activities would produce results they could use. The success and increased use of expert systems (ES) has suddenly made AI a significant concern in most major corporations. As a result of this interest, ES working teams as well as other types of AI research groups have been created in many firms.

Feigenbaum and McCorduck have defined an ES as a computer program that has built into it the knowledge and capability that will allow the program to operate at the level of a human expert. An ES typically has the following characteristics:

1) The ability to explain the line of reasoning used for both accepted and rejected reasoning-evaluated paths during the process of prediction, diagnoses, planning, and analysis.

169

2) The application of heuristic methods to allow for the use of probabilistic, inexact, and uncertain data.

3) The separation of domain-specific knowledge in the ES knowledge base from the system's domain-independent inference procedures.

The first generation of ES developed in the 1960s—such as DENDRAL, which infers structures of chemical compounds and MACSYMA, which performs differential and integral calculus—focused on solving specific problems efficiently. In most situations, these first generation systems are capable of surpassing human experts. The second generation of ES developed after 1970—such as CASNET/GLAUCOMA, which gives diagnosis of glaucoma, and MYCIN, which gives diagnosis and therapy recommendations for infectious blood diseases—presented explanations of their reasoning processes as a part of their decision-making activity. In addition to the medically related ES developed during this period, there were also second generation ES developed for business tasks, such as PROSPECTOR, which interprets soil data, XCON (R1), a configuration system for customers' orders of different VAX computer systems, and DIPMETER ADVISOR, which gives oil field log interpretations.

In addition to many off-the-shelf ES, there are also commercial building tools available for use in constructing an ES:

1) Symbolic programming languages, such as LISP (list processor) and PROLOG. These languages are used for building systems from the beginning.

2) Skeletal systems, such as EMYCIN and EXPERT. The structure of these skeletal systems permits the insertion of a knowledge base and influence rules for different tasks.

3) Procedure-oriented languages, such as ROSIE and OPS5. These languages can be used to build skeletal systems or to build expert systems directly.

LISP is a computer language developed by John McCarthy in the mid 1950s and first implemented around 1960. LISP facilitates the development of symbolic expressions in terms of lists and functions. Lists are defined as ordered sequences of numbers, symbols, expressions or other items. By defining hierarchies of lists, complex and interactive data structures can be easily created. LISP is unparalleled in its ability to express recursive algorithms which manipulate dynamic data structures. A user can either compile statements in LISP or leave them in source-code form. In more advanced versions of LISP, if the compiled form of a program is at times inconvenient, the user can uncompile the program again. These important features make LISP an excellent language tool for building ES.

Several dialects, such as MACLISP and INTERLISP, have been developed from LISP. Efforts have also been made to develop a standard version of LISP, such as COMMON LISP. A LISP machine has been specially designed to execute LISP primitives directly in order to save program execution time. This specialized machine is a favorite computer for engineers who are building very large ES.

PROLOG (Programming in Logic) is a LISP competitor. Philippe Roussel designed this computer language primarily for AI applications. PROLOG is based on the approach of defining objects and inferential relationships among classes of objects which could provide for automatic deduction. Much attention has been given to PROLOG because of its important role in Japan's fifth-generation computer efforts.

But the extent of PROLOG's utility has yet to be fully tested since there are only a limited number of PROLOG-based ES applications.

Regardless of which building tool is used, developing a substantial ES for a real-world application can take several years of effort even if the system-building team has the appropriate backgrounds and experience. Fortunately, the amount of time required to build additional expert systems decreases, because new programs can utilize the ideas and experiences incorporated in previously developed systems.

A most important factor for building and using ES successfully is selecting appropriate problems for the systems to solve. According to Kraft, applications suitable for ES are:

- those requiring a large amount of human expertise,
- those that are not mathematical model oriented,
- those for which relevant knowledge can be represented as rules or heuristics,
- those that human experts have solved well, and
- those in fast changing fields of application.

Most of the current ES are limited by the progress of developments in natural language programming. Typically, the ES systems currently implemented still require key words or template-matching in order to activate the systems. The systems do not exhibit learning. They are unable to deal with differences and conflicting views of multiple experts, and do not possess "common sense." Therefore, future ES must be developed with the capacity to learn and to automatically structure knowledge and revise rules. And most importantly, the future ES must possess common sense in order to know when to break rules in order to deal with exceptions.

Natural language and speech understanding—Current computer programming languages are designed to facilitate computer instruction. Therefore, these languages possess a rigid syntax which makes it easier for compilers to convert programming statements into computer operations. However, this rigid syntax makes the language difficult to use by individuals who do not have extensive training. Many nontechnical individuals who want access to computers are frustrated by the level of expertise required. A natural language, such as English, would make an ideal programming language. A natural language would also be a good choice as a common communication language between different computer systems.

Based on these needs, researchers have approached the problem of natural language understanding with AI concepts. These researchers generally try to model human language as a knowledge-based system for processing communications. In most natural language understanding systems, expectations about the content of the subject is normally used in a search-and-matching process in order to increase system efficiency. This expectation-driven approach is also an important method for use in understanding incomplete or ungrammatical sentences. For example, if a line of text said that "a person goes to a restaurant," the subsequent lines in the text can be expected to state that this person will

1) order food, eat, pay and leave (most likely),

2) work as a chef, waiter, etc. (less likely),

3) look for someone in the restaurant (less likely), or

4) inspect the restaurant, since he is an inspector (much less likely).

Natural language understanding systems can now deal with only a tailored version of English using a very limited vocabulary. The systems also process text sentence-by-sentence. Most of these systems, such as INTELLECT, are used as a front-end processor for database systems or expert systems. In the future, natural language understanding systems can be expected to make inferences from multiple sentences. These systems may also be able to translate among different languages because translation is closely related to natural-language understanding.

Since speech is our most natural form of communication, using spoken language to gain access to computers has become an interesting research topic. There are many advantages to using speech as a method of inputting information to computers. Speech is faster than other input methods such as using a terminal or keypunch, and with speech as the computer communication method, the hands are free for other tasks. Moreover, users would need little training in order to be able to interact with complex computer systems.

The physical aspects of speech have been well understood for many decades. Electronic speech synthesizers have been available for several years at a very low price. Currently a speech synthesizing chip can be purchased for less than ten dollars. However, understanding the spoken words is another story. Speech understanding requires technology beyond acoustic signal processing. Researchers speculate that speech understanding has close relationships with the rules of conversation, knowledge representation, and natural language understanding.

Currently, isolated-word recognizers which can recognize up to 120 words are commercially available at a reasonable price. An automobile radio panel with voice command capability has been exhibited at the 1986 Society of Automotive Engineers (SAE) conference, and similar equipment is expected to be an option available on new cars very soon. In general, current speech recognition systems have the following problems:

1. A new learning procedure is required for every speaker or even for the same speaker when the speaker's mood changes or the speaker is subject to different physical or stress conditions.

2. The systems have a very limited vocabulary of recognizable words. It should be noted, however, that even these problems are the subjects of extensive research and could be eliminated soon.

Vision—A computer vision system is an image scanning and processing system designed to understand a scene based upon its projected image. Vision is the most important source of information about the environment for AI systems. The functions performed by current computer vision systems include the recognition of objects, the perception of relationships among objects, the measurement of dimensions, the detection of surface conditions, and the guidance of mechanical manipulators.

Computer vision research has been actively pursued for many years, and considerable research has been directed toward detecting the position and orientation of a manufacturing part. Thus, computer vision systems may be introduced to eliminate the need for special part presentation devices in modern flexible manufacturing systems and in robot work stations.

Flexible manufacturing equipment could be greatly facilitated by computer vision systems. Unfortunately, many computer vision systems developed for manufacturing applications have not been used extensively on automated production lines. The problem with existing computer vision systems is that they require extensive computing capabilities, large memory storage space, and long central processing unit (CPU) processing time. All of these factors result in extremely high costs. For example, the vision system technique of using model-matching methods to establish horizontal position and orientation could require more than a million image matches before the proper decision can be made. In some vision systems, the part positioning task has been simplified by abstracting special features of scanned objects such as using the feature point method and object centering.

Others have approached the problems in vision systems applications through the use of statistical methods. Some examples are the CONSIGHT System, and the NBS Vision System. While these systems have somewhat reduced the need for large computer capacities and long computing times, they still present difficulties because of their inability to distinguish feature characteristics in a real-factory environment. Factory environments usually do not present a clear demarcation of color tones. For example, in many manufacturing plants, the colors contain predominantly brown and gray tones. Accurate feature identification requires a sharp contrast, such as black objects on a white background or vice versa. Furthermore, a primary obstacle in the analysis of pictures involving three-dimensional workplaces is the lack of precise depth information in a single picture.

One particularly successful industrial application of computer vision is in the performance of automatic inspection. Visual inspection is one of the last industrial tasks to resist automation because it requires human qualities of perception and judgment. However, with the introduction of computer technology, this barrier is beginning to fall. Recent advances in computer technology, together with refinements in image analysis techniques and image sensing devices, allow automated visual inspection systems to utilize smaller and less expensive computers to process tremendous amounts of data. The result is a vision inspection system that is remarkably accurate, as well as fast and compact, thereby making on-line, 100%-discrete part inspection possible. Computer vision inspection systems are probably the most flexible of the non-contact inspection systems available because their applications are less restricted by the shape of the part. Many particular geometric features of objects, such as threads or parts with diverse features including angles, radii, and other non-linear curves, cannot be measured by contact measurements due to the difficulties in making and maintaining precise reference models.

Automatic quality inspection and control devices that monitor the quality of in-process parts are essential for effective production. These are used to determine the acceptance or rejection of a part or a specific production lot at a workstation before the parts are fed into the next workstation. They are also used to monitor the calibration of fixtures and the conditions of cutting tools. These devices can be integrated into a feedback control system to directly influence the manufacturing process. There are many automated measurement and inspection systems available to industry which carry out such functions as automatic gauging and sorting, automatic multi-dimension gauging, computer-supported coordinate measuring, and automated visual inspection.

Vision systems have been used extensively in the inspection of electrical and electronic products such as printed circuit boards, microcircuit photomasks, and integrated circuit chips. The reason for this extensive use of vision systems is that significant technological advances in design and production of electronic assemblies have increased the speed of production while greatly reducing their physical size. Such production advances have greatly complicated the

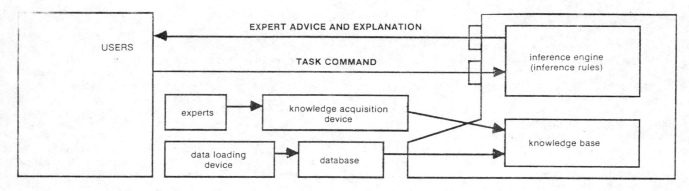

Components of an Expert System

classical manual inspection processes. As a result, the complexity of the inspection task in these advanced production systems has almost placed it beyond human capability. To resolve this difficult problem, R. T. Chin developed two methods for vision system inspection of printed circuit boards—"feature matching" and "dimensional verification."

A wide range of other industrial applications for vision systems has also been explored. Batchelor, Horaud and Charras conducted feasibility studies to automate the inspection of male screw threads. Parks introduced a simple procedure developed at the National Physical Laboratory, London, for inspecting objects such as rollers, rivets, and spindles. Coleman, Reich, Erickson, and Kelly developed an automatic inspection and reject system for small-caliber cartridge cases. This system gauges the case profile, and looks for surface flaws and the presence of a vent hole in each 5.56mm case, at the rate of 1200 cases per minute. Schlosser introduced a method, developed at Spatial Data System, Goleta, California, to inspect nuclear fuel cylinders, dentists' root canal drills, and reed switches. Chang, Goldman, Leonard, Miller and Lee developed a sampling method for on-line vision inspection systems to measure the roundness and straightness of industrial parts.

What We Can Look For

In the early years of AI research, between 1960-1970, the major research interests were in creating general problem-solving systems. Most of the commercial products currently available in AI are based on ideas and research completed during that period. These include expert systems, game playing systems, front-end natural language processing systems, vision systems, and robots. After 1970, a major portion of AI growth has been in systems upgrading and in the development of commercial applications.

Although a primary focus of AI specialists is to make computer systems smarter, some experts believe that AI development should not copy human intelligence, but rather take advantage of the unique strengths of computer systems. One of the reasons for this belief is that AI research has been eminently successful in making the computer display intelligence in those areas that require substantial effort, such as medical diagnoses, geological interpretation, and determining the molecular structure of unknown chemical compounds. However, even the best vision systems still cannot recognize a specific face from a class picture, a task which a human can do easily.

Some industrial managers may view AI as a highly specialized form of computer programming. More correctly, AI systems should be considered advanced, specialized information systems. AI researchers try to write programs that enable computers to think and to interact effectively with the environments in which they operate. For industrial managers, the task of system development is not so much to learn all of the technical details of the AI systems, but to pose the right questions for the AI system development

teams to answer. It is more important for the manager to find the right areas for AI system application than for the manager to find the right AI tools. **IM**

References

Ainsworth, W. A., *Mechanisms of Speech Recognition*, Pergamon Press, Oxford, England, 1976.

Ballard, Dana H., Brown, Christopher M., *Computer Vision*, Prentice-Hall, New Jersey, 1982.

Barr, Avron and Feigenbaum, Edward A.; *The Handbook of Artificial Intelligence*, 3 volumes, William Kaufmann, Inc., Los Altos, California, Volume II & III, 1982.

Binford, Thomas O., "Survey of Model-Based Image Analysis Systems," *The International Journals of Robotics Research*, Vol. 1-1, pp. 18-64, 1982.

Bramer, M. A. (editor), *Computer Game-Playing Theory and Practice*, Halsted Press, N.Y., 1983.

Chang, C. Alec, et al, "Locating Parts with Feature Marks for Robot Vision Systems," *Proceedings*, 7th International Conference on Production Research, Windsor, Canada, 1983, pp. 497-502.

Chang, C. Alec, et al., "A Quality Control Issue in Using Computer Vision Inspection Systems," *Proceedings*, MVA/SME Vision '86 Conference, Detroit, 1986, pp. 4.57-4.73.

Chang, C. Alec and Goldman, Jay; "An Off-line Design Procedure for the Work Station of Assembly Robots," *Robotics and Industrial Engineering: Selected Readings*, Industrial Engineering and Management Press, Atlanta, 1983.

Chang, C. Alec, Goldman Jay, and Yeralan, S.; "A Time Buffer Method for Multi-arm Operational Planning," *Robotics and Material Flow*, Vol. 3, Elsevier Science Publishers, Amsterdam, 1986, pp. 187-196.

Charniak, Eugene and McDermott, Drew, *Introduction to Artificial Intelligence*, Addison-Wesley, MA, 1985.

Chin, R. T. and Harlow, C. A., "Automated Visual Inspection: A Survey," *IEEE Transaction on Pattern Analysis and Machine Intelligent*, Vol. PAMI-4, No. 6, Nov. 1982, pp. 557-573.

Critchlow, Arthur J., *Introduction to Robotics*, Macmillan, N.Y., 1985.

Feigenbuam, Edward A. and McCorduck, P., "The Fifth Generation: Artificial Intelligence and Japan's Computer Challenge to the World," Addison-Wesley, 1983.

Fu, King-sun, "Pattern Recognition for Automatic Visual Inspection," *Computer*, December, 1982, pp. 34-40.

Harmon, Paul and King, David, *Expert Systems-Artificial Intelligence in Business*, John Wiley & Sons, N.Y., 1985.

Hayes-Roth, Frederick, et al., *Building Expert Systems*, Addison-Wesley, MA, 1983.

Hunt, Earl B., *Artificial Intelligence*, Academic Press, New York, 1975.

Kurzweil, Raymond, "What is Artificial Intelligence Anyway?" *American Scientist*, Vol. 73, May-June, 1985, pp. 258-263.

Nitzan, D., "Machine Intelligence Research Applied to Industrial Automation," Ninth Conference on Production Research and Technology, 1981.

Nof, Shimon Y., (Editor), *Handbook of Industrial Robotics*, John Wiley & Sons, N.Y., 1985.

Ralston, Anthony and Reilly, Edwin D. (Editors), *Encyclopedia of Computer Science and Engineering*, 2nd edition, Van Nostrand Reinhold Company, New York, 1983.

Rose, Frank, "Into the Heart of the Mind—An American Quest for Artificial Intelligence," Harper & Row, New York, 1984.

Rosenfeld, A. and Kak, A. C., "Digital Picture Processing," 2 volumes, Academic Press, New York, 1982.

Schroeder, Manfred R., (Editor), *Speech and Speaker Recognition*, S. Karger AG, Switzerland, 1985.

Tau, Julius T. and Gonzalez, Rafael C.; *Pattern Recognition Principles*, Addison-Wesley, MA, 1974.

Tucker, Allen B., Jr., *Programming Languages*, 2nd ed., McGraw-Hill, New York, 1986.

Winston, Patrick H. and Brown, Richard H., "Artificial Intelligence: An MIT Perspective," 2 volumes, the MIT Press, Cambridge, Massachusetts, 1979.

Winston, Patrick H., and Prendergast, Karen A., *The A.I. Business—Commercial Uses of Artificial Intelligence*, the MIT Press, Cambridge, Massachusetts, 1984.

The Promise of Artificial Intelligence

BY DR. STEPHEN J. ANDRIOLE

DR. STEPHEN J. ANDRIOLE

Dr. Andriole is the President of International Information Systems, Inc. He is formerly the Director of the Defense Department's Advanced Research Projects Agency's Cybernetics Technology Office where he was also a Program Manager. He has taught international relations, national security analysis, and applied methodology at the University of Maryland as an Assistant Professor and at the Johns Hopkins School of Advanced International Studies; he was also a Research Analyst and Project Manager at Decisions and Designs, Incorporated. Dr. Andriole also regularly teaches short courses in interactive computer-based systems design and development, command and control (C²) software systems development and evaluation, and applied analytical methodology at the George Washington University and several other locations. He is a frequent contributor to professional journals in the national security, analytical methodology, and Defense C² areas.

■ Until very recently, artificial intelligence, or "AI," was of interest to relatively few professionals. Even the parent field of computer science remained skeptical until an impressive number of basic and applied success stories could be documented. Today AI is regarded by many as a revolutionary development in the design and use of computer-based systems. Some even believe that AI systems may eventually replace human analysts, managers, and decision-makers.

Is the optimism justified? Are the goals of the AI research and development community feasible? Or desirable? Where will the impact of AI be felt? How will management be affected?

What is AI?

There are many definitions of artificial intelligence.[1] For many, AI suggests computer-based problem-solving, such as theorem proving. Others regard AI systems as "natural language processors," capable of understanding "free form" continuous language. For others, AI triggers images of "smart weapons" and "intelligent robots."

There are many definitions of AI because AI is inherently interdisciplinary with roots in virtually all of the social, behavioral, managerial, and computer sciences. The key to understanding the nature and applied potential of AI may be traced to these roots. Unlike "conventional" computer science, AI concerns itself primarily with the representation of *knowledge*. Where conventional computer programs assist in the storage, retrieval, manipulation,

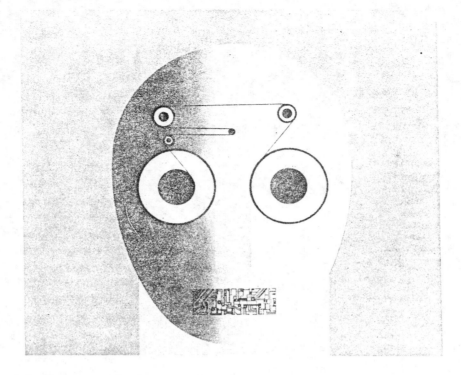

and display of data, AI programs represent knowledge and focus it at specific problem areas.

But AI systems go beyond the storage of knowledge derived from facts, data, and information. They represent and store "heuristic" knowledge, or the processes by which judgments, associations, and inferences are made. "If gold falls below $300 an ounce, then we should buy" is an example of the kind of rule-based inferences all of us make and that AI systems designers seek to incarnate in "smart" computer programs. If you can imagine a system with a thousand such rules developed after years of consultation with expert investors, then you can appreciate the potential of "expert systems," just one kind of AI system.

The process of acquiring cognitive "rules of thumb" in AI is called knowledge engineering.[2] The rules themselves often emerge after intensive consultation with experts, after the observation of expert behavior, or after the analysis of past problem-solving. It is during this process that AI systems designers borrow from the social, behavioral, and managerial sciences. Some of the very best knowledge engineers are cognitive psychologists, while linguists, epistemologists, and practitioners of operations research, pattern recognition, and logic also often play large roles in the knowledge engineering process.

A number of AI systems represent — and present access to — knowledge via *natural language* front ends.[3] Natural language systems permit users to interact with AI and conventional computer-based systems in their natural tongue. Instead of learning how to manipulate a complicated data base management system (DBMS) via a confusing query language, natural language systems permit users to simply type in (or even say) what they want in much the same way they might request information from a human associate. Many natural language systems are knowledge-based systems in their own right capable of drawing inferences and making decisions in response to free-form input. Some natural language systems like INTELLECT, permit users to query a data base in conversational English.[4] Note the difference between this and conventional query system dialogue.

Some AI Systems

There are a variety of AI systems that have recently moved from the laboratory into the field. Many of them are now in use in the military and defense establishments, but just as many are hard at work in industry. At last count there were nearly 50 different expert systems, natural language processors, and other AI-based problem-solvers performing all kinds of commercial tasks.[5]

Expert Systems

The use of expert systems has outstripped the use of other kinds of AI programs. One of the most notable success stories involves PROSPECTOR, an expert system developed at SRI International which contains about 1600 rules.[6] PROSPECTOR has been used to locate ore deposits and has already demonstrated its ability to outperform expert geologists in some problem areas. Like so many other expert systems, PROSPECTOR receives input from a user regarding geological conditions and then makes recommendations about the likelihood of specific outcomes, such as the probability of finding ore in a specific location. R1 is another expert system that has enjoyed a lot of commercial success.[7] Developed by the Digital Equipment Corporation (DEC) and Carnegie-Mellon University, R1 helps DEC configure minicomputer systems for its clients. R1 and its offspring have over 800 rules that determine the best hardware configuration given the requirements and resources of the prospective user.

Almost from the beginning, expert systems research has been applied to medical problems. The now famous MYCIN expert system, for example, is capable of diagnosing bacterial infections and even prescribing treatment (see Figure 1). PUFF works in the field of lung disorders and CADUCEUS in internal medicine.[8] As Figure 2 suggests, there are expert systems now working full-time in a number of scientific, technical, and managerial areas; new systems are being released all the time.

Natural Language Processors

Very recently IBM announced that it intended to market the INTELLECT natural language processing system. This decision was not only well received at the Artificial Intelligence Corporation, the developer of INTELLECT, but by the entire AI community because it demonstrated confidence in but one of the AI systems now in the marketplace. INTELLECT permits users to interact with large data bases in much the same way they might interact with human assistants. Instead of requesting data by means of a complicated query language that is difficult to learn and even easier to forget, INTELLECT permits "free-form" questioning. Texas Instruments has also developed a natural language interface to the Dow Jones News/Retrieval Service called NaturalLink that permits users of the service to construct English language requests by selecting the parts of sentences that the system then combines into meaningful queries. While not nearly as powerful as INTELLECT, NaturalLink is designed to operate on a microcomputer. Yet another natural language front-end system is Cognitive Systems, Inc.'s BROKER, which makes Standard & Poor's Compustat data base, an enormous data base which contains twenty years of statistical, market, and financial information on several thousand corporations, easier to access and search. Like INTELLECT, BROKER permits users to simply request data from the data base in natural, free-form language.[9]

One of the most important developments in natural language processing technology lies in the design and application of *transportable* natural language front-ends. SRI International, among other organizations, is developing a Transportable English Access Mechanisms (TEAMS) that can be used with any DBMS.[10] TEAMS "interviews" the DBMS user and then constructs a "translation mechanism" for the data base in question which, in turn, permits the user to query the data base in near free-form. The objective of TEAMS is to develop a natural language processing capability that can adapt to whatever data base it finds in need of more graceful interaction with its users. In effect, TEAMS may be viewed as a traveling charm school for unfriendly data base management systems.

Some Rules from the MYCIN Expert Diagnostic System

IF: (1) The site of the culture is blood, and
(2) The identity of the organism is not known with certainty, and
(3) The stain of the organism is gramneg, and
(4) The morphology of the organism is rod, and
(5) The patient has been seriously burned,
THEN: There is weakly suggestive evidence (0.4) that the identity of the organism is pseudomonas.

IF: (1) The infection which requires therapy is meningitis, and
(2) The patient has evidence of a serious skin or soft tissue infection, and
(3) The organisms were not seen on the strain of the culture, and
(4) The type of infection is bacterial,
THEN: There is evidence that the organism (other than those seen on cultures or smears) which might be causing the infection is staphylococcus-coagpos (.75) or streptococcus (.5).

Figure 1

	Some Expert Systems	
EXPERT SYSTEM	**GENERAL FUNCTION**	**SPECIFIC AREA**
MECHO	Analysis	Mechanical Problems
TECH	Analysis	Naval Task Force Threats
SPERIL	Analysis	Earthquake Damage Assessment
CRITTER	Analysis	Digital Circuitry
PHOENIX	Automatic Programming	Oil Well Log Modeling
PROSPECTOR	Data Analysis	Geology
DENDRAL	Data Analysis	Chemistry
CRYSALIS	Data Analysis	Protein Crystallography
ELAS	Data Analysis	Oil Well Logs
SYN	Design	Circuitry Synthesis
XCON/R1	Design	Computer System Configuration
SYNCHEM	Design	Chemical Synthesis
MEDAS	Diagnosis	Critical Care Medicine
DELTA	Diagnosis	Locomotive Troubleshooting
MYCIN	Diagnosis	Medical
DART	Diagnosis	Computer Faults
REACTOR	Diagnosis	Nuclear Reactor Accidents
INTERNIST/CADUCEUS	Diagnosis	Medical
XSEL	Intelligent Assistance	Computer Sales
CSA	Intelligent Assistance	Nuclear Power Plant Configuration
RAYDEX	Intelligence Assistance	Radiology
VISIONS	Image Understanding	Vision
IMS	Management	Automated Factory Management
CALISTO	Management	Project Management
NOAH	Planning	Robotics
OP-PLANNER	Planning	Erand planning
KNOBS	Planning	Tactical Mission Planning
MOLGEN	Planning	Molecular Genetics

Figure 2

Figure 3 presents a summary of some of the best known natural language processing systems. Note that many of the systems were developed with reference to specific problems while others are more general in application.

AI's New Role in Industry

Ten years ago discussions about AI applications were relatively rare. There were still far too many skeptics, and the systems that existed then were far from impressive. It is safe to say that the period from the early 1960s to the late 1970s was largely a period of experimentation in AI, a period which fostered the design and development of countless "demonstration systems."[11] During the last five years, however, the structure of the AI research and development community has changed. There is today considerably more interest in development than there was in the 1960s and 1970s. But much more importantly, this interest has already yielded a number of systems that have been well received in industry. One needs no more evidence to support this conclusion than the transformation that takes place every time a $500,000 under-utilized data base management system emerges as a powerful new tool via a simple natural language front-end.

There are also successes that protect and generate capital. PROSPECTOR and R1 have already saved millions of dollars during their brief lives. No doubt these and other expert systems will pay for themselves over and over again.

The record so far suggests the role that AI systems can play in the business community. At the most basic level, we should regard AI systems as "force multipliers" and "smart assistants." Force multipliers extend the power and applicability of existing information and electronic data processing resources. Natural language front-ends are cases in point. Smart assistants augment and in time may even replace human experience and judgment. Obviously this goal is now without controversy, though if we extrapolate even conservatively from the capabilities of today's expert systems the prospects for the design and application of intelligent computer-based surrogates seem very real indeed.

Some Natural Language Systems		
NATURAL LANGUAGE SYSTEM	**GENERAL FUNCTION**	**SPECIFIC AREA**
LADDER	Machine Translation/ Interfacing	Ship Identification & Location
SAM	Machine Translation/ Interfacing	Generic Story Understanding
TDUS	Interfacing	Electromechanical Repair
SHRDLU	Interfacing	Location & Manipulation of Three Dimensional Figures
EXPLORER	Interfacing	Map Generation & Display
INTELLECT	Interfacing	Data Base Management
NATURALLINK	Interfacing	Dow Jones Data Retrieval & Display
TEAMS	Generic Interfacing	Data Base Management
MARKETEER	Interfacing	Market Analysis
POLITICS	Inference Making	Ideological Belief System Simulation
BROKER	Interfacing	Standard & Poor's Data Base Management System
STRAIGHT TALK	Interfacing	Word Processing/ Microcomputer Workstations

Figure 3

Data Base Management Force Multipliers

Natural language systems like TEAMS, INTELLECT, NaturalLink, and BROKER will continue to narrow the gaps between users of very large data base management systems and the consumers of their output. Today in most large organizations data base management is considered but one arm of an otherwise enormous information management structure. Typically someone in "management" tasks someone in ADP to extract specific pieces of information necessary for some other kind of function, like planning, resource allocation, or decision-making. The first step toward bridging the gap between inaccessible data base management systems and corporate managers, analysts, and decision-makers has already been taken by the designers of "decision support systems," though decision support systems do not permit free-form interaction and, like their data base management system cousins, must be learned. Finally, what you learn about one decision support system will not help you work with another. Natural language systems that permit free-form interaction will revolutionize the use of data base management and decision support systems by extending their capabilities and by increasing access to what was previously the exclusive preserve of programmers and systems analysts.

Natural language processors will also help multiply the number of analytical problems amenable to data-based solutions. Over and over again complaints are heard today about how difficult it is to "find" data once it has been entered into a data base management system. Because of such problems many systems are under-utilized. Natural language front-ends can foster whole new ways of data-based problem-solving and make it amazingly easy to conduct "what-if" analyses.

Natural language systems will also change the contexts in which computerized data bases are applied to corporate problem-solving. Since today it often takes a lot of time to satisfy requests for information, key information is excluded from periods of corporate crisis management. Postmortems of unsuccessful corporate crisis management episodes have suggested repeatedly that if certain pieces of information had been available then the crisis might have been averted. The same postmortems also suggest that more often than not the data was available in the corporate data base management system but, for a variety of reasons, was inaccessible during the crisis management decision-making process.

The development and use of natural language processing systems will also influence the way managers, analysts, and decision-makers perceive the nature and utility of computer-based problem-solving. For years we have all listened to ADP, EDP, and IRM department managers explain just how difficult it would be to modify an unfriendly computer program even just a little, and how completely friendly systems were either too expensive to build or best left to those committed to distributed and personal computing. Natural language systems can tame even the unfriendliest systems. While today these front-ends are relatively expensive, within five years they will be a bargain. As their use becomes more and more widespread we can expect attitudes to change about computer-based problem-solving. While a "terminal on every desk" may be an unrealistic and undesirable goal, there will be many who will be well served by systems that require nothing of them but plain English, And many more who may come to depend upon literate systems for increasingly complex problem-solving.

Analysis, Planning & Decision-Aiding Assistance

Natural language front-ends can extend the capabilities of many computer-based systems. But beyond these polite smart systems are the expert and advisory systems that have already begun to affect corporate life. There are AI systems that can help with the formulation of plans, making diagnoses, project management, product design, data analysis, monitoring and forecasting, and even concept formation. There are also several targeted at decision option evaluation and selection, resource allocation, and cost-benefit analysis. Expert systems now exist or are currently under development that deal with virtually all of the analytical problems that corporate analysts, managers, and decision-makers routinely face.

The expert systems that have enjoyed success to date are relatively straightforward. Some of these include MYCIN, DENDRAL, and EL and some of their problem areas include medical diagnosis, chemical data analysis, and electronic circuitry analysis, respectively.[12] But within five to ten years we can expect the number and intelligence of expert systems to grow. There is no question that as the process of knowledge engineering improves, expert systems will be developed to deal with extremely complex analytical problems, like where to locate a new plant, where to invest excess capital, how to improve cash flow, and how to forecast advances in technology. Many believe that it will be the imagination of AI systems designers that determine the range of applications, not the depth of expert systems technology. Many of these systems will have natural language front-ends to make them even more powerful and accessible.

Current expert systems should by no means be regarded as decision-making surrogates. To the contrary, the best they can do today is serve as efficient assistants. But future systems may well replace some analysts and decision-makers, especially in areas where the problem-solving "rules of thumb" are easily identified, such as in the areas of law and accounting.

Perhaps the best example of AI systems as smart assistants may be found in the advisory systems now under development at Cognitive Systems, Inc. The goal there is to develop a set of systems capable of advising users in professional and personal problem-solving. Time of course will tell if the systems gain the confidence and trust of their users, or, like so many incompetent professionals, betray that trust at no small cost. In any case, within a few short years these systems will be available for testing.

Smart Training Systems

One of the most promising application areas is training. Almost from the inception of AI research, many have strived to develop intelligent instructional systems of one kind or another. The military led the search and has supported the development and use of a number of intelligent training systems. Bolt, Beranek, and Newman, Inc. and the Navy, for example, have developed an intelligent instructional system called STREAMER, which teaches recruits how to operate steam propulsion systems. Another smart system known as BUGGY teaches the principles of diagnosis, while GUIDON, perhaps the best known intelligent instructional system, instructs trainees about how to conduct medical diagnoses.[13] Figure 4 lists many of the best known smart training systems. Perhaps most interesting is the dual approach that AI systems designers have taken toward the development of smart training systems. Some systems, like GUIDON and SOPHIE, attempt to represent expertise in specific areas and then impart that knowledge directly to trainees, while other systems, like BUGGY and WEST, seek to model the trainee's learning skills.[14] A third thrust in the area is the development of "authoring systems" which enable in-

ICAI SYSTEM	TRAINING AREA	KNOWLEDGE REPRESENTATION
ALGEBRA	Applied Algebra	Rules
BIP	Programming in BASIC	Rules
BUGGY	Arithmetic Subtraction	Procedural Networks
EXCHECK	Logic & Set Theory	Rules with Logic Interpreters
GUIDON	Infectious Diseases	Rules & Meta-Knowledge
INTEGRATE	Symbolic Integration	Adaptive Rules
LMS	Algebraic Procedures	Rules
MENO	Programming in PASCAL	Semantic Networks
QUADRATIC	Quadratic Equations	Adaptive Rules
SCHOLAR	South American Geography	Semantic Networks
SOPHIE	Electronic Trouble-shooting	Semantic Networks with Circuitry Simulator
SPADE	Programming in LOGO	Rules
STEAMER	Steam Ship Propulsion	Device Model
WEST	Arithmetic Expressions	Rules
WHY	Causes of Rainfall	Scripts
WUSOR	Logical Relationships	Genetic Graphs (Networks)

Figure 4

structors to create new instructional materials interactively at a computer terminal. When the loop between authoring and smart instructional systems is finally closed, intelligent computer-aided instruction (ICAI) will become cost-effective and widespread.

ICAI systems will help with all kinds of training missions. As industry evolves from smokestacks to services, ICAI systems will help retrain displaced workers. As high technology attains even greater heights, ICAI systems will permit engineers and information scientists to keep abreast of developments in their fields.

In terms of the earlier description of AI systems as force multipliers and smart assistants, clearly ICAI systems will satisfy both definitions by extending the capabilities of existing unintelligent systems and by enabling trainees to master whole new areas as well.

CAD, CAM, Robotics, & Automatic Programming

AI has also affected the development and use of computer-aided design (CAD) and manufacturing (CAM) systems.[15] As these systems become perfected and distributed they will improve production dramatically. Already we can point to many examples in the robotics field, where intelligent vision and motion continue to be major AI research thrusts.[16] In addition to the automobile and appliance industries, many others will be affected by the development of intelligent CAD, CAM and robotic systems.

AI may also ease one of the most costly and pervasive bottlenecks in the entire field of high technology: computer software development. Not unlike the intelligent robot in the Japanese factory laboring tirelessly to produce yet more intelligent robots, AI-based automatic programming systems may well produce and re-produce computer-based systems merely by responding to a set of requirements supplied by management.[17] When these automated programming systems hit the marketplace we can expect enormous impact which, like the impact of ICAI systems, will be cost-effective and widespread.

Issues & Problems in Applied AI

There are a great many issues relevant to the design, development, and application of AI systems. The above has documented only a few of the AI systems now under development or in use. Hundreds of millions of dollars are being spent each year to perfect the means by which AI systems are developed and applied, and more than a few large corporations have established their own AI research and development programs.[18] There is great promise in all this effort, but there are also problems.

Perhaps the most insidious problem with the design, development, and application of AI systems can be traced to the vastly different images that all of us have about the nature and power of AI. Many of us genuinely believe that AI will revolutionize the entire business community, while others are convinced that

AI is a flash in the pan. The AI community itself is badly divided about the potential of AI.

Of course this is not the first time that misrepresentations and rhetoric have affected the evolution of new technology. Nor will it be the last. Already there are signs that advances in bioengineering and biocybernetics are suffering some of the same assaults as AI. Unfortunately, some of the problems can be traced directly to the AI community itself. The frenzied pursuit of funding has often created unrealistically high expectations about the eventual applicability of AI. If the future is to be kind to the AI community, much of this rhetoric must be toned down. In its place should be assessments anchored solidly in actual experience; speculation about future capabilities should be based upon careful extrapolations from present ones, not wild-eyed or normative. Given that AI is now receiving more attention than it ever has before, the proponents of AI must make certain that their rhetoric corresponds with reality. The lack of correspondence is especially visible during funding cycles where accomplishments and goals are often stretched to their very limits. While keen competition often dictates such a strategy, in time it will erode the funding base of the entire field.

There are also significant questions about the ability of AI systems to accurately represent human intelligence. Script versus rule-based knowledge representation suggests but one kind of question, while the difficulty of conquering the ambiguities of language in natural language processing systems raises many others. In truth, AI systems cannot reproduce human intelligence; rather the goal is to mimic it in increasingly sophisticated stages. While some systems do this very well, others are noticibly "artificial," and learning, a major component of intelligence, remains an illusive goal of AI research. Additional basic research will help resolve some of these issues, but until they have been conducted and scrutinized, AI systems should be regarded as highly intelligent compared to conventional computer-based systems, but highly unintelligent when compared to human information processing capabilities.

There are also practical problems. The first concerns the rush toward commercialization. There are many who believe that the promise of high tech profits has undermined the natural development of the field. Marvin Minsky, for example, an AI pioneer, has repeatedly cautioned against the rush to market AI systems that are not yet ready for commercial use.[19] He has also warned the community about its tendency to lure basic researchers away from the lab-

oratory and into business, suggesting that a major shortage of basic and applied AI systems designers now exists.[20] There is also a shortage of applied institutions and organizations. Nearly all of the early work in AI was conducted within academia. Even the bulk of applied research has been conducted by university-based researchers or by professors-turned-entrepreneurs. In fact, many of the corporations marketing AI systems today were founded by university professors. In order for the applied AI community to grow it will need to develop an applied research infrastructure similar to the one that now exists for basic AI research.

There are some organizational problems as well. Already the thrust toward increasingly sophisticated computer-based problem-solving systems has triggered turf battles within many management information systems (MIS) departments. In manufacturing, for example, the spectre of AI control suggests a greatly diminished role for MIS professionals, just as the use of expert systems in engineering will eventually displace some percentage of the engineering workforce. The organizational problems that will result from these technological challenges will be formidable. Just the threat of AI-inspired change will create problems in many organizations and bureaucracies. Ironically, ICAI systems may be called upon to retrain displaced professionals.

Finally, there is legitimate concern the effect AI systems will have upon the cognitive problem-solving process. A good example is corporate planning, a very complicated process that requires insight, judgment, and experience, as well as a great deal of quantitative data. When smart planning systems are perfected and linked with larger corporate data bases, will expert corporate planners come to rely too heavily upon the expertise of their intelligent assistants? Will expert systems create a false sense of security within corporate problem-solvers? There is a very real danger that our zeal to apply smart systems may shift our priorities away from the human decision-maker. The danger is by no means new. Many have critized the proliferation of interactive computer-based forecasting and decision support systems because they require very little methodological skill on the part of the "user"; others regard such systems as substitutes for difficult thinking. Hopefully, future AI systems will temper their output and provide for easy manual override. In all fairness to current expert systems, however, it should be noted that one of their strengths lies in their ability to reconstruct the logic that led to the final output, thus enabling the decision-maker to assess the consistency and comprehensiveness of the system's inference process.

There are of course other issues and problems. Cost-effectiveness, maintenance, transportability, and user-friendliness represent just a few. But there are also some promising signs that AI will make significant contributions to corporate problem-solving perhaps sooner than we think.

Prognosis for Applied AI

The success of AI will depend upon a number of interrelated events and conditions. First, AI will have to build upon its past and current successes slowly and realistically. It must guard against promising too much too soon. Systems like INTELLECT and PROSPECTOR have broken down many of the barriers that confronted AI systems marketers, but there is still a long way to go. Just as many AI systems have failed to live up to their potential and a lot of managers would rather sit on the sidelines than waste any more of their precious resources. The AI community will also have to deal with its own internal problems. Every effort should be made to expand the AI student population and the applied research infrastructure that now pales against the foundation that now supports basic AI research. But there are signs that these and other internal problems will in fact be solved.[21]

Perhaps the most important condition for success in applied AI has already been met. Whereas in the past AI was decidedly technology driven ("we should do it because we can"), today it has become much more requirements driven ("we should do it because we need to"). This shift from "technology push" to "requirements pull" has given AI a new lease on life. For the first time there are a number of new requirements, in distributed processing, telecommunications, and crisis management, for example, that conventional data processing may be unable to satisfy. As these requirements grow, more and more managers will turn to AI for solutions. If AI can deliver then its place in industry may well be defined for years to come.

Ten "Rules" for Managers

All of this suggests some guidelines for managers now confronted with decisions about AI. While all situations are different, what follows is general enough to provide some guidance to managers and decision-managers in search of some new solutions to some very old and some very new problems.

1. Remember that AI, in spite of the rhetoric, is a very young field of inquiry, and one that has yet to define its own "scope and method";
2. At the same time, there have been a number of successes in applied AI; there are also countless AI systems now under development which will soon be in the commercial marketplace;
3. The greatest successes thusfar have occurred in two areas: expert systems and natural language processing. Expert systems like PROSPECTOR and natural language processing systems like INTELLECT have convinced many about the potential of smart systems, though there are still many expert and natural language processing systems that have yet to live up to their potential;
4. Given that many applied AI systems are mature and powerful, in order to determine the utility of AI generally and AI systems in particular, requirements should dominate all evaluations. Is there an expensive data base management system whose capabilities might be multiplied by a natural language front end? Are there a variety of diagnostic problems that might be "solved" via the application of an expert system? Does your organization have a large training mission amenable to CAI or ICAI?;
5. Requirements should always be matched with existing, field-tested AI systems. If a match is impossible, then search elsewhere for the solution;
6. Test prospective AI systems at length. There is no substitute for hands-on testing, especially when the testing is guided by a clear set of requirements;
7. Following any hands-on testing, perform a cost-benefit analysis of the system under evaluation; many AI systems are still very expensive so unless your need is specific and very amenable to a particular AI system, then you should probably pass the system by;
8. Always make certain that support for the AI system exists and has a verifiable track record; it seldom pays to be the first user of either the system or its service personnel;
9. Remember that all new fields grow and that a sensible investment should be made to track progress in AI; there is a growing body of literature that should be consulted, but

make certain to distinguish between basic and applied AI. The former will no doubt intrique you, while the latter might very well solve some of your most persistent and costly professional problems.

10. Brace yourself for unanticipated and dramatic successes and failures in AI; prepare to adapt to opportunities and crises in the AI marketplace; remember that the most "vulnerable" areas of corporate activity may well prove the most resilient to progress in applied AI, while the theoretically untouchable ones — like decision- and inference-making — may well succomb to expert and other knowledge representation systems.

BIBLIOGRAPHY

Andriole, S.J., ed., *Applications in Artificial Intelligence*. Princeton, New Jersey: Petrocelli Books, Inc., 1984.

Barr, A., R. Cohen, and E.A. Feigenbaum, eds., *The Handbook of Artificial Intelligence*. Reading, Massachusetts: Addison-Wesley Publishing Co., Volumes I, II, & III, 1981, 1982, 1982.

Business Week, "Artificial Intelligence: The Second Computer Age Begins," March 8, 1982.

Carbonell, J.G. *Subjective Understanding: Computer Models of Belief Systems*. New Haven, Connecticut: Yale University, Department of Computer Science, 1979.

Duda, R.O. and J.G. Gaschnig. "Knowledge-Based Expert Systems Come of Age." *Byte Magazine*, September 1981.

Fletcher, J.D. "Intelligent Instructional Systems in Training," in S.J. Andriole, ed., *Applications in Artificial Intelligence*. Princeton, New Jersey: Petrocelli Books, Inc., 1984.

Gevarter, W.B. "Expert Systems: Limited But Powerful." *IEEE Spectrum*, August 1983.

Hayes, P.J. and J.G. Carbonell. *Natural Language Tutorial*. Pittsburgh, Pennsylvania: Carnegie-Mellon University, Computer-Science Department, 1983.

Hayes-Roth, F., D. Waterman, and D. Lenat, eds., *Building Expert Systems*. Reading, Massachusetts: Addison-Wesley Publishing Co., 1983.

Hendrix, G.G. and E.D. Sacerdoti. "Natural Language Processing: The Field in Perspective." *Byte Magazine*, September 1981.

The Institute: News Supplement to IEEE Spectrum, "Artificial Intelligence Applications Called Dead End," Volume 6, Number 10, October 1982.

Kinnucan, P. "Artificial Intelligence: Making Computers Smarter." *High Technology*. November/December 1982.

Orlansky, J. and J. String. *Cost-Effectiveness of Computer-Based Instruction*. Alexandria, Virginia: Institute for Defense Analysis, 1979.

Schank, R.C. *SAM — A Story Understander*. New Haven, Connecticut: Yale University, Department of Computer Science, 1975.

——————— and S.P. Shwartz. "The Role of Knowledge Engineering in Natural Language," in S.J. Andriole, ed., *Applications in Artificial Intelligence*. Princeton, New Jersey: Petrocelli Books, Inc., 1984.

——————— and R.P. Abelson. *Scripts, Goals, Plans and Understanding*. Hillside, New Jersey: Erlbaum, 1977.

Schutzer, D. "The Tools and Techniques of Applied Artificial Intelligence," in S.J. Andriole, ed., *Applications in Artificial Intelligence*. Princeton, New Jersey: Petrocelli Books, Inc., 1984.

Sparck-Jones, K. and Y. Wilks, eds., *Automatic Natural Language Processing*. New York, New York: John Wiley and Sons, 1983.

Webster, R. and L. Miner. "Expert Systems: Programming Problem-Solving." *Technology*. January/February, 1982.

Winston, P.H. and B.K. Horn. *LISP*. Reading, Massachusetts: Addison-Wesley Publishing Co., 1981.

REFERENCES

1. For a comprehensive look at the history and systems of AI see Avron Barr, Paul R. Cohen, and Edward A. Feigenbaum, eds., *The Handbook of Artificial Intelligence*, Los Altos, California: William Kaufman, Inc., Volumes I, II, and III, 1981, 1982, 1982.

2. *Ibid.*, Volume I.

3. See Karen Sparck-Jones and Yorick Wilks, eds., *Automatic Natural Language Parsing*, New York, New York: John Wiley and Sons, 1983; Gary G. Hendrix and Earl D. Sacerdoti, "Natural Language Processing: The Field in Perspective," *Byte Magazine*, September 1981; and Philip J. Hayes and Jaime G. Carbonell, *Natural Language Tutorial*, Pittsburgh Pennsylvania: Carnegie-Mellon University, Computer Science Department, 1983. Also see Roger C. Schank and Steven P. Shwartz, "The Role of Knowledge Engineering in Natural Language Systems," in S.J. Andriole, ed., *Applications in Artificial Intelligence*, Princeton, New Jersey, Petrocelli Books, Inc., 1984.

4. "INTELLECT" is a trademark of the Artificial Intelligence Corporation. Also see Paul Kinnucan, "Artificial Intelligence: Making Computers Smarter," *High Technology*, November/December 1982 for a more detailed look at INTELLECT.

5. This estimate assumes a broad definition of AI systems.

6. See Barr, Cohen, and Feigenbaum, eds., *Handbook of Artificial Intelligence*, Volume II; Richard O. Duda and John G. Gaschnig, "Knowledge-Based Expert Systems Come of Age," *Byte Magazine*, September 1981; and Robin Webster and Leslie Miner, "Expert Systems: Programming Problem-Solving," *Technology*, January/February, 1982 for discussions of PROSPECTOR and many other expert systems.

7. See Duda and Gaschnig, *Knowledge-Based Expert Systems*.

8. See *Ibid* and Frederick Hayes-Roth, et al., eds., *Building Expert Systems*, Reading, Massachusetts: Addison-Wesley Publishing, Co., 1983 for detailed looks at these and other systems.

9. This Figure was provided by Cognitive Systems, Inc.

10. See Kinnucan, "Artificial Intelligence."

11. Many of these "demo" systems, it should be noted, evolved into applications systems though, of course, many did not. The prototype/demo phase was critical to the development of AI, and continues to be the path many designers take toward applications.

12. See F. Hayes-Roth, et. al., eds., *Building Expert Systems*.

13. See J. Dexter Fletcher, "Intelligent Instructional Systems in Training," in S.J. Andriole, ed., *Applications in Artificial Intelligence*, Princeton, New Jersey: Petrocelli Books, Inc., 1984 for a look at these and other systems; also see Barr, et al., *Handbook of Artificial Intelligence*, Volume III.

14. *Ibid*.

15. See Barr, Cohen, and Feigenbaum, eds., *Handbook of Artificial Intelligence*, Volume II.

16. *Ibid.*, Vol. III.

17. This of course assumes that computer programming as we know it today will survive progress in software engineering, which is becoming increasingly linked with progress in hardware engineering. At the same time, there is no reason to assume that AI will not make major contributions regardless of which way the field evolves.

18. Including, but not limited to, Xerox, the Digital Equipment Corporation, and Texas Instruments.

19. Marvin Minsky, as quoted in "Artificial Intelligence Applications Called Dead End," *The Institute: News Supplement to IEEE Spectrum*, Volume 6, Number 10, October 1982.

20. *Ibid*.

21. See *Business Week*, "Artificial Intelligence: The Second Computer Age Begins," March 8, 1982.

Expert systems represent ultimate goal of strategic decision making

by Steven W. Oxman

Expert systems, knowledge-based systems, artificial intelligence systems, decision support systems, management information systems and data base management systems are related to each other because they have overlapping goals. These software systems also tend to support similar classes of users.

However, there is confusion as to what these systems are, and their goals and intended users.

Expert systems

Expert systems are computer software systems that use knowledge (rules about the behavior of elements of a particular subject domain), facts and inference (reasoning) techniques to solve problems that normally require the abilities of human experts. The goals of expert systems include substituting for an unavailable human expert, assimilating the knowledge of multiple human experts and training new experts.

If a strategic decision must be made and the strategic decision maker is not available, the expert system could be interrogated. If the expert system was properly developed, it would have not only the rules of the subject, but also the rules of the expert for whom it is substituting. In theory, the solution developed by the expert system would be technically correct and would be influenced by the decision making attributes of its substituted expert.

Expert systems can be developed to store more knowledge and facts than any single human expert is capable of storing. In so doing, these expert systems can develop inferences that would not be available to a human expert, and thereby could develop knowledge on a particular

---

Expert systems can be developed to store more knowledge than humans.

---

subject or union of subjects greater than any single human expert. Neophytes in a particular subject that is supported by an expert system could use the expert system for training. The student would be able to present the expert system with a problem and request a solution. If the student understands the solution, he or she can pose a new problem. If the student does not understand the solution, he or she can request the expert system to map out the manner in which the expert system came to the solution. This amounts to the system telling the student what rules and facts were used to develop the solution.

Expert systems will be developed in the near future to support a wide range of users, from line workers to strategic decision makers. These systems include the following components:

✓ Knowledge data base
✓ Domain data base
✓ Data base management system (DBMS)
✓ Inference engine
✓ User interface
✓ Knowledge acquisition facility

The knowledge data base contains rules about the behavior of the elements of a particular subject (domain). These rules are formatted in such a manner to be usable by the expert system. An example of a possible format is: "An accounting item is a current asset if it is an asset and if it is liquid within one year."

The domain data base contains facts about a particular subject or domain. The subject is usually limited to a single specialized problem domain. Examples would include medical diagnosis, factory automation and project management. The domain data base also uses formatting conventions to efficiently manage and utilize the data. An example of a domain fact would be: "Current asset (cash)." This fact states that cash is a current asset.

The DBMS manages the data contained in the knowledge data base and the domain data base.

The inference engine is a computer program that uses information provided to it by the domain data base and the expert system user and knowledge provided by the knowledge data base in order to infer (derive a conclusion from facts) new facts. In so doing, it is simulating the deductive thought processes of a professional.

The user interface is a computer program that allows the expert system user to enter facts about a particular situation that are relevant to the system's domain, to enter rules and general facts that are relevant to the system's domain, and to ask questions of the system. The user interface program provides responses to user requests. Any other communication that would be necessary between the expert system and the user would be supported by the user interface program.

The knowledge acquisition facility is a computer program that provides a dialogue between the expert system and the human expert for the purpose of acquiring knowledge in the form of rules and facts from the human expert. This facility then places the rules in the knowledge data base and the facts in the domain data base.

Figure 1 illustrates the components of an expert system.

Knowledge-based systems

Knowledge-based systems are software systems that derive their name from the fact that these systems include a knowledge data base. Knowledge-based systems store large bodies of knowledge; that is to say, these systems store data and the meaning of this data. These systems have the capability to infer new meanings from the existing data

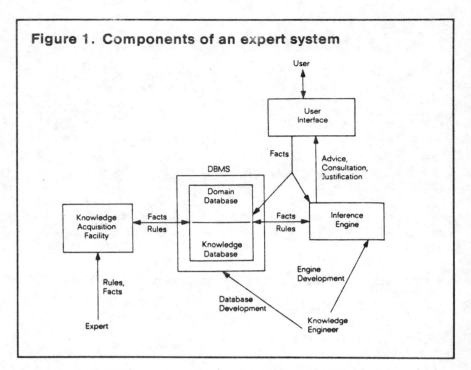

Figure 1. Components of an expert system

and meanings. There are two categories of systems today that are knowledge-based: Expert systems and natural language systems.

The natural language system is a user interface system that attempts to communicate with human users in a flexible framework that is common to the users. This flexible framework is the human language that the users are familiar with and use daily. Within the natural language communication structure, the system must allow the user to input data and data relationships, select operational choices, express operational commands and express queries.

Natural language systems attempt to allow communication between a computer system and a person who is not trained in the use of computer systems. This interface between the user and the system is used in conjunction with some other computer program. Examples of what the natural language system would interface with include expert systems and data base management systems.

Artificial intelligence

Artificial intelligence system is a general categorical term for computer-based systems that perform at high levels of competence in cognitive tasks. Artificial intelligence research has been concerned with tasks that normally require human intelligence. Examples of these tasks include symbolic reasoning and inference in problem solving. The following is a representative list of artificial intelligence systems:

- Expert systems
- Natural language systems
- Vision/Pattern recognition systems
- Intelligent robot systems
- Voice recognition systems

Artificial intelligence systems generically attempt to provide humanlike intelligence in machines. Artificial intelligence, in and of itself, is an area of scientific research rather than an end goal or product. Expert systems are an example of a product of this research.

Decision support

Decision support systems (DSS)

are computer software systems that enhance decision makers' effectiveness in making decisions while utilizing computers. DSS software generally falls into two categories: User interface support and models. The user interface support software restructures computer data before the data is presented to the user. It often allows the user to request the data in a less rigorous manner than

---

Artificial intelligence is an area of scientific research.

---

is generally required by a computer system. The data restructuring can result in graph and chart outputs instead of reams of paper filled with discrete numeric figures. These graphic reports are more understandable and natural to a decision maker than the columns of numbers.

Data query components of some DSS products allow the DSS user to ask for information from the computer data base in a manner that looks to be in the user's natural language. However, the user is still required to give certain information to the computer in the query that would not be considered natural. An example of this is the requirement to specify the computer data base name where the data resides. DSS models have been developed in many forms to solve a multitude of problem domains. There are DSS models to accomplish trend projections, seasonal analysis, trading day analysis, growth analysis, forecasting analysis and what-if analysis.

DSS is a system that supports the decision maker; DSS provides the decision maker with appropriate tools, and often, a link to information that is stored in a management information system. Decision support systems often use the computing resources and data base of the organization's management information system (MIS). However, the

intended users of the DSS are staff management and top management of the organization. DSS supports long-range, strategic decision making functions as opposed to the short-range operational support given by MIS.

DSS provides a means to interrogate the organization's data base without the need for total understanding of the underlying structure or technology. These systems provide the strategic decision maker with automation of the tools they usually use. An example of such a tool would be the "monte carlo" analysis tool. DSS responses tend to be formatted in a manner that is understandable to the problem solver. Effective DSS have the ability to provide query responses in a variety of graphic formats.

Management information systems

Management information systems (MIS) are computer-based systems that store, process, retrieve and disseminate information in support of managers. The information is stored in data bases in the form of grouped data. It is this grouping of the data that elevates the data to the information status. The components of a MIS are: The data base, the data base management system, applications programs and support programs.

The data base is the repository of the organization's data and data relationships. The data base management system manages the codified data and data relationships in the computer. The applications programs accept data from users, pass data on to the data base management system, process data at the request of a user, retrieve data and disseminate data and information to the intended users. Depending on the needs and design of the MIS, various support programs will be included in the MIS. Examples of support programs include: Telecommunications packages, report generation packages and transaction processors.

The goals of MIS include provision for input of daily operational status, timely updating of the organization's data base, generation of production reports and the provision to ask *ad hoc* questions or queries of the system. In general, the first three goals support the organization's staff people as well as certain line people. The last goal is available to support people at the line management levels.

Data base management systems (DBMS) manage data that resides in a computer data base. The data base is a collection of data of an organization. The data base is organized in such a manner as to give relationship information about the data. A DBMS is used to provide the organization's computer system with specific data management services:

- Support data definition
- Perform data manipulation
- Control data security
- Perform data monitoring
- Maintain data integrity
- Manage data distribution
- Support data recovery
- Perform data system monitoring
- Support data storage optimization
- Maintain data independence from applications

The DBMS provides these services to the computer system on which the DBMS resides. The DBMS user is usually another computer software system or computer program. Expert systems, knowledge-based systems, decision support systems, management information systems and application programs are all DBMS users. ■

About the author

Oxman is a computer scientist currently working for the US government. He is involved in data management issues related to a large geographically dispersed information system and in the development of expert system technology. —Ed.

Expert Systems for Business Applications: Potentials and Limitations

BY DR. ENGMING LIN

■ Computers have been a tool for making business decisions for almost three decades. Almost all routine, repetitive decisions that deal with quantitative data, and that have a definite decision procedure are programmed. The states of a decision, "programmed" or "non-programmed," depend very much on whether the decision is "structured" or "unstructured." An "unstructured" decision is one where there is no standard method for handling the problem or its precise nature and structure are elusive or complex.[16] Highly unstructured decisions are rarely programmed. An unstructured decision might become programmable if data can be quantified, definite decision procedures could be found, and the alternative courses of action are clear.

In business, there are routine, repetitive decisions that are made by using the "rule of thumb" or "reasoning" instead of "computing" because data are not quantifiable. Most of these decisions are "structured," but not programmed.

Recently, the success of some expert systems has caught the attention of business executives. Either with an in-house taskforce or jointly with another organization, many firms are developing expert systems. Although most of the existing expert systems are for non-business professions, some new systems are designed to solve business-related problems. With expert systems, previously non-programmed decisions will become programmable.

In the July 1985 issue of this Journal, Dr. Stephen J. Andriole discussed the promise of artificial intelligence (AI) including expert systems.[2] His article and some AI papers and books written by other authors provide the general description of expert-system applications based on the state-of-the-art of expert systems and their vision of AI technologies in the future.[1,2,11,18] As more expert systems for business become available for commercial uses, expanding the discussion of expert-system applications to include business decisions should be of interest to systems managers and data processing (DP) professionals. This article presents the potentials and limitations of expert systems for business applications based on the characteristics of managerial decision-making. "Business application" and "managerial decision-making" are synonymous in this article because making decisions is the basic function of expert systems.

Expert Systems

Expert systems are software systems that are designed to mimic the way human experts make decisions. In one sense, building expert systems is a form of intellectual cloning.[18] To create an expert system, the designer builds into the system a knowledge-base and an inference system. The knowledge-base is derived from the expert's knowledge and experience in the field. There are two types of knowledge. The first type is the "facts of domain" — the widely shared knowledge, commonly agreed among practitioners. The second type is heuristic knowledge — the knowledge of good practice and good judgement in a field. It is the knowledge that a human expert acquires over years of work.[9] This knowledge is usually contained in a set of IF-THEN rules. Knowledge-bases are not the global database that most people talk about. If a business-loan expert system is to be built, the loan officers' knowledge including all rules they use to make the loan decisions is the knowledge-base, while a loan applicant's business plan, personal and family data might be stored in a global database.

The inference system is the rule or knowledge interpreter. The knowledge-base can be thought of as a group of patterns and the inference system matches the pattern against the problem data. Built in the inference procedure is a method of reasoning (or logic) which is used to understand and match "knowledge" with the problem data. Unlike other programming techniques, an exact match is unnecessary.

The knowledge must be "mined" out of the experts' heads and be represented in a computer. The "miners" are called knowledge engineers. Mining knowledge is a very difficult task because experts can rarely define the heuristic knowledge they possess.

The expert system is an area of artificial-intelligence application that generally involve symbolic representation, symbolic inference, and heuristic search.[12] Because of these distinguishing features of artificial intelligence (AI), expert systems differ from conventional computer applications in the following ways:

  a. They are able to deal with non-numeric (qualitative) data.
  b. They allow incorporation of uncertain or incomplete information.
  c. They are capable of explaining to the user how conclusions were reached.
  d. The user interfaces with the system via "natural" dialogue.[15]

Although a variety of programming languages may be used for expert systems, most systems developed in America use the AI language LISP.

An overview of expert systems can be found in many papers or books.[1,3,4,5,8,9,11,12,18] For the most recent developments in expert systems, good sources of information are Artificial Intelligence, AI Magazine, and the proceedings of various AI conferences.

Potential of Expert Systems

Most AI researchers agree with Feigenbaum, an expert-system pioneer, that "the power of an expert system is derived from the knowledge it possesses, not from the particular formalisms and inference schemes it employs."[12] If the expertise of a human expert can be captured and embodied in the knowledge base, an expert system can be built. The potential of expert systems depends on how well humans can understand "how does the expert knowledge work?"

Routine, repetitive decisions are the best candidates for expert systems because the knowledge, judgement, and experience that are used to make these types of decisions are already accumulated and are easier to specify. Since there are more routine, repetitive decisions at the low-level management than at the high-level management, it can be predicted that many expert systems designed in the next few years will be for operational planning and control. Few systems will be designed for strategical planning that uses heuristic knowledge and is not highly repetitive.

Routine, repetitive decisions are the best candidates for expert systems.

Benefits and costs are other reasons that routine, repetitive decisions are the potential areas for expert systems. Costs of building and operating an expert system should not exceed the benefit it is expected to generate. The creation of INTERNIST, a medical expert system, took 26 man-years and PROSPECTOR, a resource-exploration expert system that evaluates sites for potential mineral deposits, took 16 man-years. Efficiency of expert system development will be improved as knowledge engineers become more experienced and better tools for design are available. Cost, however, is still higher than ordinary application software. It does not make any sense to build an expert system that will be used only once a year. For managerial decisions for which quantitative models are available and which have been working satisfactorily, expert systems that are more expensive are not needed.

Expert systems are most suited for combined problems where straightforward methods of enumeration lead to explosive numbers of possibility.[9] Feigenbaum and McCorduck use chess to illustrate this kind of problem. Many people thought computers played chess by exploring every possible move. But a chess game has 10^{120} possible moves. The fastest computer available today cannot explore all moves in a quadrillion years. Computers use the rule of thumb. In business, job-shop sequencing and scheduling belong to this kind of problem. Contracted with a group of AI researchers at Carnegie Mellon University, Westinghouse is developing an expert system for job-shop scheduling.

Expert systems are also suited for problems where decisions are based on the analysis and interpretation of an enormous amount of non-quantitative data. Many problems of this kind can be found in insurance, banking, and finance service industries. This kind of problem usually take a human expert many hours of sorting out data to make a decision. Furthermore, one must have a long period of experience in the field to become an expert. Expert systems for this type of problem can make decisions faster and more accurately than human experts. XCON and XSEL used by Digital Equipment Corporation (DEC) are expert systems for this kind of problems. DEC's VAX computers are almost always built to conform to specific customer needs. XSEL is used by DEC salespersons to assist customers in properly configuring their systems. Customer orders are then translated into detailed product specifications by XCON. Although DEC did not disclose the figure, it was estimated that XCON has saved several million dollars.

Represented in the knowledge-base may be knowledge derived from the combined experience of several experts. If the pooled knowledge is better than the individual ones, and if there is no conflict among the experts, the expert systems designed might make decisions better than human experts.

Many firms, including several major computer hardware and software companies, have entered the expert system business. Some companies have developed tool kits (or "shell" or "open-ended systems") that make it easier to build new expert systems. The ultimate goal is to let the human expert plug in his/her own knowledge. Although this goal is still many years away, some systems that reduce difficulties of knowledge engineering are already available[3,5,7,10,15,17] One example is Personal Consultant marketed by Texas Instruments (TI). The package is designed to be used on TI microcomputers or the IBM PC[15]

Limitations of Expert Systems

In their article "Expert Systems in Business," Michaelsen and Michie stated that very few expert systems developed were for business applications "because business applications involve more behavioral variables, which can slow down acceptance of such systems."[13] The AI technology itself, behavioral variables, and other characteristics of managerial decisions limit the development of expert systems for business applications.

The business environment changes very rapidly. Managers often have to handle the unanticipated. It takes more than experiential knowledge to make unstructured decisions. Mintzberg, Raisinghani, and Theoret define unstructured decisions as "decision processes that have not been encountered in quite the same form and for which no predetermined and explicit set of ordered responses exist in the organization."[14] It is very unlikely that expert systems for highly unstructured decisions can be built because experts do not have sufficient experience to provide relevant knowledge for the knowledge-base in the expert system.

An expert system usually is confined to a very narrow domain because building and maintaining a large knowledge-base is very difficult. Defining the domain is extremely important because expert systems have fragile behavior at the boundaries.[11,18] A system does not give the right answer if a problem is not confined entirely to the specific domain. Many managerial decisions are based on broad, inter-disciplinary knowledge. Designing systems for these decisions might encounter a great deal of difficulty because the domain is not narrow.

Business applications involve more behavioral variables. The heuristic knowledge that leads to the good judgement on human behavior is hard to define. As the result, mining knowledge out of the manager's head is not easy.

After the knowledge is well defined, it must be represented in the knowledge-base of the computer as a set of IF-THEN rules. But certain kinds of knowledge cannot be easily translated into the IF-THEN rule. Building an expert system for any business application with these kinds of knowledge would be very difficult.

The input/output languages used for expert systems are closer to natural language and are more "user friendly" than conventional computer applications. Some proponents of expert systems claim that users interface with the system via "natural" dialogue. The dialogue, however, is not really a natural language because users must describe problems in a strictly defined formal language.[11]

"The Commercial Application of Expert Systems Technology," a report published in 1984, listed 138 expert-system projects in the United States.[10] Very few of these projects are for management support. According to the same report, there were about 400 knowledge engineers in 1983. Although the number will increase very rapidly, the shortage of knowledge engineers is not expected to be eased for several years. With the majority of knowledge engineers participating in non-business related projects, the development of expert systems for business applications in the near future will be limited.

Solving a problem with the same available data, two human experts might come up with different answers or conclusions. Wall Street provides a very good example. Observing the same economic occurrence, one stock analyst might be bullish while another is bearish on the stock market. Whose decision rules should be represented in the knowledge-base if an expert system for stock-market analysis is to be built? Several experts may contribute to an expert-system project only if these is no conflict in their views. Knowledge engineers still do not know how to reconcile differing or conflicting views among acknowledged experts. To build an expert system, one human expert must play the role of knowledge "Czar."[11,18]

Experience is essential for good management. So is creativity. The knowledge-base has the experts' experience, but it would be very difficult to program creativity into the computer.

Business needs new ideas. These new ideas cannot come from expert systems.

Conclusion

Many expert systems for business application will become available in the next few years. Most of these systems will be for the problems that existing Operations Research/Management Science models cannot solve.

Decision-makers' knowledge must be represented in the computer. Specifying a manager's heuristic knowledge, that is essential for good decision-making, is very difficult. This might be the biggest hurdle in building business expert systems. To remove this hurdle, an extensive research on how managers' mind work will be needed. ●jsm

References

1. Andriole, S. J. ed., *Applications in Artificial Intelligence*, Petrocelli Book, Inc., Princeton, N.J., 1984.
2. Andriole, S.J., "The Promise of Artificial Intelligence," Journal of Systems Management, pp. 8-17, July 1985.
3. "Artificial Intelligence is Here," Business Week, July 9, 1984, pp. 54-62.
4. Barr, A., R. Cohen, and E.A. Feigenbaum, ed., *The Handbook of Artificial Intelligence, Vol. II*, Addison-Wesley Publishing Company, Reading, Massachusetts, 1982.
5. Davis R. and D.B. Lenat, *Knowledge-Based Systems in Artificial Intelligence*, McGraw-Hill International Book Co., 1982.
6. "DEC, Motorola, NSC Lead Joint Research Venture," Mini-Micro Systems, Vol. 16, No. 14, Dec. 1983, p. 33.
7. "Decision-support Program Boosts AI Techniques," Mini-Micro Systems, Vol. 17, No. 15, Dec. 1984, p. 46.
8. Duda, R. O. and J. G. Gasching, "Knowledge-based Expert Systems Come of Age," Byte, Sept. 1981, pp. 238-279.
9. Feigenbaum, E. A. and P. McCorduck, *The Fifth Generation*, Addison-Wesley Publishing Company, 1983.
10. Frenkel, K.A., "Toward Automating Software-Development Cycle," Communications of the ACM, pp. 578-589, Vol. 28, No. 6, June 1985.
11. Gevarter, W.B., "Expert Systems: Limited But Powerful," IEEE Spectrum, pp. 39-45, August 1983.
12. Hayes-Roth, F., D.A. Waterman, and D.B. Lenat ed., *Building Expert Systems*, Addison-Wesley Publishing Co., Reading, Massachusetts, 1983.
13. Michaelsen, R. and D. Michie, "Expert Systems in Business," Datamation, pp. 240-246, November 1983.
14. Mintzberg, H., D. Raisinghani, and A. Theoret, "The Structure of "Unstructured" Decision Processes," Administrative Science Quarterly, Vol. 21, June 1976, pp. 246-275.
15. *Personal, Consultant: Expert System Development Tool*, TechnicalR eport, Texas Instruments Inc., 1984.
16. Simon, H. A., *The New Science of Management Decision*, Harper & Row, 1960.
17. "The Smarter Computer," Newsweek, Dec. 3, 1984, pp. 89-90.
18. Winston, P.H. and K.A. Prendergast ed., *The AI Business: Commercial Uses of Artificial Intelligence*, MIT Press, Cambridge, Massachusetts, 1984.

PART VIII

CBMIS: AN INTEGRATED VIEW

INTRODUCTION

In this section we come to the end of our journey through the articles included in the text which explored the many facets of computer based information systems from a user and designer prospective. The articles selected for inclusion ranged in content from very simple to somewhat technical and there was some redundancy due to the fact that the articles were not primarily written for a textbook but developed for publication in a journal or magazine. Since no one article covered all facets of CBMIS development, the following discussion is presented to provide the reader with an opportunity to reflect on the scope and dimensions of the material covered in the text and, hopefully, serve as a review of the important points covered. The CBMIS model we introduce is a synthesis and is presented as a means of pulling the pieces together and highlighting the important concepts presented in the text.

A CONCEPTUAL CBMIS MODEL (1)

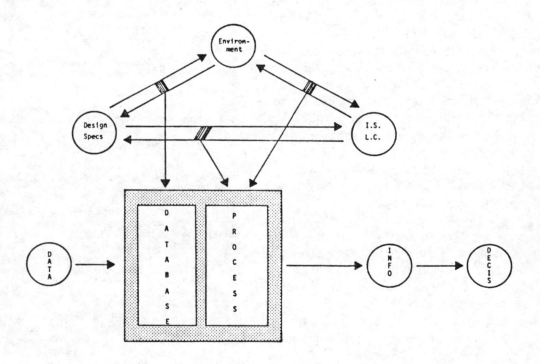

*IS = Information Systems
*IC = Life Cycle

In the following pages we briefly describe the components of this model (2).

NATURE OF DATA

In developing a CBMIS, a conceptual framework of what is needed by the user, impacts directly on the type of data used. Whether the process of developing this conceptual framework is specifically created for the CBMIS, incrementally developed from outside sources, or evolutionary in nature from an existing manual system, it reflects the mental framework of the end users.

If the organization has defined its strategic goals, organizational objectives, and critical success factors which will ensure a viable and growing organization, the data component can be structured rather easily and the CBMIS has potential for success. On the other hand, if there are conflicting goals and objectives, or the company is not aware which factors are critical to its success, a multiplicity of behavioral problems can occur which can destroy the confidence in a CBMIS or minimize its effectiveness. If the CBMIS is not designed to evolve as changes necessitate or cannot be made incrementally responsive to this change, then the system may do more damage than good.

Of course, the conceptual framework of the data ultimately resolves the questions of the sources of data, the external or internal sources of data used, and whether the data is past (performance), present (operational) or future (budget or cash flow) oriented. The urgency of need and the availability of data in many forms including aggregated or disaggregated can then be dealt with.

Disaggregated, in lieu of aggregated data, provides the opportunity to expand the horizons for decision-making and allows for a greater focus on the specific nature of the problems. This, in turn, reduces the ability of individuals to sway decisions by their position or their ability to manipulate others through emotional appeals. The need for disaggregated data is obvious when, for instance, sales are analyzed by product, territory, or salesperson and costs are analyzed by cost center or product.

CBMIS users have a need to not only receive specific output but receive it in an understandable and appropriate format or output medium for ease of use in decision making. Many individuals become very habit prone relative to what they need and how they need it. The degree of use and usefulness is based to a great extent on the perceived appropriateness of the format.

DATABASE

The conceptual framework of the data brings into focus the need for a database (data that is centrally stored). The type of database, itself, is not important, only the existence and availability or access to the database is the issue. If the CBMIS doesn't provide what the user wants, behavioral problems are created. These problems are similar to what Mintzberg (3) suggests when he observed that managers rely on gut level instinct, which is based on informal information systems. In addition, managers at higher levels have less willingness to expend valuable personal or staff time to mechanistically gather, process, and interpret available data. Thus, data needs to be treated as a common resource so that its availability, its nature, and its potential for decision making can be readily conveyed to the potential users.

PROCESS

Development of the conceptual CBMIS will generally include a wide range of transaction processing reports and some models for decision analysis. In many cases the models are built into the system in a technique mode as opposed to their integration as a process. The user, when faced with a technique mode, is severely limited in his/her ability to fully explore data structures in analyzing problem solving alternatives. Because the user has both formal and informal information available and utilizes this information in decision making, an effective and efficient CBMIS should incorporate the ability to use both kinds of information in problem solving analysis. The conceptual model of CBMIS should, therefore, include the opportunity for the user to have available a wide range of models which will support all levels of decision making. This development should include not only the ability to do inquiry and report generation but to interface with a large number of subroutines which can be linked into a selection of models. This integration and linking should allow the user to continue to adapt and become more sophisticated with the system. The ability to grow with the system will require that the initial CBMIS include features which allow the user to redefine, generate, restructure, and incorporate new information into the modeling analysis. Hence, flexibility is the essence if the user is to effectively model and utilize the information available to them in the present corporate database as well as from external sources which may be uncovered as the user matures in decision analysis. Eventually the purpose of the process component of the proposed model is generation of the most useful type of information for decision making purposes.

INFORMATION

The nature of information is determined by its usefulness to the end user and it is the usefulness that determines the success of a CBMIS. The system must be responsive to the end user in four main areas of information. It must be timely, integrated with other data and information, consistent and accurate, and be relevant. If the information lacks any of these basic features, conflicts within the organization will surely be manifested and the result will be incorrect decisions, misallocation of resources, and windows of opportunity overlooked. If the system cannot provide a minimum level of confidence, then the CBMIS will not be used or the system will be severely discounted.

Perhaps a greatest requirement for information is that it provide a fundamental base from which the end user can explore different options available, or better yet, gain an insight into the particular task at hand.

In addition to the nature of information, system user interaction or usage patterns can be of four types: subscription, terminal, clerk, or intermediary (4). In a subscription mode, the user receives information on a regular basis. This method lacks flexibility and does not consider changing user needs. A good example is monthly reports from the Computer Center. In contrast, the terminal or direct mode allows the user to use the CBMIS as it is needed, thus, the user won't be bombarded by masses of information. However, the user still needs some minimum computer training to use the system. An example of the terminal mode is the Versateller or 24 hour type teller pervading the banking industry. It is available as the user needs it and provides more ease of planning since interruptions of daily routines are reduced considerably due to after-hour access.

In clerk or off-line mode, training is not required for the user, but this type of interaction is slower. All batch processing applications can be classified within this group. Finally, in the intermediary mode, the user receives special advice about the provided information. An example of the intermediary mode is the financial analyst within the organization who interprets the financial computer output for the vice president of finance.

In other words, a system with all options for receiving or gaining access to information increases the likelihood that patterns of information availability more closely match the changing user patterns of information access and usage.

INFORMATION SYSTEMS LIFE CYCLE (ISLC)

As with all systems, the information system has a well-defined life cycle. Unless the system has a radical transformation, each information system has exploration (introduction), establishment (growth), maintenance (maturity) and decline periods. Within the system itself, each subsystem has its own life cycle. The exploration (introduction) stage is crucial to the acceptance (but not necessarily its success) of the CBMIS. The growth period may be slowed by delays in the expansion of the CBMIS, technical problems, the availability of the CBMIS to the concerned end-users or those who feel they need it, and the reluctance by the end users to accept the CBMIS. If the above delays can be overcome, the growth period of CBMIS offers a greater opportunity for CBMIS to be accepted. Finally, if the CBMIS improves the quality of the work accomplished, searches out new areas and new ways to service the end users, and actively seeks new exposure from all concerned users while lowering the cost of providing information, acceptance will also be increased.

Once these three stages are passed, the information system life cycle should concentrate on increasing the usage and reputation of the CBMIS via quality and feature improvements. Improvements include the development of new features (i.e., graphics, external databases, etc.), and greater flexibility and user enthusiasm.

The final stage in the information system life cycle is the decline period. This can be just as crucial to the company's CBMIS. If there is not a planned death or review of the CBMIS, the company may be saddled with a CBMIS which takes a disproportionate amount of the organization's resources relative to its contributions. A periodic review of the conceptual framework may force the current CBMIS to be drastically changed or eliminated in favor of a new system. The organization faces many potential behavioral problems if it avoids addressing these points.

ENVIRONMENT

Users of computer based management information systems occupy three organizational levels: (a) top, (b) middle and (c) operational. Each organizational level assumes a different role in the development and use of CBMIS.

The champagne glass phenomena as described by Thomas Whisler (5) is seen in the user structure of CBMIS. For example, at the highest level, top management has a new and powerful resource of data immediately available through the use of many and varied software packages. The question, however, is whether top management is again "over enriched" because of this data access and does this reduce rather than increase their sensitivity to occurances at operational levels?

Middle management on the other hand is experiencing undue stress as a result of the decrease in their ranks due to the reduced need to interpret data and accomplish other middle management functions. This also impacts on operational level people indirectly as promotability potential decreases.

User support must come from top management for CBMIS to be successful. Success will require formal and informal acts of support in the form of policies and encouragement from top management. The question, however, is whether top management has a felt need for CBMIS and whether they are committed to integrating the program.

General resistance to CBMIS at all levels of the organization can be seen in habit patterns, lack of familiarity with the system and feelings of insecurity regarding the system. Individuals are accustomed to tangible hard copy data regarding company policies, financial reports, progress reports, etc. Visualization of data on a CRT is inconsistent with conventional patterns and is new and unfamiliar to many people. The preference for hard copy printouts in preference to screen visualization is common.

Learning how to access the computer is also an unfamiliar activity that shakes the security needs of users. This resistance is further compounded by the boring nature of data input, extraction, and all mechanical elements associated with operating the computer.

User resistance is common since people tend to prefer the familiar over the new and unfamiliar. Punch cards are familiar and add a sense of security because the data is visual and physically available. Tape and floppy disks on the other hand are unfamiliar and add a sense of insecurity to the user because of the lack of physical contact with the data.

Security is another factor in resistance. Issues to be addressed include: Who has access to a user's data? Who has access to the data that was formally stored in the minds of decision makers? Is pirating a possiblity? Users are concerned that creative ideas and secured data may become sources of power for unauthorized individuals. Even if data is not pirated through internal or external sources it is possible that data may disappear because of software/hardware malfunctions. Have security measures been properly implemented into the system to prevent the accidental erasure of important documents?

DESIGN SPECIFICATIONS

After a careful review of the information system's life cycle and a precise definition of the environment of a particular CBMIS, the design specifications should be elaborated. Comprehensive design specifications play a crucial role in the CBMIS by creating consistency in computer utilization, by increasing the adaptability of the existing CBMIS to growing technology, by increasing the chances of acceptance by the users, and finally by serving as a guideline for CBMIS utilization. The following four factors are the most important design specification variables; types of design (task force vs. individual), provision for change (modularity in design), functional specifications and performance criteria, and system documentation. These four design specification variables are briefly discussed immediately below.

Types of Design (Task Force vs. Individual): Traditionally, a CBMIS has been designed largely by data processing personnel. As a result, the designs have not always had the full support of the users. The emerging issue of task force design emphasizes the participation of all impacted personnel in the design of the CBMIS. This particular method could increase the commitment of users and at the same time give them a chance to express their views regarding the utilization of the CBMIS.

Provision for Change (Modularity in Design): Acquisition and utilization of computer technology should not be a one-shot operation in organization; rather, it should be a continuous process. Design specifications of the proposed model should consider the ways and methods by which a particular organization might adapt to the growing technology. Modularity in design could provide such an opportunity. Modularity should be considered in relation to: hardware acquisition, software acquisition, systems design principles, and, most importantly, software development.

Functional Specifications and Performance Criteria: In order to stay within the range of the predefined objectives for the CBMIS, the designer should articulate the functional specifications of a particular system. These specifications serve as a centralizing mechanism. A continuous comparison of these specifications with the actual operation of the system will point up the deviations between predefined goals and actual performance. The smaller the deviation, the higher the achievement of goals. Functional specifications include the following:

-- time/cost and other resource estimations (roughly, how much time and money are needed to design and implement a particular CBMIS?)
-- specific objectives of the CBMIS
-- input/output specifications
-- a description of system functions and characteristics
-- accuracy of reports
-- reliability of reports
-- degree of acceptance and utilization of the CBMIS by users.

System Documentation: A comprehensive written document which describes the details and step-by-step operation of the CBMIS can be very helpful for its effective and efficient utilization. This document may also aid in improving the performance of existing systems.

NEED FOR COOPERATION AND UNDERSTANDING

As with all complex environments, the building of a successful and effective CBMIS requires the involvement of the end-user, top-management, and the information systems professional. Information technology will continue to provide the basis for enhanced CBMIS, however, to fully tap this potential, an enlightened cooperative effort between management, users, and information systems professionals must be considered as a major requisite. Without this form of cooperation, the CBMIS potential will be greatly diminished.

REFERENCES

1. Bidgoli, Hossein. A Descriptive/Predictive Model for the Employment of Computer-Based Management Information System for the Government of a Developing Country. A Ph.D. dissertation, Portland State University, 1983, pp. 64-74.

2. Barela, Bidgoli, Rudd, Stucky, and Vigen. "Improving Chances of Success in Design and Implementation of Computer-Based Management Information Systems (CBMIS): A Behavioral Perpsective," Proceedings and Abstracts, Thirtheenth Annual Conference, Western Region, American Institute of Decision Sciences, March 1984, pp. 1-3.

3. Mintzberg, Henry, "Impediments to the Use of Management Information," Society of Industrial Accounts of Canada Journal, 1978, pp. 1-23.

4. Alter, Steven L. Decision Support Systems Current Practice and Continuing Challenges, Addison-Wesley Publishing Company: Reading, Mass., 1980, pp. 111-116.

5. Whistler, Thomas L., The Impact of Computers on Organizations. Frederick A. Praeger, Inc., New York, 1970.